Postphenomenology and Media

Postphenomenology and the Philosophy of Technology

Technological advances affect everything from our understandings of ethics, politics, and communication, to gender, science, and selfhood. Philosophical reflection on technology helps draw out and analyze the nature of these changes, and helps us understand both the broad patterns and the concrete details of technological effects. This book series provides a publication outlet for the field of the philosophy of technology in general, and the school of thought called "postphenomenology" in particular. Philosophy of technology applies insights from the history of philosophy to current issues in technology, and reflects on how technological developments change our understanding of philosophical issues. In response, postphenomenology analyzes human relationships with technologies, while integrating philosophical commitments of the American pragmatist tradition of thought.

Postphenomenology and Media: Essays on Human–Media–World Relations, Edited by Yoni Van Den Eede, Stacey O. Irwin, and Galit Wellner

Diphtheria Serum as a Technological Object: A Philosophical Analysis of Serotherapy in France 1894–1900, by Jonathan Simon

Digital Media: Human–Technology Connection, by Stacey O. Irwin

Acoustic Technics, by Don Ihde

A Postphenomenological Inquiry of Cell Phones: Genealogies, Meanings, and Becoming, by Galit P. Wellner

Postphenomenology and Technoscience: The Manhattan Papers, Edited by Jan Kyrre Berg O. Friis and Robert P. Crease

Postphenomenological Investigations: Essays on Human–Technology Relations, Edited by Robert Rosenberger and Peter-Paul Verbeek

Design, Meditation, and the Posthuman, Edited by Dennis M. Weiss, Amy D. Propen, and Colbey Emmerson Reid

Postphenomenology and Media

Essays on Human–Media–World Relations

Edited by
Yoni Van Den Eede
Stacey O'Neal Irwin
Galit Wellner

Foreword by
Don Ihde

LEXINGTON BOOKS
Lanham • Boulder • New York • London

Published by Lexington Books
An imprint of The Rowman & Littlefield Publishing Group, Inc.
4501 Forbes Boulevard, Suite 200, Lanham, Maryland 20706
www.rowman.com

Unit A, Whitacre Mews, 26-34 Stannary Street, London SE11 4AB

British Library Cataloguing in Publication Information Available

Library of Congress Cataloging-in-Publication Data Available

ISBN 978-1-4985-5014-7 (hardback : alk. paper)
ISBN 978-1-4985-5015-4 (ebook)

∞™ The paper used in this publication meets the minimum requirements of American National Standard for Information Sciences—Permanence of Paper for Printed Library Materials, ANSI/NISO Z39.48-1992.

Printed in the United States of America

Contents

Foreword

Shadows and the New Media

Don Ihde

One lesson learned from now over 40 years of studying the history and philosophy of technology, is that early stages of new technologies elicit initial exaggerations of expectations: on the one side there is always utopian hype, a new technology is thought to promise more than it delivers; and equally there is dystopian hype, expressing fears that the introduction of new technologies will deskill, displace, or distort our very being-in-the-world. Yet, over longer periods of time, most newly introduced technologies "settle down" into much more taken-for-granted uses, usually more mundane than either utopian or dystopian trajectories. The second long-term lesson regarding technologies over time is that all technologies have shelf lives, but over eons these shorten, or speed up. As I have pointed out in numerous places, the 1.4 million year shelf life of the Acheulean hand axe, from 1.8 million BP to 400,000 BP is the longest life single technology known to me. If we look at the inventions and shelf lives of cellphones, perhaps the single most ubiquitous technology ever, the shelf lives of these technologies are extremely short.

As the various authors here point out, we are going through a shift in media technologies. The older and established media include print, radio, cinema, television, and more. But with the exception of print, which in the West is now approximately four centuries old, the audio-visual media are largely 20th-century developments. And yet we have come some way from early 20th-century astonishment, with radio and recording listeners astonished at how "realistic" or "lifelike" Caruso sounded, or the startled "screams" and "jumps" of Lumière cinema viewers—experiences the contemporary listener or viewer finds puzzling, given the flaws of reproduction and fidelity to our senses, and our taken-for-granted clarity now.

The new media, growing ubiquitous, now find presence everywhere to the point of intrusiveness and near-constant demand. Email, the Internet, social media, "smart" technologies of the Internet of Things, big data, driven by algorithms which seek out our every move, desire, taste. These media, electronic, often wireless, even if not literally attached or implanted, go with us everywhere. Social scientists estimate that cell or mobile phones are now accessible to 95% of the world's population, and as a resident of Manhattan the number of these devices on the Metro, in restaurants and theatres, and in our homes, is simply pervasive. Social media, too, generate arguments about how young users should be, whether or not limits should apply to children, or uses restricted for drivers. Today the tale of Thales falling into a well while watching the skies, would be replaced by a hiker falling into a manhole while jogging with an iPod. The "Thales Effect," in our time, includes distracted driving while text messaging, phantom vibrations from pocketed or even imagined cellphones, and the experience of being called at any time or place. Robert Rosenberger has taken note of widespread phantom phone vibrations among college students (see *Daily Mail* n.d.).

Postphenomenology and Media is due out spring 2017. I am writing this foreword late 2016, just after an event which paused my communications network of conversations from November 8, for approximately 10 days: the aftermath of the U.S. Presidential election. It was interesting that as communications resumed, virtually all my mostly academic interlocutors admitted the silence was related to a kind of "mourning" felt as the direction of an era reversed. The reversal, to my mind, was from a trajectory into the 21st century characterized by growing multiculturalism, urbanization, globalization, to a retro-trajectory more in keeping with the 19th century, including nationalism, revival of white dominance, insularity, racism, and worse. But it also had to do with media technologies.

Actually, the election events took place in an overlapping old and new media juncture. Newspapers played a major role, often in what now seems a more sober role of investigative reporting but also with partisan politics obvious on both sides. What those of short sight miss is the rather long history of newspapers slowly attaining standards of "objective" and "investigative" reporting. Early newspaper reporting, in the 18th and 19th centuries, was often quite crude. Television was highly present with the debates and again partisan positioning between cable news and the networks. Again, a history which included the emergence of Fox News with its notion of "balanced reporting" which often balances a 97% consensus—say on climate issues in the scientific community—on the one side with 3% often paid deniers on the other side. *Merchants of Doubt* (Oreskes and Conway 2010) revealed that the very same group of people who guided the campaign for tobacco against its negative health effects also peopled the early attacks on climate change doubts. Today fossil fuel and big sugar corporations are employing the same strategies. But, the new and social media were also pervasive. Trump's smartphone Twitter hit-backs were notorious. False news, fact checking, "pants-on-fire" ratings soared. Today's media reports are filled with attempts to correct, counter, and reform the distortions so rampant during the campaign. These new media clearly have not (yet) attained mature conventions. As I see it, this recent set of events was a dark cloud—dystopian regarding the media—contrasting with so much utopian hope about how the wider access for larger and larger numbers of people would introduce a more democratic and egalitarian politics to the world. Instead, the 21st- to 19th-century trajectory reversal introduced a darker side of media possibilities. Ironically, both sides had true insights: the actual popular vote is likely to be one of the largest ever over the founding fathers' antiquated mechanism, the electoral college. Popular democracy has now twice lost in this millennium.

I am reminded of an old ploy of mine during the Cold War. Then, it was argued, the MAD (mutual assured destruction) strategy had kept the warring sides from nuclear war. So, I fantasized placing an earth-destroying nuclear device deep underground, with every human given a button which could set it off. Here, the logic was that directly and totally democratized, we would have the ultimate MAD. My question was: Would this make us feel safer? An ultimate, democratized MAD? Here the question relates, in a similar way, to the ultimate democratization of media for news. What if everyone could publicize a storyline, globally? For example, one piece of false news targeted a pizza parlor, claiming it was a front for a child abuse ring funded and directed by the Clintons. This was a blog from a single individual. The owner of the pizzeria received many death threats, yet the news was totally false, circulated on Facebook. Nevertheless, I remain bothered by the implications which could lead towards a dystopian weighting. How does one gain wider media democracy, yet restrict false news which has distinct harms? Clearly the extreme thought experiment, while capturing part of the expert/non-expert arguments for media use, does not address a broader need for checks and balances and mature use conventions. Widely public use of even radio is still today short of a century old. The social media are much younger.

All the above points to a more generalized ambiguity which characterizes any technology. In postphenomenology, a more precise notion relates to *multistability,* or to a range of multiple uses and developmental trajectories. Print, a now "old" medium, very deeply structured into our lifeworld, is just beginning to shift stabilities. A new development, only a few decades old, is 3D printing. Here, very unlike standard print technologies which have been dominantly 2D, the objects "printed" are three-dimensional. The simplest of these machines usually uses some powder-like substance to "build up" a pre-designed object—let us imagine something like a 3D snowflake. The predesign can be very complex; examples of student projects in our Stony Brook

Engineering College are often exhibited in hallway displays. Note several things about this process: 3D objects are not print-linguistic, but are fully 3D objects, at the least visual-tactile. Then, in an easily imagined step, one develops such objects in size—many new 3D printing technologies already make large objects, including handguns and projected automobiles. And in medical applications, artificial esophagus and bone printing of joints are imagined on the horizon. Many flesh, blood vessel, and body parts are envisioned.

Work backward now; 2D printers traditionally and dominantly have printed linguistic objects—texts. Our "Gutenberg Revolution" led to books, newspapers, pamphlets, and print. But today, large 2D printers are used for printing out circuits, solar panels, flexible film and a whole series of non-linguistic print objects, a very different stability than earlier uses or designer intent. All this could be something like a second printer revolution. One of my favorite examples is a new, layered solar panel. Current panels are able to turn sunlight into electric current only from a limited range of the optical spectrum—but new techniques promise capturing a wider range of the spectrum, which calls for various layering processes, all possible from a 2D+ printer.

In my most recent state-of-the-art articles, I have been pointing to the preponderance of micro processes in the new technologies. Nanotech, ICT (information and communication technology), biotech, the new biologies, femto-photography, the new microscopies, surface science, all employ nano processes. And while there are some large developments—for example biomimetic slippery-skinned submarines and torpedoes—most such technologies take a micro trajectory. Even attack drones are much smaller than B-52s and many are bumblebee size. Surveillance devices detect micro vibrations through laser reading processes and a whole range of acoustic detectors find ways to penetrate ground surfaces, foliage and the like to produce clearer images. My *Acoustic Technics* (2015) points to medical diagnostic acoustic processes which acoustically display sounds which differentiate between healthy and malignant cells. Optic-acoustical surveillance technologies can even detect cement column vibrations to project what goes on inside a building. My physics colleague, Harold Metcalf, recently just missed a Nobel for his work in "trapping" individual atoms—he was the fourth on a team and Nobels can only be split three ways. Micro visualization is pervasive. Pill-sized cameras are used medically: swallowed and then these devices photograph the entire digestive track. Similarly in low-angle photography adumbrated with infrared, micro X-rays are used to examine paintings to determine how many times they have been retouched. And for affordable prices, one may buy an infrared attachment for a smartphone to photograph heat loss—my son-in-law just showed me how the biggest losses from his 18th-century house were from the basement sill area. These are all imaging media which as the dominant trajectory has it, are usually visual or audio-visual. See also Galit Wellner's *A Postphenomenological Inquiry of Cell Phones* (2016).

One can see here the temptations for techno-utopians. "Apps" such as the infrared photo device for a smartphone camera to detect heat loss are practical. But "enhancement" apps are also available, running from fantasy creatures in Pokémon games to "enhanced reality" apps for other forms of voyeur-about-town activity. Yet the very old and very mundane money-making activity drives much of this trajectory, epitomized in the recent meeting of business and political interests of the election.

With new media, multistability accelerates: the cellphone has audio capacity—a telephone—visual capacity—camera—text, Internet, many "apps" ad infinitum. As many have pointed out, it is a sort of electronic rather than mechanical "Swiss Army Knife." The just now developing Internet of Things, with more new media, opens the way to more ways to interfere—hacking possibilities multiply. Think of the intrusion-control possibilities for any sort of autonomous machine, like driverless cars or drones. Any watcher can also be watched. Any listener can also be heard. Or, anything which can be "controlled" can be counter-commanded by others.

But this is actually nothing new—at least in principle. In my own case, I grew up on an isolated Kansas farm. We did not get electricity until after WWII, but we did get a hard-wire, battery-powered phone line earlier, a community line. Our ring was one long three shorts, but we knew that anyone on the line could pick up and "listen in," and in keeping with rural culture everyone knows what everyone is doing, knew that certain people always listened in. Much later, after my undergraduate days, I spent a summer in Chicago in an urban studies project. I was hired by the Illinois Bell Company in a post-college job which entailed both manhole and pole wire work. One of my tools was a probe which could be stuck into the bundles of copper wires and if some wire had a conversation in progress, I could hear it. Of course one purpose of the tool was to avoid working on any "live" wire and work only on silent ones—but, like unintentional hacking, I could, in principle, listen in. From both these experiences a lesson was learned: this wire medium is not really private, it may at any time be heard by another. The same obviously applies to the Internet—so a reasonable question would be: Why would one ever treat such a medium as "private" and thus put on it any embarrassing or incriminating evidence? Yet, in the early days of the Internet, one also recalls the proliferation of "flaming" incidents still prolific in tweets and social media. Again, this past campaign illustrates profusely precisely this lack of caution and sense of consequence.

Look briefly at a spectrum of social media affects: sexting, selfies, earlier flaming, tweets, and all the sharing moves associated with these uses. In each case there is an exaggerated exhibitionism tendency. I have always been an anti-determinist regarding technologies. Technologies do not *make us do things as such*, but I have taken note of what I have called "inclinations." Technologies in use make certain actions easier than not. Older flaming: email makes the quick response easier. Not only is a quickly typed response easy, our emotions, if angry, are immediate and on the surface, it is easy to flame. Similarly, selfies with the camera cellphone are easy. Indeed all the phenomena listed are immediate and easy, and if somehow there is an inclination toward exhibitionism, then these inclinations are understandable. Escalate a level up: video selfies, in action, are only one step harder. They entail a minimal kind of casting. Take the adolescent drinking selfie video. A young person takes a self-video of himself or herself draining a bottle of alcohol—maybe thinking "cool" but not cautionarily thinking "future employers might not think 'cool.'" And then we reach what is hard. All these social media actions are easy and easy to record—but they are difficult to remove, particularly if already sent to a cloud storage or other permanent resource. Europe now rages with a right to remove items from the Internet, a right to be forgotten. Easy to get on, hard to get off; an asymmetry.

What emerges is a pattern of asymmetries and interrelations. Overall, electronically powered media exhibit many reciprocal interrelations. If you can hear or see the other, then it is possible also to be heard or seen. Asymmetries include the easy to get on, hard to get off phenomena, or also easy for one to broadcast widely, whether true or false, or the asymmetry used in this election cycle, tweets asymmetrically overwhelming traditional news sources. I have hinted in this foreword that while many of the new media remain immature, without balancing conventions, and thus easily enhance various exaggerations, it seems unlikely that any kind of restraining conventions will soon appear or overwhelm the distortions. Thus I wish to turn to a back-up notion: *the critical user*.

In its simplest form, a critical user is a self-aware user who is like a "buyer beware" while shopping. This is to be critically aware of what is asymmetrical and what is reciprocal. For those who like rules or guidelines, to know that to hear and to see entails the reciprocity of being heard and seen. To be hacked in some form is an ever-present possibility. At a higher level, one can develop sensitivities to any manner of "sales pitch" and can carry a sense of fact checking as part of one's media awareness. But, a warning—all critical awareness carries a resistance to instantaneity which characterizes new media.

Yet this is no different from the role of philosophy in any new enterprise. There is some degree of the cautionary in any critique. Yet this can also be a responsible burden of doing critique.

REFERENCES

Daily Mail. (n.d.). "Robert Rosenberger Describes Phantom Phone Vibration." MailOnline Video. http://www.dailymail.co.uk/embed/video/1240524.html

Ihde, D. (2015). *Acoustic Technics*. Lanham: Lexington Books.

Oreskes, N. and E. M. Conway. (2010). *Merchants of Doubt: How a Handful of Scientists Obscured the Truth on Issues from Tobacco Smoke to Global Warming*. New York: Bloomsbury Press.

Wellner, G. P. (2016). *A Postphenomenological Inquiry of Cell Phones: Genealogies, Meanings, and Becoming*. Lanham: Lexington Books.

Acknowledgements

What is it like to have our being in the midst of our technology? This is a central theme of postphenomenological work, and certainly this volume is no exception. *Postphenomenology and Media: Essays on Human–Media–World Relations* is largely about being in the midst, because today's world always seems to be in the midst of some kind of media technology.

But there are other ways we can be in the midst—in the hub, the focus, the core, and the thick of things. Immersion into a community or collaboration of like-minded individuals is also a way of being in the midst. This acknowledgement serves to recognize those who have allowed us to study at the hub of postphenomenology for some time now and to honor the many conversations and contributions we have been in the midst of, as we experience and try to build this growing philosophical movement.

The collective we fondly call the Postphenomenology Research Group is somewhat formally clustered around the "Postphenomenology and the Philosophy of Technology" book series but also informally gathered at conferences and research homes for many of its scholars. It is at the informal gatherings, often, after formal presentations have been given and drafts have been shared, that the authentic work of thinking through the postphenomenology framework occurs, and for this we are grateful. First, we'd like to thank Distinguished Professor of Philosophy, Emeritus, Stony Brook University of New York, Don Ihde, in big and small ways, for his foreword to this volume, and his work as an Executive Editor of the series. But more importantly, his vast knowledge, deep understanding, warm friendship, and continuous encouragement have meant the world to us. Not only Don encouraged us but also Robert Rosenberger, as a colleague and as the Editor-in-Chief and co-founder of the postphenomenology book series. In addition, Executive Editor Peter-Paul Verbeek has been an exemplary scholar in our postphenomenological circles and a source of inspiration to further expand the limits of postphenomenology. We have also had the good fortune to be in the midst of the group of scholars that came together from many countries and continents to form this volume. Many thanks for your stellar contributions Lars Botin, Pieter Lemmens, Nicola Liberati, Shoji Nagataki, Robert Rosenberger, Fernando Secomandi, Robert N. Spicer, Daniel Susser, and Heather Wiltse.

We would also like to thank Marc Veyrat, Société i Matériel, 2017 Artiste and Associate Professor in Digital Art at Université Savoie Mont Blanc, for the cover art for this volume. Explains Marc, "This i+D/sign (information + Design/sign) is what we could call a semantic terminal arc, that is to say a linguistic arc creating an undeniable visual tension between several signs. For each constituent element (each primary key) of the i+D/sign, the placement is achieved by bonding signifying associations; these being progressively operated through various attributes (color, signifying or informational potential, logotype). There is thus always a semantic functional dependence on a sign between two attributes (a) and (b) of this sign when the knowledge of a value of the attribute (a) makes it possible to find a value of the attribute (b). On this signifying junction table producing the semiosis of this i+D/sign, the key identifying these attributes; what allows us visually to identify them depends on the signifying potentiality of the links put in form—between (a) and (b)—by this linguistic collage." The image has pulled together nicely the emergent themes in this volume.

Obviously this book could not have been realized without the good work of the staff of Lexington Books, especially Jana Hodges-Kluck and her staff.

And finally, we would like to thank our media technologies that enable us as part of the Postphenomenology Research Group to meet online and continue the face-to-face discussions in many other digital ways.

Introduction

"What Media Do"

Yoni Van Den Eede, Stacey O. Irwin, and Galit Wellner

Not so long ago, typical illustrations about the use of contemporary media would go like this:

> You get up in the morning, put on clothing, and pour yourself a cup of coffee. Then you start checking your phone for messages, put on the TV, check your e-mails, read the news online,….

This little stage setting, of course, is meant to underscore the ubiquity of digital media and information and communication technologies (ICTs) in our lives. Nowadays we're more and more forced to adjust our illustrations, for instance as follows:

> You get up in the morning. Or no, wait, before you get up, you have already checked your phone for new messages. Or no, wait, before waking up, you might have been tracking your sleeping patterns via your smartphone or a dedicated device. That device might even have woken you up at the right moment in your sleep cycle….

There seems to be a movement "inward" here. In a literal-physical sense, media are moving into our bodies, or at least into our bodily activity and behavior. They are getting "closer." It takes less and less deliberate action on our part to engage with media or ICTs. No longer do we need to place ourselves behind a computer to go online; we carry "the online" constantly in our pockets or on our wrists. It is always there, at our fingertips.

This is exhilarating, but we might easily forget that corresponding to this process is also a movement "outward." And if that is not really manifest just yet, a near-future illustration might unfold like this:

> Your sleep-monitoring device, connected to your home Wi-Fi network, tells your coffee machine you will be woken up in the next phase of light sleep—time to start percolating. The heating system has already switched itself on based on that same information. But wait, at that very moment a traffic accident happens on your route to work. Algorithms start calculating the projected traffic jams for the next three hours. The cloud, organically pouring into your home network, transmits that info onto your devices, while you are still blissfully asleep. You will never be able to arrive at your morning appointment on time, the system determines for you, so an automatic cancellation message is sent to your contact (explaining in detail the reasons and proposing another date for the meeting). But wait, your extended machinic consciousness notes now that you have been building up some sleep deprivation in the last couple of days. Since there is really nothing else to do at this time, the system "decides" to let you sleep for another series of cycles. Percolating and heating are put on halt. Somewhat later, you wake up, feeling refreshed. A computer voice tells you your schedule has been rearranged....

The scene may appear like science fiction, but developments of this type are on the horizon. In fact, the illustration might be obsolesced even quicker than we think, as self-driving cars may someday—ideally—make road accidents rare.

What does this tell us? Media creep upon us. But they also spread their tentacles. They flow "in between," are woven throughout our existence. *Where* are they actually? *What* are they actually? How do they relate to, impact upon, withdraw from human action, experience, awareness? These are all complex questions with which we are confronted in our contemporary world and can expect to be dealing even more intensely in the future.

In this volume we investigate these issues by deploying the framework and insights of postphenomenology.

POSTPHENOMENOLOGY AND MEDIA

Postphenomenology is a branch in philosophy of technology that has in recent years attracted ever more attention among a variety of scholars who have found in its concepts and images ways to fruitfully express their insights. Postphenomenology, as developed first and foremost by Don Ihde, stays grounded in classic phenomenology, hermeneutics, and pragmatism, and so still revolves around central notions such as perception, embodiment, practice (or praxis), experience, and interpretation. But it "updates" these notions in order to put them to work for the philosophical study of technologies and their usage. Technologies are seen to transform things such as perception and interpretation in particular ways. Our experiences are "technologically mediated," our lifeworld is "technologically saturated," and the empirically oriented methodologies of postphenomenology are crafted to map the specificities of this saturation and mediation.

Yet it is striking that postphenomenology has up until now, notwithstanding a few exceptions and beginnings (more on them shortly), paid relatively little attention to the developments in *media* hinted at above. Certainly given the core theory of technological mediation, one could suspect a more direct focus on *mediation*, as "what media do"—to paraphrase Peter-Paul Verbeek's book title, *What Things Do* (2005). Instead, postphenomenology has focused first and foremost on technologies, with media perhaps being implicitly considered a technology. But the distinctions between these terms, if they were ever clear, are blurring, as was demonstrated in the foreword and as we will shortly explicate. Moreover, we might be in need of, paradoxically, at the same time a clearer *and* a wider definition of media as such, in terms of these developments.

We believe thus that "mediation theory"—as the postphenomenological conceptual framework is sometimes referred to[1]—should shed its light on media more specifically. While media and their current evolution may confuse us, postphenomenology might bring order in the chaos and can provide a theoretical framework for media and technology. The postphenomenological toolbox holds many conceptual instruments that can be put to good use here: human-technology-world relations, the transparency versus opacity distinction, embodiment, multistability, focus-field-fringe distinctions, and more. Postphenomenology may contribute to existing approaches to media by invoking new questions that push forward our understanding of the effects of contemporary media on humans and our surrounding world. But in parallel, and in a self-reflexive moment, we can and must also ask: How well is postphenomenology suited for a substantial treatment of media? To that extent, thinking about media is also a way of taking postphenomenology further.

In this introduction we will provide a short overview of some basic concepts in postphenomenology. We will discuss the beginnings of media analyses in the postphenomenological literature. These will serve as a springboard to consider some directions to push postphenomenology forward and hint at the possible contribution of this book. Finally, we will outline the central issues with which the contributors to the book are engaged.

BASICS: THE POSTPHENOMENOLOGICAL TOOLBOX

There are excellent introductions to the postphenomenological research field available (Rosenberger and Verbeek 2015; Ihde 2009); no need to reiterate these in all-too great detail here.[2] Still, we do want to put in place a few orientation points for the investigations, and describe some of postphenomenology's central concepts as most of the authors in this volume engage with them.

Postphenomenology, as said, originates in Ihde's oeuvre. Ihde has crafted postphenomenology as a combination of phenomenology, pragmatism, and empirical studies of technology such as STS (Science and Technology Studies). The result is a framework that is, in his words, antiessentialist, interrelational, and non-subjectivistic (Ihde 2012; Ihde 2009; see also Rosenberger 2016). As its starting points it nevertheless takes some central notions of classic Husserlian phenomenology: intentionality, bracketing, and variations. In opposition to the modernist contraposition of subject and object, phenomenology assumes observer and observed to be basically interrelated. However one chooses to frame the relation between a conscious thinking being and the world, at any time that consciousness is and must be aimed *at something*. Consciousness always has something as its content. This characteristic, called intentionality, Ihde terms the "*foundational correlational rule* of phenomenology" (1998, 16; original emphasis). Simply put, it accounts for how observer and observed "go together," how the "subject" is related to the "object": consciousness and world are "correlates."

That does not mean that the subject or observer could achieve something like a clear or neutral view on the observed. On the contrary, our perception is always shaped and determined by socio-cultural conditions, presuppositions, and learned habits, and these in fact often harbor remnants of our modernist, for a large part Cartesian heritage. The phenomenological technique of bracketing or *epoché* is meant to put aside exactly these "ordinary assumptions and sediments" (Ihde 2012, 74), the complex of which is known as the "natural attitude." Leaving behind the natural attitude and acquiring the phenomenological attitude instead, nonetheless, requires effort. Paradoxically, it involves looking for and describing as many as possible aspects of a phenomenon.

In this sense, doing phenomenology entails something of a playful, creative exercise, although one should go about it in a principally rigorous way. Ihde outlines four rules of conduct in *Experimental Phenomenology*: (1) attend to experiential phenomena as they appear; (2) describe instead of explain; (3) equalize or horizontalize all phenomena in their immediate givenness, that is, treat them all as equally real; and (4) find invariant or structural features of the phenomena (2012, 18–22). Nevertheless, in order to find structural invariants, one must in the first instance explore variants or variations—like when one walks around a house and tries to take in as many aspects and dimensions of it as possible, with the aim of grasping precisely the idea of *this* very house.

This last point is crucial, as here the Ihdean framework departs significantly from Husserlian orthodoxy. In distinguishing what is variant from what is invariant, Husserl claims to be able to determine "essential structures" or "essences," but Ihde purports to find something altogether different: multistability. Here we are reminded of his famous exercises in looking for variations in phenomena such as the Necker cube (Ihde 2012, 63–76). Traditional experiments in psychology usually outline two variations, that are in Ihde's terminology "passive": they appear without much effort on the observer's part. In the case of the Necker cube, this concerns the—three-dimensional—gestalt switch between a "top" and a "bottom" view. When one, however, applies a more "active" form of observation, Ihde proposes, more variations become possible. For instance, the Necker cube may also be perceived two-dimensionally as an insect trapped in a hexagon. The exploration of such variations that exceed the binary possibilities to which passive perception stays confined, often requires some work of the imagination: some story needs to be told in order to let the image "appear." Nevertheless, once variations have been discovered, one can relatively easily switch between them, while each, as such, can be held in view on a fairly stable basis—hence the multistability of experiential phenomena.

This project of finding surprising variant gestalts is of great importance as it shows the "hidden potential" of phenomena. "Variations 'possibilize' phenomena" (Ihde 2012, 23). But even more importantly, the notion of multistability is central in Ihde's philosophy of technology. In putting phenomenology to work in the context of technologically enhanced perception, for instance in the case of scientific imaging technologies like the telescope, Ihde eventually finds that technologies *mediate* the human-world correlation. Here the addition of pragmatism and empirical technology studies to the framework becomes crucial. First, technologies are always embedded in some practical situation, in a praxis, that usually involves some level of embodiment. Even the handling of a purely "visual" instrument such as a telescope requires some bodily technique or incorporation. Second, technologies are no neutral means or media because they shape our perception and the ways in which we experience the world. But, that does not mean that they wholly determine us, as more classic philosophers of technology would have it: they are "non-neutral." This we learn by looking at specific practices in which technologies may be deployed for certain usages, but are soon readapted, by users for example, to suit other purposes. All across the human-world correlation, to put it in grand terms, multistability reigns: praxes as well as technologies, by the logics of variational theory, harbor multiple different forms, of which one or another at any time may become at least temporarily stable.

All of this, in Ihde's work as well as in phenomenology, is in the first instance grounded in an ontological analysis. Of course, the framework has epistemological and practical consequences, but these sprout from this ontological base: human/subject/noesis and world/object/noema are essentially interrelated. None exist as autonomous entities. What is more, their (inter) relation—through for instance the mediation of technologies—constitutes them, and not the other way around. The *mediation makes the mediators*, not vice versa. However, the ontological differs from the methodological, and so the principal methodological guideline from phenomenology is: "[t]he analysis begins with *what* appears (noema) and then moves *reflexively* toward its *how* of appearing [i.e., noesis]" (Ihde 2012, 31; original emphasis). In other words, in following the rule of conduct that we attend exclusively to the phenomena that present themselves to consciousness, we always find the world first. The subject is enigmatic (ibid., 11). Only "reflexively" we discover the thinking "I." (Notice that this entails the exact opposite procedure of Descartes' "methodic doubt" of the *cogito*, that poses a thinking ego as certain and from there deduces the rest of the world.) In this way, (post)phenomenology is non-subjectivistic and non-introspectivist.

***

There are obviously different accounts of the human-world interrelation and different branches of phenomenology that provide different angles—cognitive, praxical, existential, or linguistic-hermeneutic. Ihde, in a pragmatist spirit, blends all these angles in an approach that perhaps has as its pinnacle the famous analysis of diverse forms of human-technology-world relations known under the rubric of the "phenomenology of technics" (Ihde 1990, 72ff.). For, it is not only a choice of theory which aspect gets most highlighted: some technologies happen to relate more to our bodies, others function mostly on a hermeneutic basis, and so on—hence Ihde's distinction between four relations: embodiment, hermeneutic, alterity, and background relations.

In embodiment relations one "incorporates" the technology. The technology is embodied, such as in the case of glasses. As someone who wears them knows well, glasses—luckily!—mostly disappear from view. One focuses on the things, on "world" instead. The intentionality is directed at world, while user and technology become "merged" to an extent, at least phenomenologically speaking.

This is different in hermeneutic relations. There the visible/invisible border shifts, so to speak, in the direction of technology and world. The technology is positioned for a human being to interpret, to "read" world. One example concerns the dashboard of a car. By definition one simply cannot perceive what happens in or around the car's engine, especially while driving. So one "reads" the situation on the meters and dials in the dashboard. Intentionality is now aimed at the technology (the metering instruments) *through* which one learns something about world (the engine). But in a phenomenological sense, technology and world are hardly distinguishable; they become merged.

It should be clear that in the description of these different types of relations, it does not only matter what the human subject *does* with a technology in relation to a world: embodying or interpreting. Just as important is what appears and disappears. Ihde in *Technology and the Lifeworld* conceptualizes this in terms of transparency and opacity—and as we will see, these notions are about to play a crucial role in this volume. There is always a balance between transparent and opaque elements in a human-technology-world relation, like communicating vessels: where transparency diminishes, opacity increases, and vice versa. For the wearer of glasses, the instrument is transparent, but the world is opaque (one cannot see "through" it as one does with the glasses). For the reader of dials, the technology-world unit is opaque. One does not get a clear perception of the car's engine; any perception of it is always enmeshed with the instrument. But in between instrument and world (the engine), some kind of transparency comes about: one sees indeed *through* the instrument. It cannot be stressed enough that Ihde's analysis of human-technology-world relations must (also) be seen as an investigation of such transparency-opacity ratios, situated on a spectrum of sorts in which however pure transparency can never be realized.[3]

This is made even clearer by looking at the other two relation types that Ihde outlines. With alterity relations, the transparency-opacity ratio is different again. One interacts with a technology as if it were an "other," such as with an ATM machine. World disappears here almost completely from view. The interaction is exclusively with the machine as such. Technology becomes opaque, world transparent.

In the case of background relations, finally, the technology becomes transparent, while world takes on an opacity again. The prime example is a central heating system, that just sits there without us noticing it except maybe for a hum sometimes or when the temperature is off. We just mind our business while these background technologies (another example is a refrigerator) do their work unnoticed.[4]

In classic phenomenological terms this spectrum can also be made sense of by way of the terms figure, field, and fringe, as Ihde points out (Ihde 2012, 40; see also Rosenberger 2014). Figure is what we focus on, the target of intentionality. However, a figure always relates to a wider ground or field within which it is situated. There is never a figure in isolation. But the focus on a figure (opaque) presupposes the invisibility of a ground (transparent). We can nevertheless try to get that environing context, the field, in view by practicing variational analysis. But in turn the field ravels out into an even wider context: the horizon or fringe, what is situated really on the border of our perceptual grasp. Here, too, we can attempt to widen our perception, and get a grasp on the fringe, but it takes great effort. This three-component structure helps to point out that it is often not just a matter of balancing *two* (in)visibilities. When one invisibility is put into focus, another one looms—literally—on the horizon. And, this structure can be made instrumental in the context of an investigation of media as well.

BEGINNINGS: POSTPHENOMENOLOGICAL RESEARCH INTO MEDIA

As mentioned, the investigation and analysis of media have remained in the fringes of postphenomenology. Yet Ihde himself already for example in *Technology and the Lifeworld* discusses media as we commonly know them—for example, mass media, television—to a considerable extent. Looking somewhat more closely, one notices a tight interwovenness between his mentions of media such as television on one hand, and the conceptual dichotomy he makes between microperception and macroperception on the other hand. Microperception is what his "phenomenology of technics" is centrally concerned with: the immediately given in the "here" and "now." But this "here and now" is always affected by larger socio-cultural contexts: macroperception. And the two types of perception are essentially intertwined. A good part of *Technology and the Lifeworld* is actually devoted to the scrutiny of that intertwinement. And implicitly a lot of the contributions in this book build on Ihde's analysis of micro vs. macro dynamics, looking at what goes on "beyond" immediate use. A focus on media, we will find, in a sense forces us to do so.

The beginnings of a postphenomenological approach to media can be found in several corners of the postphenomenological household, so to speak. The editors of this volume have done and are doing work in this area. Yoni Van Den Eede (2012) fuses postphenomenology with among others the media theory of Marshall McLuhan, an exercise resulting in an encompassing "medial" ontological outlook; an effort he continues and extends in his chapter in this book. Galit Wellner with her *A Postphenomenological Inquiry of Cell Phones* (2016) has crafted the first comprehensive postphenomenological study of the cellphone, diving also deep into ontological waters and showing how the cellphone as a technology dovetails with some of our most essential metaphysical assumptions. Stacey O. Irwin, then, focuses full-force on digital media in her book of that title, *Digital Media: Human–Technology Connection* (2016). Exploring and mapping the "technological texture" with which digital media overlay our lives nowadays, she collects an array of case studies informed by postphenomenology.

Of course these are not the only ones. As editors we selected the contributors to this volume on the basis of an interest we knew they have in media or of work they are doing in the area. All authors have related their research in one way or another to media, and the investigations in this volume can be seen as either a further surfacing of what were maybe already dormant foci, or a consolidation and elaboration of clearly present conceptual angles.

PUSHING FORWARD: THE POSTPHENOMENOLOGY OF MEDIA

The reader might ask: What makes media such a special case that we should delineate it/them from the "ordinary" treatment of technology by postphenomenology? Is it appropriate and proportional to reserve a special place for media, as this book does? This leads us straight to the fundamental question: What are media in fact?

Traditionally media—also "the media"[5]—are defined as "means of communication": press, radio, television, and so on. In everyday discourse, media are still largely thought of in this way. Yet Marshall McLuhan, usually regarded as one of the first media theorists (if not the first), already in the 1960s widened this classic definition substantially. His *Understanding Media* (2003) from 1964 is filled with case studies of all sorts of "media" such as clothing, housing, roads, clocks, weapons—things many people would rather categorize under, if anything, "technology." Indeed, McLuhan simply equates the terms medium and technology (the logical implication also being that his famous phrase "the medium is the message" thus counts for technologies just as much). By the end of his career, McLuhan even winds up defining media as all things made by humans: all artifacts—material as well as immaterial. Coffee pots, electric guitars, consumerism, the state—all of these "things" are "made" by humans. Hence they are media. Hence, and most importantly, they *act* as media: they do "what media do."

The McLuhanist definition is so broad that it might provide little conceptual leverage. If everything is a medium, what's the use of a definition at all? Nonetheless, from a certain viewpoint, some recent technological developments have been validating McLuhan's approach (this is also one of the main reasons for the revival of his thought in the last years). If many things were not already media in the fundamental-philosophical sense that McLuhan was envisioning, then they became or are now becoming *medial* in—if only—a practical-technical sense.

Media as we know them are starting to become "blurred." We already referred to this evolution at the beginning. With the onset of mobile communication technology, media are no longer "over there"; they are moving toward us, into us. Looking at the history of media, one perceives almost the evolution of an organism becoming more and more complex, diverse, and ubiquitous. While only half a century ago well-defined media dominated our lives—books, newspapers, radio, television—now media are becoming increasingly invisible, transparent, "seamless," interactive, and predictive (they "guesstimate" our next move). Thanks to contemporary technologies such as the cellphone, media have become not only what we read, hear, and see but also what we constantly have around us.

In parallel, things that were not usually perceived as media are now acquiring an "information and communication" or ICT character by taking on traits formerly reserved for media in the classic definition alone. Think of developments such as Internet of Things, "smart" homes, and location-based services. Through the incorporation of new technologies like radio-frequency identification (RFID) tags, sensors, and microchips, previously "dumb" things such as household appliances, medical tools, automobiles, or even clothing are acquiring a form of "intelligence" as they are taken up in a data network and made to transmit and process information, algorithmically react to events, or generally act and decide "on their own." Here then is a movement "outward."

As a result, media are becoming a significant part of our everyday lives in very real, very tangible ways, but paradoxically, we cannot be so sure anymore about what they are (if we ever were). Instrumental in this context is obviously the shift from analog to digital. It is "the digital" that has made a lot of these technological developments possible from the start. Media by way of omnipresent digital networks become fused with our everyday lives to the extent that they are indistinguishable from it, but simultaneously—because of this invisibility—we partly lose our grip on them. This is a problem tailored to the phenomenological outlook, and surely, the instruments provided by classic phenomenology already offer a useful toolbox for the study of media; witness the important work done by such organizations as the Society for Phenomenology and Media in the last decade and a half (see Majkut and Canán 2010). But postphenomenology is eminently placed to make sense of these developments, given how it is specifically oriented toward an analysis of transparency-opacity ratios, multistability, multiple types of human-technology-world relations, perception and understanding, micro- and macroperception dynamics.

***

So what are the central issues for a postphenomenology of media, then? As such, this kind of investigation cannot but bring several different angles together. There are fundamental reflections: How to define media? Is there a difference between media and technology(/ies)? Can media ground an ontology? What role do media play in the production of knowledge (media as, to use Ihde's term, "epistemological engines")? Of course we need to look into typical phenomenological themes: perception, understanding, interpretation;

media and the senses, media and ("expanded") hermeneutics. There should be a substantial consideration of those aspects that have started to characterize our contemporary media environments: What is the status of "the digital"? Is the digital something new? How should we look upon the history of media from a postphenomenological standpoint? Thus shifting toward a more comprehensive inquiry of societal implications, we can begin to ask how media—in whatever sense—are related to morality, culture(s), politics, to name a few. And of course, the postphenomenological framework can be deployed for the analysis of specific contemporary problems in relation to media (perhaps rather in the more classic sense), such as surveillance, user empowerment, and the (online and/or "quantified") self. All across these thematic angles, we will find the central thread of multistability. This also means that we do not, perhaps, need clear-cut, unified, linear definitions. We might just find that most of these issues might be multistable in themselves, as are the technologies and media environments under scrutiny.

In a truly (post)phenomenological spirit, though, we should begin by attending to the phenomena that impinge themselves upon us in a direct fashion: our current media environments—their most striking features including ubiquity, digitality, and seamlessness. Immediately, one is confronted then with those hotly debated issues such as privacy, the impact of digital media—for example e-readers—on cognitive skills, social-psychological effects of social media use, the Anthropocene, and the like. The postphenomenological toolkit can be put to good use to cast a new light on these issues by way of an encompassing analysis of how these media environments are actually constituted and constituting, and generally how they "work."

In their ubiquity, subsequently, and as said, contemporary digital media tend to disappear from view to a certain extent. What "part" of media do we perceive, and which other characteristics go unnoticed? Exactly the finding that some things escape our grasp seems to be one of the most important problems we are facing today in our usage of media. As already suggested, postphenomenology's transparency-opacity ratio analysis can be put to work in the context of understanding media's visible vs. hidden aspects. Moreover, it can help to delineate how not only perception, but also action is shaped by this dynamic, how media extend human capacities, and how this extension feedbacks upon those capacities.

This theme then organically flows over another central issue: as we extend ourselves into media, we need to ask how media impact upon our bodily constitution, on bodily experience, and on perception. We thus should ask, along the lines of Ihde's "phenomenology of technics," which kinds of human-technology-world relations do media take part in, and conversely, can (contemporary, digital) media teach us something about human-technology-world relations? Are they changing the nature of those relations? What kind of "hybrids" are we, or have we become, exactly? Even taking a step further, we might ask whether the body is not, or is at least becoming, a medium itself.

And so as we move gradually from the "world" component, via technology/media, to finding at last the "I" of the investigating subject, we should dive still deeper, toward ontological and metaphysical depths. This is moreover a good way of weaving together and synthesizing some of the insights developed in thinking about the issues above. Questions at stake here are: what *are* media actually, on the most fundamental level? To what extent should we regard them as building blocks of reality? And which take does postphenomenology develop on this matter? Moreover, inversely, do we need to adapt or fine-tune the postphenomenological framework on the basis of the analyses deployed here in function of media (in either a generic or a contemporary-digital sense)?

OVERVIEW OF THE VOLUME

The volume is divided into three parts. Part I looks at our current digital media environments somewhat from a distance, in order to get a general feel of the issues we're dealing with. As such, by scouting the perimeters of the domain under scrutiny, this part provides a framework for the rest of the investigation. Part II then goes into more detail and develops, true to the postphenomenological mission, case studies of specific technologies/media. This part of the collection offers some reflections on digital media with which many people are familiar. Following this, we become a bit more theoretical and self-reflexive, and ask in Part III to which extent postphenomenology as a conceptual toolbox itself should be fine-tuned and/or expanded to be able to adequately deal with media, digital media/ICT and media environments.

Part I Heather Wiltse sets the tone by attempting to grasp an essential aspect of new media technologies: as they surpass mere human intentionality, we need new ways of understanding them. Her notion of "mediating infrastructures" is meant to make sense of the way in which these media are starting to live a life of their own, so to speak. Working toward the formulation of that notion, Wiltse explores the boundaries and overlaps between media, technology and—introducing an important term for the study of media—environment, to arrive at an intriguing matrix that seeks to map the complex interactions between those realms.

Continuing the spirit of critical distance, Daniel Susser looks at a crucial difference between the physical and the digital world. While the physical world is opaque—our bodies literally bump into it—the digital world is transparent: unlike the action-reaction patterns we know from physical reality, the effects of our digital actions often stay hidden. But this has far-reaching consequences for the possibilities of developing good behavior online. Susser analyzes the situation meticulously and offers possible solutions that are set to (re)introduce feedback processes into the digital "flow," coercing users into awareness and self-reflexivity.

The following two chapters elaborate these themes further, but each in their own way. Shoji Nagataki's chapter zooms in on the body, deploying the notion of the "body as medium" and asking how in—impending—times of human enhancement the body will play a role in constituting a sense of self. Will robots or humanoids be able to have a real sense of identity? Nagataki provides, via a survey of some instances of science-fiction literature through the (post)phenomenological lens, a challenging answer: the identity of a person is constituted by having memories of oneself, but also by memories of one's environment, and by others having memories about the person.

Nicola Liberati then closes off this part by taking a closer look at the transparency-opacity dichotomy, coupling it to the concept of magic. He does this by way of Arthur C. Clarke's third law of technology—"any sufficiently advanced technology is indistinguishable from magic"—and helpful illustrations from fantasy and magic performances. New digital media, Liberati proposes, have the effect of appearing as "magical" to their users. On the one hand this is because of the way their workings stay invisible—transparent—and appear like "sleight of hand." On the other hand, the "magic" is also grounded in an opacity: we do not understand the way those media work.

Part II Continuing the discussion on transparency and opacity, and at the same time kicking off the second part that revolves around case studies of specific media technologies, Robert Spicer investigates three cases: the Apple Watch, drones, and virtual reality. These may not have much to do with each other at first sight, but superposed onto each other—Spicer talks of them in terms of concentric circles—their analysis exquisitely demonstrates how different media technologies play out differently with regard to transparency-opacity ratios, in function of their distance from "us." On a fundamental level, it helps to describe how digital media relate to the visible/invisible dichotomy.

Stacey Irwin neatly continues this thread, with a case study of the mobile GoPro camera from the perspective of the evolution of "mediamaking" and its tight relation to multimedia. Multimedia in a sense instantiate multistability as such, an idea Irwin conceptualizes through the notion of "multimedia stabilities." The concept, together with the notion of the postphenomenological pivot (elaborated in recent times by Kyle Whyte), can help to clarify how contemporary multimedia technologies—cameras, visual editing tools, et cetera—take their place in the historical trajectory they have been and are tracing.

The chapter by Fernando Secomandi takes the discussion on media multistabilities further. He studies the interaction with the visual interface of a service designed by the Dutch corporation Philips to help people self-track their fitness activities. Secomandi observes the work of designers and programmers "from the inside," at the stage in which the interface is still being designed, developed, and tested. This makes him eminently placed to map the multistability of digital images in relation to (actual or anticipated) user experience during design practice. What becomes clear is how pertinent the notion of intersubjectivity is in this context.

Robert Rosenberger concludes this part with a study of e-readers from the perspective of Ihde's analysis of human-technology-world relations, complemented by his own work on how technologies mediate a user's field of awareness. As a counterpoint to his argument, he engages with Anne Mangen's critique of "hyperlink-laden text." Arguing against the technological determinism inherent in that critique, Rosenberger explicates how reading practices cannot be just the effect of the technological device, but are also rooted in long-developed, sedimented habits, and can thus be potentially changed.

Part III The third part takes stock, and entails sometimes critical, sometimes self-reflexive inquiries. Authors here examine the postphenomenological framework itself and/or supplement it with new approaches or perspectives, as ignited by thinking on media. Lars Botin in a wide-ranging, provocative exploration asks how we should relate to the ongoing acceleration of media environments. Prominent voices on this theme, such as Paul Virilio's and Hartmut Rosa's, often tend to be pessimistic. In line with postphenomenology, that would claim that technologies are not harbingers of doom—they are malleable and open to positive change—Botin searches another way, through an exploration of the notion of the sublime. From this angle, ever-accelerating media can be seen as forms of "sublimating" ourselves in a constructive manner.

Pieter Lemmens also moves "beyond" and critically approaches postphenomenology as a theory, superposing the work of French philosopher of technology Bernard Stiegler onto it. Unlike postphenomenology, Lemmens argues, Stiegler is able to make sense of the concept of technology *as such*, as that which conditions our existence. And that can exactly be brought out by zooming in on digital media, or with Stiegler, "mnemotechnologies." Lemmens lays bare how the two frameworks dovetail with each other and how they diverge, showing that an analysis of media may press postphenomenology into critically scrutinizing its ontological underpinnings.

Still another kind of "going beyond" is offered by Galit Wellner. Observing that the discussion on media has been dominated by attention to hermeneutic issues and thus the "reading phase" of media, she proposes to supplement this viewpoint with a thorough investigation of their writing or recording modalities and histories. Employing amongst others the "phenomenology of technics" and extensions of it by Verbeek, Liberati, and Wiltse,

Wellner's chapter weaves together a lot of the threads developed throughout the volume. In the process she, too, helps to make clear how digital media urge postphenomenology to "adapt."

Yoni Van Den Eede, finally, continues this synthesizing effort as well as the "expanding" exercise by looking again at the definition of media and valuing the notion of "everything as a medium." His starting point is the challenge recently posed to postphenomenology by Diane Michelfelder to attend more to the "world" component in human-technology-world relations. In order to meet that challenge, Van Den Eede suggests, postphenomenology can join forces with two other frameworks that are actually much less removed from it than one would expect: McLuhanist media theory and Graham Harman's object-oriented philosophy.

NOTES

1. Especially Verbeek (2005) uses this term, but the concept of mediation by technology (or technological mediation) is already elaborated in Ihde's *Technology and the Lifeworld* (1990).
2. See also for helpful collections showcasing the diversity of the field, the companion volumes Friis and Crease 2015 and Rosenberger and Verbeek 2015b, and Selinger 2006.
3. An important lesson in itself; see Ihde's admonishments with regard to the wish for "total transparency" (1990, 75).
4. Additional relations have been developed based on the I-technology-world formula, as for example in the work of Verbeek (2008).
5. Or media used in the singular form: "media *is*" instead of "media *are*."

REFERENCES

Friis, J. K. B. O. and R. P. Crease (eds.). (2015). *Technoscience and Postphenomenology: The Manhattan Papers*. Lanham: Lexington Books.

Ihde, D. (1990). *Technology and the Lifeworld: From Garden to Earth*. Bloomington: Indiana University Press.

———. (1998). *Expanding Hermeneutics: Visualism in Science*. Evanston (IL): Northwestern University Press.

———. (2009). *Postphenomenology and Technoscience: The Peking University Lectures*. Albany (NY): State University of New York Press.

———. (2012). *Experimental Phenomenology: Multistabilities*. Second Edition. Albany (NY): State University of New York Press.

Irwin, S. O. (2016). *Digital Media: Human–Technology Connection*. Lanham: Lexington Books.

Majkut, P. and A. J. L. Carrillo Canán (eds.). (2010). *Phenomenology and Media: An Anthology of Essays from Glimpse, Publication of the Society for Phenomenology and Media, 1999–2008*. Bucharest: Zeta Books.

McLuhan, M. (2003). *Understanding Media: The Extensions of Man*. Critical Edition. Corte Madera: Gingko Press.

Rosenberger, R. (2014). "The Phenomenological Case for Stricter Regulation of Cell Phones and Driving." *Techné: Research in Philosophy and Technology* 18 (1–2): 20–47.

———. (2016). "Notes on a Nonfoundational Phenomenology of Technology." *Foundations of Science* Online First (January): 1–24. doi:10.1007/s10699–015–9480–5.

Rosenberger, R. and P.-P. Verbeek. (2015a). "A Field Guide to Postphenomenology." In R. Rosenberger and P.-P. Verbeek (eds.), *Postphenomenological Investigations: Essays on Human–Technology Relations*. Lanham: Lexington Books, 9–41.

——— (eds.). (2015b). *Postphenomenological Investigations: Essays on Human–Technology Relations*. Lanham: Lexington Books.

Selinger, E. (ed.). (2006). *Postphenomenology: A Critical Companion to Ihde*. Albany (NY): State University of New York Press.

Van Den Eede, Y. (2012). *Amor Technologiae: Marshall McLuhan as Philosopher of Technology—Toward a Philosophy of Human-Media Relationships*. Brussels: VUBPRESS.

Verbeek, P.-P. (2008). "Cyborg Intentionality: Rethinking the Phenomenology of Human–Technology Relations." *Phenomenology and the Cognitive Sciences* 7 (3): 387–95.

———. (2005). *What Things Do: Philosophical Reflections on Technology, Agency, and Design*. Trans. R. P. Crease. University Park (PA): The Pennsylvania State University Press.

Wellner, G. P. (2016). *A Postphenomenological Inquiry of Cell Phones: Genealogies, Meanings, and Becoming*. Lanham: Lexington Books.

Part 1

Exploring Media Environments with Postphenomenology

Chapter 1

Mediating (Infra)structures

Technology, Media, Environment

Heather Wiltse

When asked recently if Facebook is an "editor" of news, founder and chief Mark Zuckerberg responded: "No, we're a tech company, we're not a media company."[1] He went on to say that although Facebook builds the "tools," they "do not produce any of the content." But he also later described social media as "the most diverse form of media that has ever existed" (Fiveash 2016). In light of these comments, one might be excused for being rather confused about what, exactly, Facebook is. Yet this distinction can actually have crucial consequences for how Facebook operates. Zuckerberg's insistence that Facebook is a technology company came in the context of European leaders calling on it to police extremism by quickly removing hateful and illegal posts; but if it does this and is thus labeled a "publisher" it would then be open to domestic libel laws (Fiveash 2016).

Choosing to think in terms of technology, media, or something else also has implications for analysis and understanding, for highlighting certain aspects and dynamics while leaving others in the unexamined background. And, as evidenced by Zuckerberg's comments, many of the things we now live with can be viewed in multiple ways; there is no obvious, given, or unproblematic starting point. Yet there do seem to be significant aspects of our technologically textured lifeworld that call for responsible and response-able (Haraway 2015; Wiltse et al. 2016) accounts of the increasingly pervasive and sophisticated things that can be described using words such as digital, computational, media, networked, sensing, responsive, customized, active, and smart; and for which "use" might involve actions such as clicking, liking, sharing, curating, monitoring, remixing, collecting, sending, reading, creating, profiling, collaborating, perceiving, configuring, tracking, tagging, finding, interpreting, embedding, targeting, customizing, and connecting.

Of course, these sociotechnical practices *are* studied and accounted for in many different ways; and since they involve and implicate many different cultural forms and practices, technologies, application areas, and so on, there is a confluence of many different perspectives that are brought to bear. In fact, the present book is an example of such a confluence, combining the perspectives of postphenomenology and media. With all of this attention and combination of perspectives it might seem that there should be, in total, quite thorough coverage of contemporary technological things and the practices they support. Yet one potentially troubling consideration is that analytic lenses come "pre-loaded" with basic conceptions of the nature of their objects of study, ones that have been developed in relation to earlier cultural forms and practices and which may thus not be best suited for highlighting qualitatively different aspects of newer ones. For example, Heidegger's (2010) famous tool analysis and example of the hammer, how it becomes present-to-hand or ready-to-hand through use, has been highly influential and is still relevant in many ways; and yet the transparency of a technology that can occur in skilled use and occlude awareness of it as such is of a somewhat different order when we consider digital tools that not only recede from awareness in use, but are actually inaccessible.[2] Another concern is that although different perspectives may relate to some of the same terminology or ostensive objects of study they may in fact have quite different conceptions of what these objects actually are, making their simple combination potentially problematic. For example, a smartphone is something that is possible to point to as an object of study; but whether it is conceived of as a medium for communication or as a technological tool has implications for the conceptual and analytic frames that are used. This will be further elaborated later.

There are also more fundamental reasons to care about the consequences of the concepts we use. One is that they inevitably draw our attention to certain things while occluding others. As Deleuze and Guattari put it, "a concept always has components that can prevent the appearance of another concept or, on the contrary, that can themselves appear only at the cost of the disappearance of other concepts" (Deleuze et al. 1994, 31). Going even further, according to Barad's agential realist account, the material and the discursive are intra-actively constituted. As she says, "*discursive practices are specific material (re)configurings of the world through which local determinations of boundaries, properties, and meanings are differentially enacted*" (Barad 2003, 820–821; original emphasis). This means in turn that we are all accountable—whether technology executives, philosophers, designers, engineers, technologists, citizens, critical theorists, or researchers—for the particular material discursive practices that produce the things and phenomena with which we intra-actively engage (Barad 2003, 2007).

The goal in this chapter, then, is to explore what different ontological/analytic perspectives point us toward when it comes to what might be called "media technologies," and to probe for blind spots and openings for further investigation. Specifically, it will begin by considering three strong candidates for what these things might be like and how they might then be studied (and which are already suggested by the focus of the present book): *technology*, *media*, and *environment*. It will then look at how they can intersect in ways that might bring into focus certain key dynamics of contemporary networked computational things. Finally, the analytic concept of *mediating (infra)structures* will be developed as a way to synthesize and develop these matters that have been foregrounded, and to point toward new analytic directions and sensitivities that are required in order to adequately and incisively account for them.

The underlying argument of this investigation is that it is crucially important to (re)consider the intellectual tools that are brought to bear on phenomena and practices involving contemporary networked computational things. These are things that are often very active and interconnected; and they have functions and behaviors that are hidden beneath user-facing surfaces and may even be very different from the functionality and character a person experiences during interactions with and through them. This state of affairs calls for new conceptual and analytic lenses that build on the strengths of existing ones, but also recognize the inadequacies of existing perspectives and thus develop in the new directions that are required.

TECHNOLOGY, MEDIA, ENVIRONMENT

Inquiring into the roots of notions that seem appropriate for considering the things we encounter can be instructive in terms of highlighting specific aspects and dynamics of interest, and also for being conscious of how those notions and their histories can set us out on a particular analytic path. In postphenomenological terms, we might think of this as the various kinds of multistabilities we are able to brainstorm and explore. While this will by no means be an exhaustive or definitive study, even a relatively straightforward and commonsense survey can be informative.

However, it should be noted that this brief survey will inevitably be reductive and simplistic, and will not do justice to the richness and nuance that can be found in these traditions. The reason for zooming out to such a high level is in order to see something else that is more to do with basic conceptions and ideas of what things are, what dynamics are at play, and what is at stake.

The three terms that will be explored here as lenses that frame certain types of things are *technology*, *media*, and *environment*. No doubt others could be chosen, although some of these other terms will also make appearances in the discussion of technology, media, and environment. These three terms were chosen because they seem to be some of the most commonly used and relevant ones when it comes to addressing contemporary computational things; and because they entail corresponding conceptions of basic orientations toward how humans relate to them. *Environment* is perhaps a less obvious candidate than the other two, but there seem to be compelling reasons to include it that will be explicated later on.

TECHNOLOGY

Terms already in common use (and which emerged in Zuckerberg's comments) are *technology* and *media. Technology* commonly implies some kind of tool that is actively and intentionally used, typically by a human. In fact, technology-use has been said to be one of the things that makes us human (Nelson and Stolterman 2012). Moreover, technology is often seen as being used in an instrumental fashion for some particular purpose.[3] This purpose is often in focus in design processes in which specific objects, applications, and systems are created with certain forms in order to serve particular functions and use cases. Of course, once these designed things are released into the world the designers' intentions may not be followed by those who use them (cf. Akrich 1991), as the multistability of any given thing allows for achieving a variety of relations to it (Ihde 1990). But even then there is still a purposeful design—just one that comes from the side of use (Redström 2008).

Technology has historically been strongly associated with (masculine) projects of domination and control (Wajcman 2000; Faulkner 2001), and specifically with science. The academic field of science and technology studies grew out of the sociology of science as the result of the perceived need to extend analyses to the technological tools of applied science (Bijker, Hughes, and Pinch 1987; Collins and Pinch 1998). The roots of postphenomenology are also connected to this tradition (Ihde 2008), and a number of postphenomenological cases are scientific tools. Examples include microscopes and telescopes (Ihde 1990), obstetric ultrasound (Verbeek 2008), visual renderings in science (Hasse 2008), and the Mars rover (Rosenberger 2013). Owing to its roots in phenomenology, postphenomenology considers how the world and humans are mutually present to each other, but with a special emphasis on the technologies that often mediate human-world relations. The focus is on mediated *perception* of and access to the world, and *action* in it. While it would by no means be claimed that humans can have access to the world in any direct or unproblematic way, and there is a decidedly non-foundational orientation (cf. Rosenberger 2016), there is also a sense (particularly through the connection to science) that what is at stake has to do with how we can connect to, know something about, and engage with what is "real."

When speaking of technology, human agency is typically in focus. Technology is at the heart of Western narratives of progress, from the first time an early human picked up a bone and turned it into a weapon or other kind of tool, to the Industrial Revolution, to any of the more recent technology-based "revolutions." Breathless predictions of the "coming age of [insert specific advanced technology here]" have become commonplace. Other predictions take the form of dystopic visions of robots that become smart enough to rebel against their human creators; these thus flip the script of technologies being subject to human agency and control, yet through doing so also play off of and reinforce typical conceptions of technologies as tools (or perhaps servants, in the case of anthropomorphic robots) created by and for humans. Somewhat less dramatically, popular and widely accessible social media technologies that enable the relatively easy creation, manipulation, and sharing of media content are regularly blamed for making us dumb, distracted, unable to converse with each other, and generally disconnected from the "real world." This is particularly intriguing and noteworthy given the traditional role of technologies in science as instruments that connect to and reveal the world, rather than detract from it. But the perspective of media can provide more illumination here.

MEDIA

Media is a term associated with communication, messages, content, social practices, and creation.[4] These practices can be characterized by their performative character: in other words, what people communicate and create can be seen as culturally shaped and embedded *performances* of self and identity (Goffman 1959). Participation and collaboration are also key aspects of more recent sociotechnical developments and media practices (cf. Jenkins 2006; Löwgren and Reimer 2013; Meikle and Young 2011). Here what is in focus are cultural practices that are enabled by and enacted through media, and the ways in which those practices also shape the development of the associated media technologies.

More recently, media technologies have been considered from a postphenomenological angle in order to elaborate the multistable human-technology relations they enable and support. For example, Irwin (2016) considers the texture woven by sociotechnical practices around things such as dubstep mashups, photo manipulation, self-tracking, and earbuds; while Wellner (2016) explores relations to and through cellphones.

But this combination of a perspective honed on technologies (postphenomenology) with media as object of study has inherent internal tensions. While (especially scientific) technology relates to what is "real," media is "not real" (or at least not *necessarily* real). Or rather, while the existence and effects of media might have a very real character, there is no direct, stable, or reliable connection between signifiers and signified. Already before the advent of the Internet Baudrillard argued that modern society is ordered by simulation and can be characterized by a play of simulacra—signs with no originary points of reference (Baudrillard 1994). This could be seen also in at least the early Internet that was regarded as a place to play with identity (Turkle 1997), which was made possible because of the dissociation of physical body and communicative capability that enabled performances of self unencumbered by the realities of physical presence and embodiment (Hayles 1999).

In more recent years, however, there has been a trend away from online-only identities separate from those in "meatspace," and toward online accounts that are accurate and "verified" in various ways (meaning: connected to offline, more or less official identities). The "verified account" badge on Twitter is one example. Another is Facebook's policy on identity, as set out in its terms of service. It is interesting to note the number and variety of ways in which these seek to maintain and enforce a connection between online and "real" identities:

> Facebook users provide their real names and information, and we need your help to keep it that way. Here are some commitments you make to us relating to registering and maintaining the security of your account:
>
> 1. You will not provide any false personal information on Facebook, or create an account for anyone other than yourself without permission.
> 2. You will not create more than one personal account.
> 3. If we disable your account, you will not create another one without our permission.
> 4. You will not use your personal timeline primarily for your own commercial gain, and will use a Facebook Page for such purposes.
> 5. You will not use Facebook if you are under 13.
> 6. You will not use Facebook if you are a convicted sex offender.
> 7. You will keep your contact information accurate and up to date.
> 8. You will not share your password (or in the case of developers, your secret key), let anyone else access your account, or do anything else that might jeopardize the security of your account.
> 9. You will not transfer your account (including any Page or application you administer) to anyone without first getting our written permission.
> 10. If you select a username or similar identifier for your account or Page, we reserve the right to remove or reclaim it if we believe it is appropriate (such as when a trademark owner complains about a username that does not closely relate to a user's actual name).
>
> (https://www.facebook.com/legal/terms)

Of course it is technically possible for users of the Facebook technology to not follow these terms, but it is worth noting that there is a strong legal and social pressure to maintain a stable link between online and offline identities. And, significantly, this cannot be enforced entirely through the technology, which is why legal frameworks are brought to bear in order to regulate behavior.[5] The combination of "authentic" identity and "performed" content presents a tension along the same lines as that between the conceptual lenses of technology and media (i.e., scientific tool that reveals some aspect of reality versus means for socially situated performances of self), and is one that will be further explored later.

ENVIRONMENT

Another, relatively more recently used, concept for describing the role and character of contemporary networked computational technologies is *environment*. That is to say that these things have become so pervasive that they have come to constitute something that is more like an environment we live in than isolated tools we pick up and use but then put down and leave (Meikle and Young 2011; Deuze 2012)—even if it is an environment that is more messy and less seamless than those envisioned in traditional narratives of ubiquitous computing (Dourish and Bell 2011). These networked computational technologies can not only function as environments themselves (Wiltse and Stolterman 2010) but can also shape experiences of "real" space (Coyne 2010). To use Puech's (2016) term: we live in a *technosphere* of ambient, pervasive technologies, and ones that increasingly sit at the interface between self and world.

In addition to resonating with common experiences of a life that is thoroughly textured and mediated by these technologies, the environmental lens also suggests some more aspects that are illuminating. Specifically, an environment is something that is always there, and often in the background. It is something with which we typically have a "background relation," to use Ihde's (1990) terminology, just as it is also something we can navigate and leverage more intentionally.[6] An environment involves infrastructures, foundations on which other structures are built and which often remain hidden to a greater or lesser extent. This can be noted from even a commonsense survey of manifestations of infrastructure: things such as phone and power lines, utility holes, roadways, plumbing, and similar kinds of pervasive, systemic resources that typically do not warrant second thought (as long as they continue to function normally). But infrastructures are always there, and often active in the case of infrastructural services that are always running. Infrastructures also imply interwoven and continuous structures, even as they are composed of many smaller components.

Importantly, environments are things that surround us, that we can move around in to varying degrees and get out of only by entering another environment. Even leaving a particular local environment entails a process of tracing a connection between it and wherever else one arrives at. There are no clean edges, firm boundaries, or absolutely exterior positions. An environment is not something we pick up and use like a tool, but rather something that surrounds and incorporates us.

The relatively recent tendency to view contemporary networked computational things in terms of environment might relate to some of these qualities. These technologies are something we cannot get "out of," as they are all around. Even many basic transactions of everyday life are now made through them, such as managing finances; communicating with colleagues, friends, and family (and indeed strangers); playing games; making purchases; reading the news; keeping personal records; and many more. And rather than the free play of identity that was thought to be enabled by a boundary between real and virtual lives, online and physical interactions are increasingly enmeshed—as are the technological systems themselves. Looking beneath the surface, we might also recognize the existence of lower-level infrastructures—everything from the protocols used for information exchange on the Internet to cloud computing service providers to APIs that turn applications into resources for other applications.

Environments are thus underneath and all around, and we are in relation to them, whether we like it or not.

COMBINING, PROBING, DETERRITORIALIZING

For each of the "things" referenced by the terms technology, media, and environment we can identify corresponding (and correspondingly simplified and general) human activities that are involved and that are at the heart of why each of them matter. Media can be said to be about *communication*, about exchanging information, expressing oneself, and, perhaps most of all, connecting and being present with and for others. Technology relates to *action and perception*, what people can do and perceive, their ways of being and acting in the world. Environment is about *dwelling*, how people inhabit and navigate their everyday material lifeworlds and the possibilities they afford and constrain, and how they flourish through connection with an environment (Puech 2016).[7] These activities and core concerns can provide the lenses through which we view the significance of the things in question (see Figure 1.1).

Now, the purpose here is not to reduce and mangle rich areas of investigation and scholarship beyond recognition, but rather to get to a point where it

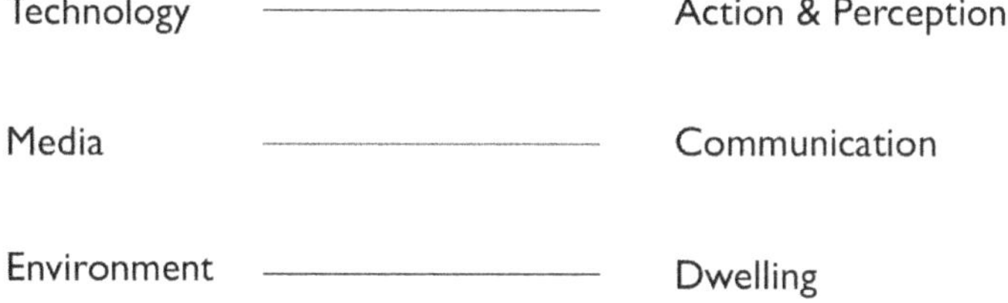

Figure 1.1 Thing and activity lenses.

might be possible to recognize basic orientations and assumptions that are not necessarily easy or possible to see while in the thick of that richness. It is also for the purpose of what follows, which is an intentional exercise in disturbing, perturbing, deterritorializing, and looking for new lines of flight.

Roles, Relations, Agencies

Adding to the simple table above, we can also note that in each of the activities and relations, human involvement and relative position can be in different *modes*: active or passive, sending or receiving, creating or interpreting, navigating or following, and so on. For example, in terms of media, a person can at different times be a creator or a recipient of messages, a producer or a consumer, encoder or decoder, and so on. In relation to technology, we can see that humans make use of technologies to mediate their perceptive access to the world, but they can also be in the position of "world" (in the sense of the basic *I-technology-world* relation of postphenomenology) that is made perceptible to another human through the mediation of technology. And when it comes to environment, a person can actively navigate and utilize it as a resource, or just inhabit and be in it more passively.

So we can see this mode as a sort of modulator that affects the character of the activity in question, and that can be used to articulate the perspective from which relations are analyzed and perhaps also to identify a relevant

Technology ———— *(Subject/Object)* Action & Perception

Media ———— *(Sender/Receiver)* Communication

Environment ———— *(Active/Passive)* Dwelling

Figure 1.2 Thing, mode, and activity lenses.

converse perspective (see Figure 1.2). It is also worth noting that the more passive modes indicate a significant difference from what is typically considered from the perspectives of user experience, phenomenological intentionality, and so on. What is there to see if we look for what is going on with and through things outside of these frames that place humans in the active role?

Opening Up the Matrix

Another possibility for charting potentially interesting territory is to combine the "things" in question with an activity lens more typically associated with a different conceptualization of its object of study. We can try this out by opening up the first simple chart such that rather than "things" and "lenses" corresponding directly to each other, they each become an axis that opens up a matrix that includes the typical conceptions but also new possibilities. The point here is not to literally fill in this matrix, but rather to use it as a conceptual tool for teasing apart complex dynamics and as a lens for opening up other relevant vantage points that can be used for finding other trajectories and territories worth exploring (see Figure 1.3).

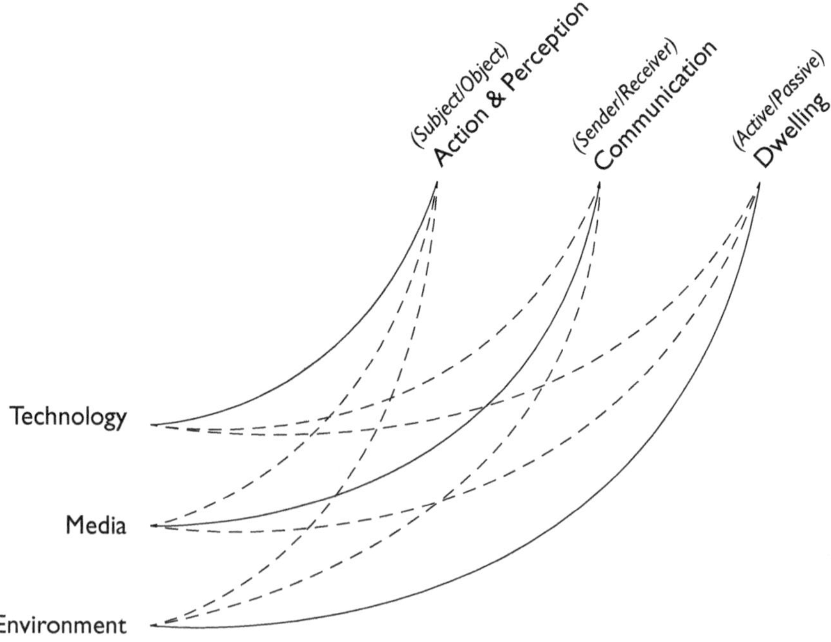

Figure 1.3 Opening up the matrix.

In some ways this is straightforward: it might seem obvious that media (thing) can mediate perception of the world (activity lens), for example. But it gets more interesting when we note that media are not neutral tools, but rather involve communicative performances; a hermeneutic strategy for understanding the workings of a technology and how they shape its output[8] is significantly different from one for understanding the contexts and meanings of a cultural text. We can also go back to the distinction between the active and passive modes and see that a person might enter into a relation with technology in which she or he is in the "world" position as that which is made available for another person to perceive, and that this might take the form of media that is created. For example, a digital photo that can be easily seen as media is also the result of a technological process that leaves traces (Wiltse 2014) of its production that are more along the lines of a "neutral" scientific instrument. These might include location, date and time, equipment used, et cetera that typically show up in photo metadata. Thinking of even a simple action of digital media consumption, when viewing a webpage the very act of loading that page becomes visible to the owners of the site. Through the "back end" of even consumer website creation and management platforms one can see how many people visited certain pages, when, from which countries, through referral from which sources, and so on. Indeed, through separating these things, activities, and modes it becomes easier to see that in many cases there is an overlapping and intertwining of them—and disentangling them can be a productive (and indeed important) analytic exercise when the goal is to understand the character of the human-technology-world relations that are at play in particular cases.

Applying the lens of technologically mediated action and perception to environment, we can begin by simply noting that these technologies have become so pervasive that they have become integrated into and taken on the character of an environment. In one sense this means that there is now a wide variety of commonly available tools at our disposal, and there may be technological resources actually embedded in environments. One might think of the open Wi-Fi networks that are widely available in many urban areas, for example, or even sensors that allow for opening doors or turning on water taps. But if we once again switch to considering the passive mode of action and perception, it becomes possible to see that many of the technologies we use and live with also turn us into objects of perception and even surveillance and control, both actual and potential. In urban areas we are physically monitored by surveillance cameras that may even have facial recognition capabilities. When using the Internet we are tracked, monitored, and profiled, across sites, platforms and devices, to be later targeted with advertising content. Here we can see the interconnected structural character of this environment. As one of Google's advertiser-facing pages explains one of their products:

"Audience Center 360 brings together all your data—analytics, campaign, search, email, and CRM—and enhances it with third-party and Google exclusive data. The result helps you understand who your most valuable customers are across channels, devices, and campaigns" (https://www.google.com/analytics/audience-center/capabilities/). These technologies allow for not only targeting, but micro-targeting and excluding.[9]

These sociotechnical practices point to interesting and arguably quite significant and pressing areas for investigation from the perspective of technologically mediated action and perception. What is the "world" that is made available and accessible to those who do the tracking and surveilling? What is the character of this relation, how is it perceived (or not) and experienced by both parties involved (tracker and tracked), and what possibilities do they each have (or not) to configure it?

More fundamentally, in the context of these underlying and interconnected infrastructures, what exactly is the character of the technology in terms of what and how it mediates? Put more concretely, and to take one example: when a person accesses a web service, where and how is that action registered, and with what consequences? What chain of actions is propagated, what effects does it have, and at what time scales? What other networked technologies are involved and activated? What kinds of data are produced and stored, where, and by what entities? Who can access the data, and under what conditions? These questions take on increased practical, legal, and ethical importance in an age of pervasive and highly sophisticated government surveillance, and potential for personal activity data to be used to configure differential access to information, services, and other resources.

Moving on, we can use the lens of communication to look at technology as an object of study. Of course there is again the straightforward case of media technologies: those that are used to mediate communication. But if we take a somewhat broader angle we can also consider how technologies facilitate connection and mutual presence in other ways. For example, the sociotechnical practice of using hashtags on social media makes it possible for people to connect, communicate, and simply become aware of each other's presence around a common topic. It is a practice of creating and consuming media, but also of technologically mediated perception.

This technologically mediated perception is also, more specifically, a case of digital material mediation (Wiltse 2014) in which the presence and activity of these other people are attested to not only by the claims of the media content itself, but also by the underlying technological infrastructures. The messages are not free-floating, but rather connected to a particular account identity with a particular history of activity; and each message typically has some kind of associated metadata, such as a time stamp, that is not freely performed/created by the sender but is rather added "objectively" by the technology. In these cases we can see both performative communication in the sense of the content created and sent, but also technological mediation of a relation between sender and receiver in which the sender—or, more specifically, the action of creating and sending a message—is recorded and made visible by the technological platform. Interpretation of the message on the part of the receiver thus entails both typical textual hermeneutics and a hermeneutics of the functionality of the mediating technology. To take a very simple example of the latter: a time stamp of 10:31 a.m. can be read as an indication that the sender of the message clicked the send button at or around 10:31 a.m. However, particularly if the account owner is a brand, a savvy user might (quite rightly) suspect that the content was scheduled in advance to be published at 10:31 a.m. through a social media marketing platform rather than actually manually posted at that moment. It gets even more complicated in the case of Twitter bots (and no doubt other scenarios that could be added here as well).

Now, it can certainly be said that such readings of traces of technologically mediated activities are quite common and unremarkable. Yet this is also precisely why they call for attention. These traces of activities and the technological infrastructures in and through which they are produced have come to constitute and reveal our environments, and to reveal us to each other. They provide a means by which we can find out and more generally get a sense of what is going on. They can be used for surveillance and as evidence in judicial contexts. These dynamics point toward the environmental characteristics of being always there in the background, potentially active, generally less than transparent, and not entirely (or even at all) under our control. At a more intimate scale, we might also think of what it could mean to live with computational things that are designed to reveal the ways in which we engage with them in their sociomaterial contexts through traces of use (Robbins, Giaccardi, and Karana 2016).

Indeed, and moving on to consider things through the lens of dwelling, we can ask: What does it mean to dwell with mediating technologies turned environment, and environments permeated by interconnected technologies? What are the implications of living with these over time, having traces of our activities build up as sedimented history and as datafied standing reserve available for future use? How do we come to move, act, perceive, understand, perform, and communicate in these environments? How does the presence of these things and their potentials affect how we conceive of our own possibilities and the kinds of selves we become (Kiran 2012)? What forms of life should we cultivate as "technosapiens" (Puech 2016)? And how can we develop incisive accounts of these matters that do justice to what is at stake?

As part of an analytic toolkit for such an enterprise, I suggest the conceptual lens of *mediating (infra)structures*.

MEDIATING (INFRA)STRUCTURES

The preceding analysis highlighted the fact that our contemporary landscape is populated by things that do not fit neatly into single stable categories, and that often entail multiple kinds of functionalities that enable a wide variety of sociotechnical practices and relations. Just as it is necessary to do detailed analyses to get beneath the surface of things in order to see the full spectrum of dynamics that are at play, it is also important to zoom out in order to get a sense for the connections between things and underlying infrastructures.

I suggest the term *mediating (infra)structures* as a pointer to these matters of concern discussed in the previous section, and an associated theoretical and analytic enterprise that seeks to grasp the texture, dynamics, and implications of mediating technologies (i.e., technologies that mediate action, perception, relations, communication) become infrastructural. It involves structures that mediate communication, action, and perception and that are often *infra*—hidden beneath the surface. Mediating (infra)structures are also always around and potentially doing things we did not ask them to do and mediating relations we did not intentionally initiate, perhaps even serving others without our awareness or permission. They are technology, media, and environment; and they are implicated in action and perception, communication, and dwelling (see Figure 1.4).

In order to begin to flesh out what mediating (infra)structures entail, it will be helpful to briefly highlight a few more characteristics, dispositions, and sensibilities that seem to be key matters of concern (and which have also emerged in relevant current discussions). Characteristics considered here are *infrastructure*, *proliferating relations*, *ecosystems and fields*, and *fluid assemblages and their multi-instabilities.*

Infrastructure

Perhaps one of the most significant aspects of the technologies that now populate our collective landscape is their infrastructural character. As architect and writer Keller Easterling (Easterling 2014, 11) says:

> The word "infrastructure" typically conjures associations with physical networks for transportation, communication, or utilities. Infrastructure is considered to be a hidden substrate—the binding medium or current between objects of positive consequence, shape, and law. Yet today, more than grids of pipes and wires, infrastructure includes pools of microwaves beaming from satellites and populations of atomized electronic devices that we hold in our hands.

These technologies are infrastructural in the sense that they are and/or rely on networked and pervasive enabling resources (Bowker et al. 2010) running on

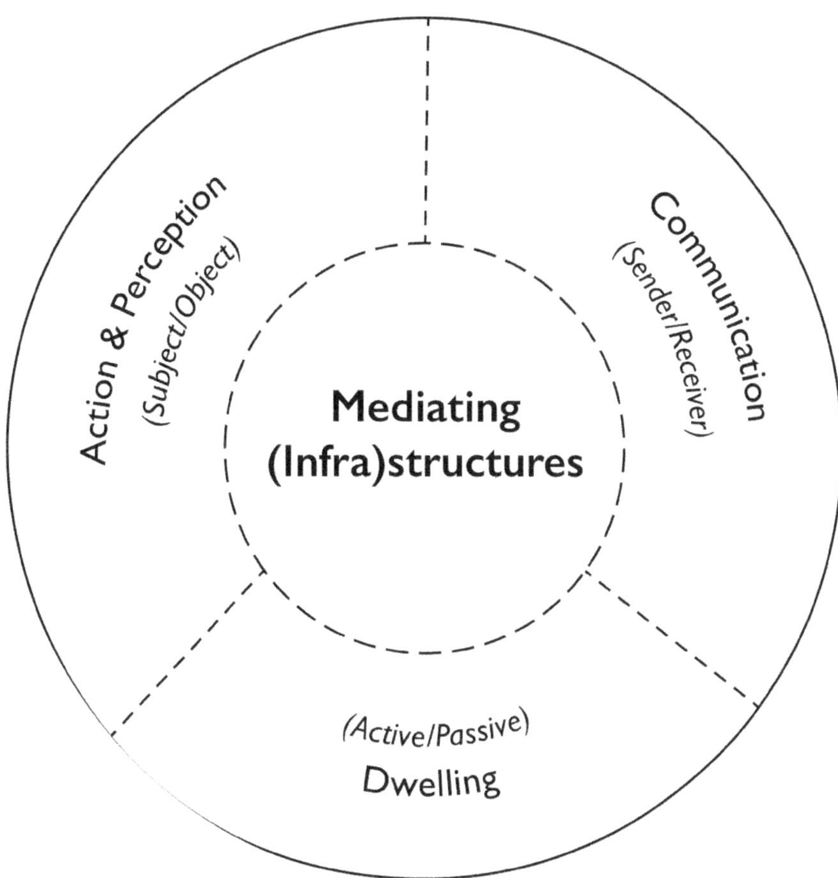

Figure 1.4 Mediating (infra)structures.

widely shared protocols, platforms, and formats. Interacting with and through even a single device that one can hold in one's hands thus often entails interacting with many layers of interconnected infrastructure and platform components,[10] often with only a vague awareness of them. The various trackers that are loaded as part of most webpages now are one simple example of this, as is any smartphone app that uses the Internet and location services.

Technological infrastructures exist beneath the surface, at levels typical users cannot easily access (if at all). Moreover, we as humans may not even be capable of comprehending the structural character of our networked reality (Van Den Eede 2016). This means that when considering the role of these technologies in the world it does not suffice to begin and end exploration with the ways in which humans can experience and intentionally relate to them.

Proliferating Relations

As already indicated by the brief discussion of infrastructure, technological relations seem to be only proliferating—and this includes *relations among technologies themselves*. This is perhaps most clearly seen in paradigms such as Internet of Things, but can be seen in other ordinary interactions: when another person's smartphone shows up in the list of available networks on one's own smartphone, when taking a photo at a restaurant causes Google to request that it be uploaded to Google Maps, when a card with an RFID chip must be held up to a card reader in order to access a facility, and so on. Things can be active and interconnected, performing actions and communicating with each other in ways that do not necessarily or directly involve us. In other words, they fall outside of our own intentionality and experience.

Thus, it seems there is a need to cultivate a sensitivity for *alien phenomenology* (Bogost 2012), for recognizing that objects and infrastructures can have their own agencies, relations, potentialities, and dispositions (Easterling 2014). Analyses of lived experience are not sufficient for understanding objects (or machines, to use Bryant's term) that are operationally closed or withdrawn (Bryant 2014)—even as they may have quite significant and far-reaching consequences in the world of human experience.

Ecosystems and Fields

The continually increasing complexity of computational artifacts and systems presents both opportunities and challenges when it comes to interaction design. New technologies present new possibilities for interfaces; yet at the same time the increasing functional complexity of artifacts, along with possibility to decrease size, mean that "the interface is in a tight squeeze" (Janlert and Stolterman 2014, 516)—there are only so many buttons that can fit on a single device. Janlert and Stolterman, design theorists working in the context of human-computer interaction (HCI), consider this problem in detail (Janlert and Stolterman 2014). Considering the term "interface" in a literal sense to "apply to real surfaces and surface-bound interaction," they are able to make the argument that "*interaction* does not necessarily require an *interface*" (523; original emphasis). Surface-free modalities include "hearing, sound production (voice, et cetera), smell, heat, wind, breath, balance, posture, and so forth, and free gestures" (524). These are opposed to the surface-bound modalities that we can see and touch and that have until now been most commonly utilized as interface modalities. They call these surface-free interactions "faceless." Based on the characteristics of these interactions, they suggest that interaction designers may come to think and design more in terms of ecologies, force fields, and contexts than single artifacts.

Examples of this approach can already be seen in always-on, voice-activated personal assistants such as Amazon's Echo, Apple's Siri and Google Home. More disturbingly, and to take a more concrete example, marketers could also trigger devices with always-on voice detection through ultrasound signals that are impossible for humans to hear:

> The technology, called ultrasonic cross-device tracking, embeds high-frequency tones that are inaudible to humans in advertisements, web pages, and even physical locations like retail stores. These ultrasound "beacons" emit their audio sequences with speakers, and almost any device microphone—like those accessed by an app on a smartphone or tablet—can detect the signal and start to put together a picture of what ads you've seen, what sites you've perused, and even where you've been. (Hay Newman 2016)

This development combines the aspects of infrastructure and proliferating relations mentioned earlier, but also adds a more explicit ecological and systems perspective (i.e., involving components that relate to each other and work together in some kind of coherent way). How should we then conceptualize and analyze human-system-world relations, when it is really an entire system that does the mediating of multiple relations in a particular context? How can we develop an ecological understanding of contemporary technologies (Van Den Eede 2016) and a corresponding wisdom about how to responsibly design and dwell in them?

Fluid Assemblages and Their Multi-Instabilities

Adding to the problematics already identified, we can also note the increasingly context-bound character of digital, networked, computational things. Even an application that can appear and function in quite thing-like ways (e.g., a digital music player such as Spotify) is actually called into being as a particular (provisional) thing for a particular user in a particular context (Redström and Wiltse 2015b). These kinds of things are assembled on the fly from a variety of components[11] and infrastructural services. Their character and behavior can change as these components and software are updated. They can thus perhaps be better thought of as *fluid assemblages* than as traditional things: fluid in the sense that they are continually changing, and assemblages in the sense that they are assembled from a variety of components (Wiltse, Stolterman, and Redström 2015; Redström and Wiltse 2015b).

This state of affairs poses a challenge for postphenomenological (and other kinds of) analysis. Variational analyses of possible multistabilities are based on brainstorming various relations that can be had to a technology—but the technology itself remains stable. However, it is now possible to identify many cases in which a technology itself actually achieves a certain customized form, or stability, in relation to a particular human; and in which the technologies themselves are "unstable" and constantly changing in terms of their appearance, structure, function, connections, and so on, in ways that may or may not be apparent or accessible to people who relate to them.

Just as multistability is an important counterpoint to claims of technological determinism and essentialism, a sensitivity to *multi-instabilities* (Redström and Wiltse 2015a) might be necessary to counter premature closure regarding conceptualizations of what things actually are and do. An important aspect of this sensitivity must be an attunement to the constant becoming of the changing things that are (manifestations of) fluid assemblages. They are not just made, but rather *always in the making*. To use a fluid assemblage is to participate in its ongoing design and configuration. Fluid assemblages are not stable, standardized things that sit ready for use and analysis, but rather things that are called into particular forms of being and relations through use. In order to properly care for the consequences these changing things have in terms of human experience, it is thus essential that we find ways to engage and account for the complexities of their ongoing assembling and the multiple, proliferating, and shifting relations this assembling entails.

DISCUSSION

Building on the matrix exercise and discussion of mediating (infra)structures, we might identify some key problematics that call for critical engagement. One involves the question of what to do about things that are not just sitting politely and waiting to be picked up and used by humans, but that also have their own (programmed) agencies and intentionalities.[12] These are *active, non-transparent, connected, computational things*. What they do exceeds the usual parameters of non-computational technologies that mediate certain relations on the basis of their forms and functions, but not their own active behavior. Would we even need to occasionally put these technologies in the active, intentional, "I" position in the I-technology-world schema, in order to understand how they relate to other technologies, and to us as "world"? Relatedly, it seems that there is a need to carefully consider *what is active and what is passive*, to recognize that it is not only always humans in the active position and technologies in the passive position, but that it can in fact be the other way around as well.

Another dynamic of mediating infrastructures is that mediations on the basis of traces of activity do not necessarily occur at the time they are produced. There is an uncoupling between the means by which traces are created and the means by which they are made visible, and this can also involve a significant spatial and temporal uncoupling (Wiltse 2014). Put in more practical terms: our activities are now logged, tracked, datafied, processed, and stored. This collected data, both big and small, is already put to use in many ways, but is also now (continually) created and made available for future use. We do not know the kinds of uses to which they might be put in the future, but we can already see that interpreting them responsibly in order to mediate understanding will require careful textual and technological hermeneutics. Developing such an understanding and practice could be an important—and very politically relevant—joint task for media and technology studies.

Finally, this current situation also points to a fundamental tension between media and technology mentioned earlier: the *tension between "real" and "not-real."* There have been many critiques about media-saturated contemporary culture being "not real," and about information coming to stand in for reality rather than point to it (Borgmann 2000; Baudrillard 1994). Yet at the same time the real constantly intrudes, pushes back, and calls for our attention in various ways. And sometimes it does this through the mediation of technologies. When considering mediating (infra)structures, it is crucially important to follow the relations that are actually at play. Because in this context the relevant question is not *whether* it involves the real or the not real, but rather *when*, *where*, and *how* it involves both.

CONCLUSION

This chapter has considered the character of contemporary networked, computational, digital things. Because conceptions of what things are provide the analytic lenses that determine or at least shape what we can see, it is important to revisit these foundational orientations and assumptions—especially when bringing different perspectives together. The goal of this chapter has not been to provide a thorough analysis, but rather to zoom out to a high enough level that it is possible to more clearly see tensions between perspectives that seem relevant and that may actually point to areas that call for further attention. The investigation of some of these intersections and the concept of *mediating (infra)structures* have been intended not so much to present results, but to point to and begin to open up territory for future exploration.

In relation to mediating (infra)structures we need to go back to and expand that question that serves as a persistent leitmotif in postphenomenological work: *what do these things do* (Verbeek 2005)?

But no, really, what do these things *actually* do? What do they do when we are not watching? What do they do that we did not ask them to do? What do they do with each other? What do they do that we do not know about? What kinds of worlds do they show us? What kinds of stories do they tell us? What kinds of stories do they tell about us?

And what should we do about it?

NOTES

1. My thanks to Johan Redström, Erik Stolterman, Yoni Van Den Eede, Galit Wellner, and Michel Puech for insightful comments on earlier drafts of this chapter, and to Monica Lindh Karlsson for help with producing the figures.

2. Harman's (2011) reworking of Heidegger's tool analysis that emphasizes the withdrawn reality of objects is particularly relevant in this context.

3. For example, one such formulation can be found in Hugues' description of technological systems: "An artifact—either physical or nonphysical—functioning as a component in a system interacts with other artifacts, all of which contribute directly or through other components to the common system goal" (Hughes 1987, 51).

4. See, for example, Gitelman's definition of media: "I define media as socially realized structures of communication, where structures include both technological forms and their associated protocols, and where communication is a cultural practice, a ritualized collocation of different people on the same mental map, sharing or engaged with popular ontologies of representation" (Gitelman 2006, 7).

5. See Lessig (2006) for a discussion of this kind of interplay of regulatory forces.

6. For example, see de Certeau's famous analysis of walking in the city (de Certeau 1984).

7. Puech's discussion of dwelling in a "technosphere" is quite relevant here: "Dwelling means attachment bonds, memories, belonging, and a sense of flourishing in connection with an environment. The fundamental harmony with contexts is expressed in the human mode of *dwelling*. Coevolution conveys a broader image of dwelling: we dwell in nature and in technology; our agency in dwelling constantly reconfigures the natural and technological environment. We dwell naturally in technology and we dwell technologically in nature: this constitutes the specificity of human dwelling" (Puech 2016, 53; original emphasis).

8. See Rosenberger (2008) on hermeneutic strategies for technologically produced scientific imagery.

9. Worryingly, Facebook has even allowed advertisers to do the latter on the basis of ethnicity, which, in relation to advertising for housing at least, is actually illegal (Angwin and Terry 2016).

10. For more on the differences and synergies between theories of infrastructures and platforms, see Plantin et al. 2016. Use of the term infrastructure here is not meant to declare allegiance to the tradition of infrastructure studies over platform studies, but rather to at a very basic level point to the structures that exist beneath the surface—*infra*-structures. And these structures can often be very accurately and productively characterized as platforms.

11. Examples of components in this sense might include third-party services that are used for ad targeting and serving, social media services, analytics, and services

that provide metadata and other information (for example, Spotify uses a third-party system for track listings, artist information, album reviews, and so on).

12. For related discussions of technological intentionality, see, for example, Verbeek (2008) on cyborg intentionality and Wiltse (2014) on the intentionality of digital materials.

REFERENCES

Akrich, M. (1991). "The De-Scription of Technical Objects." In W. E. Bijker and J. Law (eds.), *Shaping Technology/Building Society: Studies in Sociotechnical Change*. Cambridge, MA: MIT Press.

Angwin, J. and T. Parris Jr. (2016). "Facebook Lets Advertisers Exclude Users by Race." *ProPublica* October 28. https://www.propublica.org/article/facebook-lets-advertisers-exclude-users-by-race

Barad, K. (2003). Posthumanist Performativity: Toward an Understanding of How Matter Comes to Matter. *Signs* 28 (3): 801–831.

———. (2007). *Meeting the Universe Halfway: Quantum Physics and the Entanglement of Matter and Meaning*. Durham: Duke University Press.

Baudrillard, J. (1994). *Simulacra and Simulation*. Ann Arbor: University of Michigan Press.

Bijker, W. E., T. P. Hughes, and T. J. Pinch (eds.). (1987). *The Social Construction of Technological Systems: New Directions in the Sociology and History of Technology*. Cambridge, MA: MIT Press.

Bogost, I. (2012). *Alien Phenomenology, Or, What It's Like to Be a Thing*. Minneapolis/London: University of Minnesota Press.

Borgmann, A. (2000). *Holding on to Reality: The Nature of Information at the Turn of the Millennium*. Chicago: University Of Chicago Press.

Bowker, G. C., K. Baker, F. Millerand, and D. Ribes. (2010). "Towards Information Infrastructure Studies: Ways of Knowing in a Networked Environment." In J. Hunsinger, L. Klastrup, and M. Allen (eds.), *International Handbook of Internet Research*. Dordrecht/Heidelberg/London/New York: Springer.

Bryant, L. R. (2014). *Onto-Cartography: An Ontology of Machines and Media*. Edinburgh: Edinburgh University Press.

de Certeau, M. (1984). *The Practice of Everyday Life*. Trans. S. Rendall. Berkeley/Los Angeles: University of California Press.

Collins, H. M. and T. J. Pinch. (1998). *The Golem at Large: What You Should Know About Technology*. Cambridge, UK: Cambridge University Press.

Coyne, R. (2010). *The Tuning of Place: Sociable Spaces and Pervasive Digital Media*. Cambridge, MA: MIT Press.

Deleuze, G., F. Guattari, G. Burchell, and H. Tomlinson. (1994). *What Is Philosophy?* London/New York: Verso.

Deuze, M. (2012). *Media Life*. Cambridge, UK/Malden, MA: Polity Press.

Dourish, P. and G. Bell. (2011). *Divining a Digital Future: Mess and Mythology in Ubiquitous Computing*. Cambridge, MA: MIT Press.

Easterling, K. (2014). *Extrastatecraft: The Power of Infrastructure Space*. London/New York: Verso.

Faulkner, W. (2001). "The Technology Question in Feminism: A View from Feminist Technology Studies." *Women's Studies International Forum* 24 (1): 79–95.

Fiveash, K. (2016). "'We're a Tech Company, We're Not a Media Company,' Says Facebook Founder." *Ars Technica,* August 30. http://arstechnica.com/tech-policy/2016/08/germany-facebook-edit-hateful-posts-zuckerberg-says-not-media-empire/#p3

Gitelman, L. (2006). *Always Already New: Media, History, and the Data of Culture*. Cambridge, MA: MIT Press.

Goffman, E. (1959). *The Presentation of Self in Everyday Life*. New York: Anchor Books.

Haraway, D. (2015). "Anthropocene, Capitalocene, Chthulhucene." In H. Davis and E. Turpin (eds.), *Art in the Anthropocene: Encounters Among Aesthetics, Politics, Environments and Epistemologies*. Ann Arbor: Open Humanities Press.

Harman, G. (2011). *The Quadruple Object*. Winchester, UK/Washington, USA: Zero Books.

Hasse, C. (2008). "Postphenomenology: Learning Cultural Perception in Science." *Human Studies* 31 (1): 43–61.

Hay Newman, L. (2016). "How to Block the Ultrasonic Signals You Didn't Know Were Tracking You." *Wired,* November 3. https://www.wired.com/2016/11/block-ultrasonic-signals-didnt-know-tracking/

Hayles, N. K. (1999). *How We Became Posthuman*. Chicago: University of Chicago Press.

Heidegger, M. (2010). *Being and Time*. Trans. J. Stambaugh. Albany: SUNY Press.

Hughes, T. P. (1987). "The Evolution of Large Technological Systems." In W. E. Bijker, T. P. Hughes, and T. J. Pinch (eds.), *The Social Construction of Technological Systems: New Directions in the Sociology and History of Technology*. Cambridge, MA: MIT Press, 51–82.

Ihde, D. (1990). *Technology and the Lifeworld: From Garden to Earth*. Bloomington: Indiana University Press.

———. 2008. "Introduction: Postphenomenological Research." *Human Studies* 31 (1): 1–9.

Janlert, L.-E. and E. Stolterman. (2014). "Faceless Interaction—A Conceptual Examination of the Notion of Interface: Past, Present and Future." *Human–Computer Interaction* 30: 507–539.

Jenkins, H. (2006). *Convergence Culture: Where Old and New Media Collide*. New York: NYU Press.

Kiran, A. H. (2012). "Technological Presence: Actuality and Potentiality in Subject Constitution." *Human Studies* 35 (1): 77–93.

Lessig, L. (2006). *Code: Version 2.0*. New York: Basic Books.

Löwgren, J. and B. Reimer. (2013). *Collaborative Media: Production, Consumption, and Design Interventions*. Cambridge, MA: MIT Press.

Meikle, G. and S. Young. (2011). *Media Convergence: Networked Digital Media in Everyday Life*. Basingstoke/New York: Palgrave Macmillan.

Nelson, H. G. and E. Stolterman. (2012). *The Design Way: Intentional Change in an Unpredictable World*. Second edition. Cambridge, MA: MIT Press.

O'Neal Irwin, S. (2016). *Digital Media: Human–Technology Connection.* Lanham/New York/London: Lexington Books.

Plantin, J.-C., C. Lagoze, P. N. Edwards, and C. Sandvig. (2016). "Infrastructure Studies Meet Platform Studies in the Age of Google and Facebook." *New Media & Society.* http://doi.org/10.1177/1461444816661553

Puech, M. (2016). *The Ethics of Ordinary Technology.* New York/London: Routledge.

Redström, J. (2008). "RE:Definitions of use." *Design Studies* 29 (4): 410–423.

Redström, J. and H. Wiltse. (2015a). "On the Multi-Instabilities of Assembled Things." In *4S 2015, Denver, Colorado, USA.* http://doi.org/10.13140/RG.2.1.2649.1924

———. (2015b). "Press Play: Acts of Defining (in) Fluid Assemblages." In *Proceedings of Nordes 2015: Design Ecologies.*

Robbins, H., E. Giaccardi, and E. Karana. (2016). "Traces as an Approach to Design for Focal Things and Practices." In *Proceedings of the 9th Nordic Conference on Human-Computer Interaction.*

Rosenberger, R. (2008). "Perceiving Other Planets: Bodily Experience, Interpretation, and the Mars Orbiter Camera." *Human Studies* 31 (1): 63–75.

———. (2013). "Mediating Mars: Perceptual Experience and Scientific Imaging Technologies." *Foundations of Science* 18 (1): 75–91.

———. (2016). "Notes on a Nonfoundational Phenomenology of Technology." *Foundations of Science.* http://dx.doi.org/10.1007/s10699–015–9480–5

Turkle, S. (1997). *Life on the Screen: Identity in the Age of the Internet.* New York: Simon and Schuster.

Van Den Eede, Y. (2016). "The (Im)possible Grasp of Networked Realities: Disclosing Gregory Bateson's Work for the Study of Technology." *Human Studies.* http://dx.doi.org/10.1007/s10746–016–9400-x

Verbeek, P.-P. (2005). *What Things Do: Philosophical Reflections on Technology, Agency, and Design.* University Park, PA: Pennsylvania State University Press.

Verbeek, P.-P. (2008). "Cyborg Intentionality: Rethinking the Phenomenology of Human–Technology Relations." *Phenomenology and the Cognitive Sciences* 7 (3): 387–395.

———. (2008). "Obstetric Ultrasound and the Technological Mediation of Morality: A Postphenomenological Analysis." *Human Studies* 31 (1): 11–26.

Wajcman, J. (2000). "Reflections on Gender and Technology Studies: In What State is the Art?" *Social Studies of Science* 30 (3): 447–464.

Wellner, G. P. (2016). *A Postphenomenological Inquiry of Cell Phones: Genealogies, Meanings, and Becoming.* Lanham/New York/London: Lexington Books.

Wiltse, H. (2014). "Unpacking Digital Material Mediation." *Techné: Research in Philosophy and Technology* 18 (3): 154–182.

Wiltse, H., E. Stolterman, and J. Redström. (2015). "Wicked Interactions: (On the Necessity of) Reframing the 'Computer' in Philosophy and Design." *Techné: Research in Philosophy and Technology* 19 (1): 26–49.

Wiltse, H., M. L. Karlsson, K. Lindström, A. Pawar, and Å. Ståhl. (2016). "Non-Local Situations: Speculating about Future Response-Abilities of Postindustrial Design (Research)." Conversation presented at *DRS 2016*, 27–30 June 2016, Brighton, UK.

Wiltse, H. and E. Stolterman. (2010). "Architectures of Interaction: An Architectural Perspective on Digital Experience." In *Proc. of NordiCHI 2010*, 821–824.

Chapter 2

Transparent Media and the Development of Digital Habits

Daniel Susser

Our lives are guided by habits. Most of the activities we engage in throughout the day are initiated and carried out not by conscious thought and deliberation, but through an ingrained set of dispositions or patterns of action—what Aristotle calls a *hexis*. We develop these dispositions over time, by acting and gauging how the world responds. I tilt the steering wheel too far and the car's lurch teaches me how much force is needed to steady it. I come too close to a hot stove and the burn I get inclines me not to get too close again. This feedback and the habits it produces are bodily. They are possible because the medium through which these actions take place is a physical, sensible one. The world around us is, in the language of postphenomenology, an *opaque* one. We notice its texture and contours as we move through it, and crucially, we bump up against it from time to time.

The digital world, by contrast, is largely *transparent*. Digital media are designed to recede from view. As a result, we experience little friction as we carry out activities online; the consequences of our actions are often not apparent to us. This distinction between the opacity of the natural world and the transparency of the digital one raises important questions. In this chapter, I ask: How does the transparency of digital media affect our ability to develop good habits online? If the digital world is constructed precisely not to push back against us, how are we supposed to gauge whether our actions are good or bad, for us and for others? What's more, can it be constructed otherwise? Can we build opacity into our digital environments, and thereby better inhabit them? I argue that we can.

In the first section, I look at habits generally, and the development of good habits specifically, in non-mediated contexts. Next, I discuss technological mediation and the various modes of transparency it produces. In the third section, I bring together the insights from the first two: I examine the effects of transparency on the development of technologically mediated habits, focusing in particular on digital media. I argue that the digital world conceals from us the "internal effects" of our actions upon the technologies we engage with—traces of our clicks and keyboard presses, transmissions of our personal information, and so on—and it provides only selective feedback about the effects of our digital actions upon other people. Our digital habits are therefore responsive only to some of the effects of our actions, and they are blind to others. But this, I argue in the final section, is something we can change. By designing digital media to reveal some of what it presently conceals—designing for what I call *strategic opacity*—we can generate the feedback necessary to form good digital habits.

DEVELOPING GOOD HABITS

It has long been observed that we act the way we do for the most part out of habit.[1] Whether that is a good thing or bad thing is a matter of some debate. Clare Carlisle has surveyed a number of discussions about habits in the Western philosophical tradition and found widely diverging views. For some, habits are indispensable guides both to knowledge and action. For others, they are obstacles to overcome. "Aristotle thinks that habit lies at the heart of moral life," writes Carlisle, "Spinoza argues that it leads us astray and prevents us from perceiving the deep intelligibility of nature. Hume regards custom as 'the great guide of human life,' since it helps to make our world orderly and predictable. Kant suggests that it undermines our innate moral worth, making us 'ridiculous' and machine-like" (2014, 3). Habit is like Plato's *pharmakon,* Carlisle says: "both a poison and a cure" (ibid., 5).

The good and the bad of habit both stem from the fact that habits allow us to act without thinking. Having done something sufficiently many times, we need not pay much conscious attention to the task at hand when setting about doing it again. As Ed Casey writes, habitual actions are "on tap" (2013, 213). They are "ready to activate: so ready that conscious deliberation or decision is not called for" (ibid.). When I wake up in the morning I do not plot my route to the bathroom, think about where I store my toothbrush, deliberate about how long to spend brushing, and so on. I simply do these things, unthinkingly, out of habit. "Muscle memory" guides me along the right path and through the right motions, leaving my conscious attention free to contemplate other things. I can think about where I left off in my work the previous evening and what I need to accomplish today. I can listen to the weather report and think about what to wear. Being able to act out of habit means being able to multitask. It means being able to plan tomorrow's lecture while cooking dinner, being able to type out notes while the boss is talking, and being able to carry on a conversation with one's passengers while driving. If we had to consciously deliberate about everything we did, all of our time would be spent contemplating trivialities.[2]

At the same time, acting unthinkingly can obviously be a problem. For Kant, it makes us "machine-like" because freedom is precisely a function of thinking—acting freely is acting after deliberation and in accordance with rational law. Habit "deprives even good actions of their moral worth because it impairs the freedom of the mind" (Kant 2006, 40). Indeed, one need not go as far as Kant does to arrive at the issue. Simply consider the difficulty of correcting *bad* habits. Perhaps my morning routine involves leaving the water running while I brush my teeth, wasting a precious resource. I might, on conscious reflection, decide I want to act differently. But when I go to brush my teeth I do so automatically, out of habit, repeating my error without thinking. "A bad habit," writes John Dewey, "suggests an inherent tendency to action and also a hold, command over us. It makes us do things we are ashamed of, things which we tell ourselves we prefer not to do. It overrides our formal resolutions, our conscious decisions" (1922, 24).

Since we rely on our habits and are in many ways beholden to them, it is important to cultivate good habits. I use the term "good" expansively here, to mean habits which are either morally good or those which are merely good for oneself. Habits are, as Hobbes says, "motion[s] made more easy and ready by [...] perpetual endeavor, or by iterated endeavors"—that is, we develop them through repetition.[3] We thus develop *good* habits when we are rewarded for acting well and punished for acting poorly. The former inclines us to repeat the good behavior, thereby carving a path we'll tend to travel down again. The latter steers us away from it.

Sometimes the rewards and punishments are administered intentionally by those trying to instill good habits in us. We are *taught* good habits when our parents tell us to sit up straight and to eat healthy foods, when our teachers force us to rewrite essays, and when our partners nudge us to clean the house. Aristotle suggests that to develop the right set of habits—the right *hexis* or character—we must be raised the right way from childhood. "One who is going to listen adequately to discourse about things that are beautiful and just, and generally about things that pertain to political matters," he says, "needs to have been beautifully brought up by means of habits" (2002, 4). If our habits are shaped early in life by attentive parents and upright teachers, later in life we will recognize and tend toward the good.

In addition to having good habits cultivated in us, we develop good habits through trial and error. We act and gauge how the world responds. Children are constantly experimenting in this way—figuring out what they are capable of and how much they can get away with. They put things in their mouths that ought not to be eaten and the taste encourages them to spit it out. They pull their friends' hair and wait to see if their own hair gets pulled back. The effects of our actions—on ourselves, on others, and on the physical world—incline and disincline us to repeat them. The *feedback* we get from the world indicates that we are acting well or poorly, to our benefit or detriment, pro- or antisocially.

Crucially, the process of internalizing this feedback is bodily. We don't (predominantly) choose how to act by recalling the feedback we have received from acting in various ways in the past, weighing in our minds the pros and cons of acting that way again, and then calculating the cost-benefit ratio.[4] Rather, the feedback we receive from acting in the world accrues in our bodies, as the disposition to act a certain way in response to similar situations down the road. Whether it is the glare of an angry parent or the physical jolt from a car driven too near the edge of the road, the memory that feedback leaves behind is not representational memory, but rather a kind of muscle memory. It produces not intellectual or propositional knowledge, but rather, as Merleau-Ponty says, "knowledge in the hands" (Merleau-Ponty 2002, 166). Describing the habits of moving around his apartment, Merleau-Ponty writes: "My flat is, for me, not a set of closely associated images. It remains a familiar domain round about me only as long as I still have 'in my hands' or 'in my legs' the main distances and directions involved" (2002, 150).[5]

Dewey points to the bodily dimension of habits by comparing them to basic physiological functions like breathing and digesting food, and describing both as products of bodily organisms interacting with environments:

> Habits may be profitably compared to physiological functions, like breathing, digesting. The latter are, to be sure, involuntary, while habits are acquired. But important as is this difference for many purposes it should not conceal the fact that habits are like functions in many respects, and especially in requiring the cooperation of organism and environment.... [N]atural operations, like breathing and digesting, acquired ones like speech and honesty, are functions of the surroundings as truly as of a person. They are things done *by* the environment by means of organic structures or acquired dispositions. (1922, 14)

Put another way, the feedback we get from acting in the world is not merely a resource to draw from, to consider later when we find ourselves in similar situations. When we interact with our environments the feedback it relays to us *shapes us*, producing or ingraining the habits which then determine (in part) how we act. Reflecting on Dewey's position and, in a sense, expanding Merleau-Ponty's view, Shannon Sullivan argues that "whether the activity is riding a bicycle, walking in high-heeled shoes, or interrupting people while they talk, habits are constituted in and through a dynamic relationship with the world 'outside' them ... [Walking in high-heeled shoes] isn't an activity that is contained within a person's feet and legs. It is located, so to speak, between feet, legs, shoes, floors, and gendered expectations" (2013, 258).

If habits are a function of both persons and their environments, the question arises as to how habits form in environments filled with digital technologies. Our natural environment—the physical, sensible world—constantly pushes back against us. It generates feedback about the effects of our actions, indicating to us whether they are behaviors we ought to repeat or retire. The digital technologies that mediate much of our contemporary lives are designed, by contrast, to operate silently and invisibly, so that we can focus our attention on the activities we want to do through them. They are designed to be *transparent.*

TRANSPARENT TECHNOLOGIES

When we engage with technologies and they work, when they perform their functions fluidly and without incident, the technologies themselves tend to withdraw or recede, so that we forget we are even using them. Heidegger famously drew attention to this phenomenon with the image of a hammer. When we encounter a hammer, he says, we don't encounter a *thing*—an object, simpliciter. We encounter what he calls "equipment" (*Zeug*), which is to say, a tool embedded in potential use contexts. "Equipment," writes Heidegger, "is essentially 'something in-order-to'" (1962, 97). Because what is salient to us about tools is the work they are meant to help us do (the "in-order-to"), that is what we attend to. We ignore the equipment and focus on the work. Tools "must, as it were, withdraw in order to be ready-to-hand quite authentically," Heidegger says (ibid., 99). Or as Hubert Dreyfus puts it: "Precisely when it is most genuinely appropriated equipment becomes transparent" (1991, 65).

Transparency is lost, on the other hand, when tools break or malfunction. When the hammer fails to drive in the nail we are forced to confront its objectness, to question what about it is keeping it from doing its job. We are drawn out of what Dreyfus calls "absorbed coping" (1991, 69) and the tool becomes, so to speak, opaque. Robert Rosenberger points to a familiar contemporary example of this shift from transparency to opacity: encountering a slow-loading webpage. Ordinarily, a skilled computer user does not attend to the computer itself. They are able to type on the keyboard, manipulate the mouse, and interpret the digital interface instinctively, so that their full attention is focused on the content presented on-screen. It is only when the computer fails to act as expected that their attention shifts to the computer *qua* object:

> [T]he sudden and unexpected occurrence of a slowly-loading webpage can be jarring. It is more than an inconvenience with regard to one's work; it changes

> the character of one's relation to the technology. The slowly-loading webpage can cause a drop in transparency. The particular ways one interfaces [sic] the computer—the keyboard, mouse, on-screen icons and buttons—reemerge into the forefront of experience. The user becomes explicitly aware of her or his own situation as a user. The computer itself appears in terms of its stubbornly limited options for interface; it is suddenly unable to mediate one's experience in a meaningful way. (Rosenberger 2009, 178)

Rosenberger's description illustrates the fact that transparency is not simply a side effect of tool use; it is required in order to become absorbed in one's work. We aren't just annoyed when a webpage fails to load, we are jolted out of our "flow." Forced to turn our attention away from the goal of our work (the "in-order-to"), and attend instead to the tool mediating it, we might lose our train of thought or forget what we were looking for in the first place. Transparency is thus both product and precondition of effective tool use: when tools function properly they withdraw or recede from conscious attention, and they must remain withdrawn in order to remain useful.

As Yoni Van Den Eede has shown, the idea of transparency can be found in discussions about technology across many different fields. In addition to Heidegger's account, Van Den Eede finds technology's withdrawal from conscious attention thematized in the work of media theorist Marshall McLuhan (2003), sociologist Bruno Latour (1992), social psychologist Sherry Turkle (1995; 2005), cognitive scientist Donald Norman (1999), and philosopher Don Ihde (1990), among others (Van Den Eede 2010). In each field, a different facet of technological transparency takes center stage. McLuhan, for example, is interested in how the "form" of media—which of our senses it is meant to stimulate, and how that stimulation is structured—is invisible to most media consumers, despite the fact that, according to McLuhan, the form has a greater effect on us than its content (ibid., 144–45).[6] For Latour, on the other hand, what eludes our attention is the historical context in which the technologies we use were developed, and the moral and political values that shaped their design (ibid., 147–48).[7]

The most systematic account of technological transparency comes from Ihde, and from those working in the field of postphenomenology, which he initiated.[8] Drawing from both phenomenology and the American pragmatist tradition, postphenomenologists ask: How do technologies mediate our experience of ourselves, each other, and the world? And how does technological mediation transform that experience?[9]

According to Ihde, we relate to and through technologies via four different "human-technology relations." We *embody* technologies (producing "embodiment relations") when they extend or amplify our basic perceptual capacities—such as when we wear eyeglasses or a hearing aid. By contrast, when we use technologies like clocks and dashboard speedometers we pay attention to the technologies themselves, which *represent* the world through readouts or other symbolic displays. Since they require us to engage in interpretive work, Ihde terms these "hermeneutic relations." In other cases, we relate to technologies as though they are quasi-human, such as when we ask questions of virtual assistants like Apple's Siri or Microsoft's Cortana. These Ihde calls "alterity relations." And finally, some technologies operate wholly out of sight, without soliciting any interactions from users. Our relations to technologies like air conditioners and the electric grid Ihde calls "background relations" (Ihde 1990, 72–123). In what follows, I pay special attention to embodiment and hermeneutic relations, though my arguments may bear on alterity and background relations as well.[10]

Transparency and opacity function differently in these different relations, with human, technology, and world coming in and out of view in different ways. When we embody technologies, the instruments themselves recede and we experience the world *through* them. In order to work my eyeglasses have to be (literally) transparent enough for me to see through them, while the world on the other side of them remains opaque. The same is true for non-visual technologies: a hearing aid is embodied aurally, a cane tactilely. "Once learned," writes Ihde, "cane and hearing aid 'withdraw' [...] I hear the world through the hearing aid and feel (and hear) it through the cane" (1990, 73–4). What's more, we can embody more complex technologies than eyeglasses, hearing aids, and canes. Merleau-Ponty, whose theory of embodiment Ihde draws from in developing his own account, describes embodying a mechanical typewriter: "When the typist performs the necessary movements on the typewriter, these movements are governed by an intention, but the intention does not posit the keys as objective locations. It is literally true that the subject who learns to type incorporates the key-bank space into his bodily space" (2002, 167).

In order for this to happen, for the technology to become incorporated into the user's "bodily space"—their pre-reflective sensorimotor orientation to the world—and thus recede from view, the technology has to generate feedback about the world, which the user can feel, and which accurately orients them to it. Ihde illustrates this by describing the devices used to manipulate radioactive materials:

> [T]he mechanical arms and hands which are designed to pick up and pour glass tubes inside the shielded enclosure have to 'feed back' a delicate sense of touch to the operator. The closer to invisibility, transparency, and the extension of one's own bodily sense this technology allows the better. Note that the design perfection is not one related to the machine alone but to the combination of machine and human. The machine is perfected along a bodily vector, molded to the perceptions and actions of humans. (1990, 74)

In other words, what makes us able to embody technologies, and therefore what allows technologies to become transparent enough to withdraw from our attention, is the connection they maintain between our perception and the world we are experiencing through them. Embodied technologies have to be reliable sensory conduits. If my glasses are too dirty for light to pass through them it is the glasses I will attend to, not the view beyond.

Hermeneutic relations work differently. Rather than extending our sensorimotor experience, technologies we relate to hermeneutically represent the world to us symbolically. When I look at my watch, the directions the hands face visually represent the time. When I listen to a Geiger counter beeping sounds aurally represent the presence or absence of radiation. Braille represents text through touch. Hermeneutic relations thus require interpretation—I must learn to read the hands of a clock, the beeps of a Geiger counter, and the bumps of braille. As with embodiment relations, once I've learned to read these technologies well they too begin to recede. Only the transparency that is produced is different from the transparency of eyeglasses and hearing aids.

To perceive the temperature outside through the thermometer I can see out my window, the instrument itself must remain opaque enough for me to attend to its display. Of course, once I am sufficiently accustomed to reading it, I need not attend to the display all that carefully. As long as the readings are accurate, some degree of what Ihde calls "hermeneutic transparency" allows me to forget that I am looking at a device at all, and to simply gauge the temperature through it. But this form of technological withdrawal is different from the withdrawal that occurs in embodiment relations, for the ultimate object of perception is not the world but a representation of it. "You read the thermometer, and in the immediacy of your reading you *hermeneutically* know that it is cold," writes Ihde, "[…] But you should not fail to note that *perceptually* what you have seen is the dial and the numbers, the thermometer 'text.' And that text has hermeneutically delivered its 'world' reference, the cold" (1990, 85; original emphasis).

For technologies we relate to hermeneutically to recede from view, they must—like embodied technologies—produce a reliable connection between user and world. They must generate perceptual feedback. The feedback is different from that produced in embodiment relations, since hermeneutic relations connect us to the world only abstractly. But in both cases, with embodiment relations and hermeneutic relations, it is the feedback technologies generate or transmit, the connections they facilitate between user and world, that allows the technologies themselves to recede from view. Transparency derives from perceiving the effects of my actions upon the world instead of upon the technology through which I experience it.

Importantly, Ihde stresses that no matter how fully we embody technologies, nor how skilled we become at interpreting their displays, the transparency that results is always partial. And as a consequence, the world we experience through mediating technologies is always a world transformed. It is, as Ihde says, "non-neutral" (1990, 75). Indeed, though we may dream of perfectly transparent, fully embodied technologies, we can see upon reflection that we adopt technologies precisely *for* the transformations they afford. Eyeglasses would be useless if they didn't bring our vision into focus. We would have no need for thermometers which failed to transform the feeling of ambient temperature into an abstract, numerical representation. "The desire [for fully transparent technological mediation] is, at best, contradictory," Ihde writes, "[...] Such a desire both secretly *rejects* what technologies are and overlooks the transformational effects which are necessarily tied to human-technology relations" (1990, 75; original emphasis).

At the same time, these transformational effects aren't arbitrary—they have a particular structure or form, which Ihde describes as a "magnification/reduction structure" (1990, 76). Perceiving the world through technology means having some aspects of that world magnified or emphasized and other aspects reduced or "placed aside." Eyeglasses, for example, focus our attention on what is directly visible in front of us, reducing our sensitivity to peripheral phenomena. Similarly, hearing aids are designed to magnify sounds associated with human voices and to reduce background noises, like strong winds or the din of construction. Technologies we relate to hermeneutically produce a magnification/reduction structure as well—a function of which aspects of the world a particular technology has been designed to represent, and what form that representation takes. For instance, analog clocks represent time in relational terms, while digital clocks represent time in discrete, measurable units. Reading the time in these two different ways is experienced differently: "The person who awaits the train, who once could glance at his watch and *see* that it was yet ten minutes until arrival time by *seeing* the relation between the pointers and the span, now sees only the number and must infer or calculate the span" (Ihde 1983, 38–39; original emphasis).

Now, having thus far emphasized the differences between embodiment and hermeneutic relations, it is important to point out that many complex technologies afford relations of both kinds. To return to the example of slow-loading webpages, we can see that this is certainly true in the case of computers. We interact with computers, and other digital technologies, both through physical interfaces, like keyboards and mice, and representational interfaces, such as monitors and LED displays. As we become skilled at manipulating the physical interfaces, we learn to embody them. Just as Merleau-Ponty embodied his mechanical typewriter by "incorporating" it into his bodily space, we incorporate electronic keyboard and mouse into our bodily spaces. We need not think about where and how to maneuver the mouse in order to click on objects of interest on-screen. Once we've used a computer mouse for long enough, the screen simply becomes an extension of our spatial field. The same is true of hermeneutic relations to computers: once we become accustomed to interpreting the visual metaphors and other on-screen signifiers—"files," "folders," "windows," "scrollbars," et cetera—the representations recede and we are able to simply see and do our work through them. Just as I'm able to navigate my physical desktop without paying conscious attention to each item on it, I'm able to navigate my computer desktop without giving it a thought.

Our ability to navigate computers and computer interfaces is, of course, a product of habituation—of developing bodily and interpretive habits. "Through the development of expectations and bodily habits," writes Rosenberger, "one comes to embody the computer as it is used" (2013, 291). But the habits we develop around our computers and other digital technologies are not as straightforward as the non-mediated habits discussed in the previous section. For, as we've seen, technologies transform the way we experience the world, and the effects of our actions upon it. Since we develop bodily habits by gauging such effects, the habits we develop toward and through technologies reflect those transformations.

DIGITAL HABITS

In order to understand precisely how habits develop when our activities are technologically mediated we must examine two things. First, we have to look at what exactly recedes from view when technologies become transparent. To that end, I distinguish between *internal* and *external effects*. Second, since technological transparency is always partial, we have to look at how the things that don't recede from view are presented to us. I describe this in terms of *selective feedback*.

Internal and External Effects

When we embody technologies, what recedes from view is, again, the technology itself—the material instrument or device. Depending on the nature of that device, however, more or less may escape our attention.

Consider once more Heidegger's hammer. When I use a hammer to strike a nail into the wall, I feel the nail through the hammer. I sense whether the nail is meeting any resistance, and if so, how much. If it meets only a little bit of resistance I can tell I've only penetrated sheetrock. If I feel slightly more, I know I've hit a stud. Because the feedback I receive through the hammer is feedback about the nail and the wall—rather than about the hammer—the hammer itself withdraws from conscious attention and I am able to concentrate fully on my work. Now, in this case, what has receded from view is an inert object. There is nothing interesting going on *inside* the hammer; it is just a slab of metal and wood that enables me to more capably transfer force from my arms onto objects around me.

Now consider Merleau-Ponty's typewriter. When I type on a mechanical typewriter, I feel it through my fingertips as the typebars strike the page. I sense whether or not they have traveled the appropriate distance. I see letters appear, confirming that my typing is going as expected. Like Heidegger's hammer, Merleau-Ponty's typewriter transmits feedback. And since it is feedback about the end product of my activity—in this case, ink on paper—rather than about the typewriter itself, the instrument withdraws from attention and I become absorbed in my work. Unlike Heidegger's hammer, however, Merleau-Ponty's typewriter is a complex mechanical device. It contains hundreds of parts, large and small, which fit together in just the right way. When I type I not only affect the page I'm focusing on, but the entire series of gears and levers extending from each key to each letter plate. As long as I type properly I receive little feedback about the effects I am having on the typewriter itself—what I will call *internal effects*. For the typewriter has become transparent in use and withdrawn from conscious attention.[11]

Finally, consider using a digital technology, such as a personal computer. When I type on the computer's keyboard and move the cursor with the mouse, I receive feedback about the effects of my actions on the monitor. As I feel my fingers strike the keyboard I see letters appear. As I drag the mouse across my desk I see the cursor glide across the screen. The feedback I receive is, again, feedback about what I am working on—in this case, the content on the screen. It is feedback about *external effects*, rather than about what is happening inside the device. And as a consequence of this feedback the device is once again able to withdraw from conscious attention and I can focus on the work at hand. The difference, however, between hammer and mechanical typewriter on the one hand, and digital computer on the other, is that in the case of digital technologies like computers, what is happening inside the device is enormously complicated. When I interact with a keyboard and mouse I produce multitudinous internal effects. Electronic signals pass from interface device to computer processor, where they are stored and processed as data. That data is then passed through countless layers of software, which register and transform it. What I perceive on my screen as the effects of my actions—characters appearing, cursor moving—are only the very last stages in long series of events.

Yet computers generally do not alert us to the fact that we are producing all of these internal effects. Which, from the perspective of computer interface design, is a good thing. If we received constant feedback about what was happening inside of our computers it would be difficult to focus on the work we wanted to do *through* them. Transparency, as we've seen, is necessary for effective tool use. The last thing technology designers want to do is draw us out of absorbed use of their tools. As Donald Norman suggests, well-designed technologies should be "invisible" (Norman 1992). We should also notice, though, what this transparency means for our habits. If we develop habits by gauging the effects of our actions, and a large subset of those effects—the effects internal to our devices—are invisible to us, then our habits are partially blind. They are geared to the effects we have on the world through our devices, but are non-responsive to what goes on inside them. We are forced, as Sherry Turkle puts it, to take our devices at "interface value" (1995, 23).

This is cause for concern, since what goes on beneath the surfaces of our computers can have very important consequences. For example, say I open a harmless-looking email attachment, purportedly from a colleague, and a computer virus quietly installs itself on my machine. Perhaps it includes a keystroke logger—software that records each keyboard press. Now, when I type, the data about my keystrokes is intercepted before it can reach the open document I'm editing, and is transmitted to the virus's creator online. It could record me entering passwords to sensitive websites, like my bank or health insurance company. If I were at work it might record me discussing tightly held trade secrets. Since none of this would generate feedback (at least until much later), I wouldn't know—and more importantly, wouldn't *feel*—that I had done anything wrong. Nothing would chasten me for opening the email attachment without verifying its origins, and bad behavior that I ought not to repeat would continue unabated.

The same is true for good behaviors that ought to be reinforced. For instance, it is good practice to frequently update computer software, since updates generally make software more reliable and secure. Most computers users fail to do this, however, because doing it produces no positive response. If we remember to upgrade once, we don't sense the enhanced reliability and security of our system, at least not directly. So nothing reinforces the behavior and inclines us to do it again.

To develop good habits we need positive feedback in response to good behavior and negative feedback in response to bad behavior. But the feedback we get from interacting with digital media is designed to impress upon us only *some* of the effects of our actions. Specifically, digital feedback is designed to indicate external effects, so that the media itself recedes from view and our attention stays focused on the activities we're using it *for* (Heidegger's "in-order-to"). The transparency of digital media therefore makes it difficult to develop good digital habits—habits which are responsive to the full range of effects our actions have on and through technology.

Selective Feedback

In fact, the situation is even worse than that. Not only don't we receive feedback about most internal effects of our actions, we also only receive partial feedback about the *external* effects. Technological mediation is, as Ihde says, "non-neutral": the world we experience through technology is a world transformed. And the particular structure of that transformation, as we saw above, is that technologies magnify some aspects of the world and reduce others. When we interact with digital media, its magnification/reduction structure thus shapes how we perceive the effects of our actions on the world. Certain facets of those effects are brought to the fore, while others are relegated to the background. We receive *selective feedback* about the former, while remaining unaware of the latter.

Take, for instance, our interactions with other people. When we interact face-to-face with friends or colleagues what we say and do affects them, but not always in the ways we intend. Maintaining healthy interpersonal relationships therefore requires gauging how others react to us and modulating our behavior in response. Friendly advice can come across as patronizing. What is intended as a joke might trigger or offend. Some people—"no-nonsense" types—respond better to directness. Other people prefer to be eased into difficult conversations. Face-to-face interaction produces a wide variety of feedback, which allows us to determine, with great subtlety, how our words and actions affect others. People can react verbally, of course, and tell us that we are making them unhappy or uncomfortable. But they might also simply look away or adopt a hushed tone. If we are trying to cheer up a friend who has fallen on hard times, we can detect that it's working if they smile a little or move more airily around the room. This nuanced information registers as positive and negative feedback, which shapes our social habits. We become habituated to social norms, like courtesy and civility, in part by acting rudely and intolerantly and discovering how people respond.

Now consider social interactions that take place through digital media. Just like in face-to-face interaction, when we interact with other people through social media technology our actions can have an impact on them. Clever tweets can make other people laugh or cry. Facebook posts can intrigue or bore them. A text message can enrage or console. But how do we gauge our impact? In all of these cases our connections to other people are mediated through hermeneutic relations—the feedback we get about our effects on them is representational feedback, usually text or images. Understanding and internalizing how our Facebook post or text message was received therefore requires interpretive work. It requires decoding text or evaluating images, and those representations are necessarily incomplete. Rather than being able to assess the totality of an interpersonal interaction—not just the words another person speaks or the face they make, but their body language and gestures, whether communication is fluid or stilted, the overall gestalt or “feeling in the room”—we must draw our conclusions from words or images on a screen. Oftentimes we lack even a name or face to give textual feedback context, as much of our digitally mediated activity is anonymous.

This kind of multidimensional feedback is especially important in heated or tense exchanges. When we are angry or indignant we sometimes lash out, saying things we hope will hurt or offend. Debates about politics can become snarky or demeaning. In arguments with family members we might dredge up painful episodes from the past. Yet when we see the effects of our words on our interlocutors, that feedback can stop us in our tracks. Realizing that we have hurt or offended someone is often enough to steer us toward a different course. What’s more, we remember the negative feedback. We internalize it, make it muscle memory. And the next time we are in a similarly heated exchange we might be less disposed to let our anger get the best of us.

There are fewer ways to detect these effects when we interact through digital media. Given the technical constraints of social media technologies, the selective feedback we receive generally takes the form of written or graphical responses. This not only privileges (or “magnifies”) written text and images over other (“reduced”) modes of expression, such as tone of voice, bodily gesture, tempo of speech, and so on, it privileges intentional expression over all manner of unconscious response. Though what we indicate or emote without consciously knowing it is often far more expressive and impactful than the words we use to describe how we feel, that feedback is not usually relayed through digitally mediated interactions. And again, the habits we develop in a world of digital media reflect this. They reflect the fact that we are only partially attuned to how we impact others, that many facets of their reactions remain invisible to us. It shouldn’t be surprising, as a result, that good social habits—tendencies toward kindness and civility—are rarer than they should be online.

CONCLUSION: DESIGNING OPACITY

As the examples in the previous section illustrate, we develop different kinds of habits around digital media. Like non-digitally-mediated habits, some of these habits are what we might call *self-regarding*, while others are *other-regarding*. Which is to say, in some cases we are the beneficiaries of our good habits and the ones who suffer from our bad habits, while in other cases it is others who benefit from and bear their consequences. Examples of good self-regarding digital habits are protecting your own privacy and online security. Good other-regarding digital habits might involve things like civility in online comments sections. In addition, growing accustomed to digital media means developing *technology-regarding* habits—patterns of action which either preserve or deteriorate the tools themselves—such as keeping on top of software upgrades.

The transparency of digital media prevents us from learning many of these habits through trial and error. So unless we are explicitly taught to develop good digital habits (which we ought to be), many of us won't develop them. This raises the question: If the problem is transparency, can we make our media more opaque? Can we design the tools which mediate much of our lives to give us more feedback? Should we be drawn out of our technological absorption more frequently, and forced to reflect on what we're doing? While this is largely a question for technology designers, models for creating what I will call *strategic opacity* already exist. I conclude by briefly describing two.

First, the standard computer interface design strategy for conveying feedback to users: the text alert. Since the development of the earliest personal computers, software designers have used text feedback to give users information about the internal states of their computers and their options for altering them. If my web browser detects that I am about to send sensitive information over an unencrypted server, it asks me if I want to proceed. If I try to close a document without saving it, my word processor produces a text prompt encouraging me to think twice. These alerts are designed to interrupt our normal "flows," to bring particular aspects of our technologically mediated activities into focus—to make them, in the language of this essay, more opaque.

This strategy can be used to interrupt bad habits. The designers of a website familiar to many philosophers employed it to considerable effect. Philosophers on the academic job market often visit the "Philosophy Jobs Wiki,"[12] a website where users can note whether or not particular jobs have been filled. At the height of job market season, job candidates have been known to sit on the Jobs Wiki, refreshing it over and over again, desperate to learn about any changes to their odds. In response, the website's owners built in a text alert. Now, if a user visits or refreshes the page sufficiently many times in a given period a text box emerges at the top of the page reading: "We notice you've been coming here a lot. Maybe you'd be better off if you blocked yourself from looking at the wiki for a while. Then you could go do something more productive, like getting up to speed on a new philosophical topic." A little bit of negative feedback to make people think explicitly about otherwise unthinking digital habits.

At the same time, many have recognized the limits of text-based alerts. A common method for forcing website visitors to consciously consider whether or not they consent to a website's legal terms has historically been to present them with a "clickwrap" agreement—a statement of terms which must be accepted (by clicking "I agree" or "I accept") before they can proceed. Over time, people have become habituated to this process, to the point where most people click "I accept" without bothering to read the terms. The agreements have become transparent.

In response to this problem, some scholars have turned their attention to how we might counteract this bad habit—how we might induce users to pay more conscious attention to privacy and other legal implications of their online activities. Legal scholar Ryan Calo, for instance, advocates an alternative to text-based forms of legal notice, which he calls "visceral notice" (2012, 1027). "Language is not the only means to convey information," Calo writes, "Nor is it always the most efficient" (ibid., 1034). Rather than presenting website visitors or software users with written policies, Calo suggests that website and software designers generate user *experiences* that make the choices they face opaque. He points to examples of computer programs generating sounds or attention-getting images, and websites showing users the particular pieces of information about them that they have collected and are preparing to transmit (ibid., 1034–44). "[T]he experience of [online] commenting could be made to feel more like an in-person conversation by graphically representing that a comment to a post is also a comment directed at the author," Calo writes (ibid., 1041).

These are just a few examples of how technology designers might create strategic opacity. Whether it takes the form of text alerts or more visceral feedback or some other form entirely, our digital media can be designed to demand more of our attention. They can reveal to us the internal effects we are having on our devices, and give us a more robust sense of the external effects we are having on other people. In other words, we can construct our digital environment to be more like our natural one—an environment in which we feel the effects of our actions. If we want to promote cherished values, like privacy, security, and civility online, this is the kind of environment we will have to build. For the activities we undertake through digital media are driven by digital habits, and those habits are blind without it.

NOTES

1. It has also been observed that we *think* the way we do for the most part out of habit. In what follows I focus almost entirely on habits of action, rather than habits of thought, but my arguments about the former pertain to some degree to the latter as well.

2. For an accessible discussion of neuroscience research showing that the brain is less active while executing habitual activities than novel ones, see the first chapter in Duhigg 2014.

3. Cited in Carlisle 2014, 8.

4. Of course we do in fact go through this process on occasion, but those are the exceptions, not the rule.

5. Or as Ed Casey puts it, describing Merleau-Ponty's view: "In brief: no habit or past without body; no body without habit or past" (2013, 214).

6. See McLuhan 2003, cited in Van Den Eede 2010.

7. See Latour 1992, cited in Van Den Eede 2010.

8. Ihde first developed many of the ideas which follow in *Technics and Praxis* (1979). However I will refer mostly to their more mature formulations in his *Technology and the Lifeworld* (1990).

9. For an excellent, detailed overview of the central concepts of postphenomenology, as well as its philosophical origins and trajectories, see Rosenberger and Verbeek 2015.

10. In particular, my observations are likely relevant for thinking about how we comport ourselves in relation to the range of sensors beginning to be embedded in our built environments.

11. If I type too quickly, though, and two typebars get crossed, the internal effects present themselves immediately and transparency is lost.

12. http://phylo.info/jobs/wiki.

REFERENCES

Aristotle. (2002). *Nicomachean Ethics*. Trans. J. Sachs. Newburyport, MA: Focus Publishing.

Calo, R. (2012). "Against Notice Skepticism in Privacy (and Elsewhere)." *Notre Dame Law Review* 87 (3): 1027–72.

Carlisle, C. (2014). *On Habit*. London: Routledge.

Casey, E. S. (2013). "Habitual Body and Memory in Merleau-Ponty." In T. Sparrow and A. Hutchinson (eds.), *A History of Habit: From Aristotle to Bourdieu*. Lanham, MD: Lexington Books.

Dewey, J. (1922). *Human Nature and Conduct*. New York: Henry Holt and Company.

Dreyfus, H. (1991). *Being-in-the-World: A Commentary on Heidegger's* Being and Time, *Division I*. Cambridge, MA: MIT Press.

Duhigg, C. (2014). *The Power of Habit: Why We Do What We Do in Life and Business*. New York: Random House.

Heidegger, M. (1962). *Being and Time*. Trans. J. Macquarrie and E. Robinson. Oxford: Blackwell Publishers Ltd.

Ihde, D. (1979). *Technics and Praxis*. Dordrecht: D. Reidel Publishing Company.

———. (1983). *Existential Technics*. Albany, NY: State University of New York Press.

———. (1990). *Technology and the Lifeworld: From Garden to Earth*. Bloomington, IN: Indiana University Press.

Kant, I. (2006). *Anthropology from a Pragmatic Point of View*. Trans. and ed. R. B. Louden. Cambridge, UK: Cambridge University Press.

Latour, B. (1992). "Where Are the Missing Masses? The Sociology of a Few Mundane Artifacts." In W. E. Bijker and J. Law (eds.), *Shaping Technology/Building Society: Studies in Sociotechnical Change*. Cambridge, MA: MIT Press.

McLuhan, M. (2003). *Understanding Media: The Extensions of Man*. Corte Madera: Ginkgo Press.

Merleau-Ponty, M. (2002). *Phenomenology of Perception*. Trans. C. Smith. London: Routledge Classics.

Norman, D. (1999). *The Invisible Computer: Why Good Products Can Fail, the Personal Computer Is So Complex, and Information Appliances Are the Solution*. Cambridge, MA: MIT Press.

Rosenberger, R. (2009). "The Sudden Experience of the Computer." *AI and Society* 24: 173–80.

———. (2013). "The Importance of Generalized Bodily Habits for a Future World of Ubiquitous Computing." *AI and Society* 28: 289–96.

Rosenberger, R. and P.-P. Verbeek. (2015). "A Field Guide to Postphenomenology." In R. Rosenberger and P.-P. Verbeek (eds.), *Postphenomenological Investigations: Essays on Human-Technology Relations*. Lanham, MD: Lexington Books.

Sullivan, S. (2013). "Oppression in the Gut: The Biological Dimensions of Deweyan Habit." In T. Sparrow and A. Hutchinson (eds.), *A History of Habit: From Aristotle to Bourdieu*. Lanham, MD: Lexington Books.

Turkle, S. (1995). *Life on the Screen: Identity in the Age of the Internet*. New York: Simon and Schuster.

———. (2005). *The Second Self: Computers and the Human Spirit*. Cambridge, MA: MIT Press.

Van Den Eede, Y. (2010). "In Between Us: On the Transparency and Opacity of Technological Mediation." *Foundations of Science* 16 (2): 139–59.

Chapter 3

Body, Technology, and Humanity

Shoji Nagataki

Human beings have changed their environmental world in various ways.[1] They have designed different types of dwelling in order to make a living space comfortable. Most notably, the advancement of science and technology after the Scientific and Industrial Revolutions has been transforming our living world drastically. More light would be shed on these changes with the aid of the (post)phenomenological insight that the world given to us is mediated by the body—a medium through which we recognize, work on, and physically transform the world.

While the environmental world has been historically changed to a great extent, the body itself has not undergone much change regarding the physical constitution. Though medical advancement and the amelioration of public health have succeeded in keeping our body healthier than before and extending the length of life, they have not extended our physical abilities per se. Our desire for comfort has not been directed to the body, but to the world around us and things in it, including different kinds of media.

The situation, however, is changing in the new millennium. As manifest in the concept of enhancement, it looks increasingly likely that technology intervenes directly in the human body and reinforces its physical ability. While medical treatment mainly aims at restoring physical functions to the normal level, enhancement intends to satisfy a desire for abilities beyond it. Genetic engineering, tissue engineering, and cyborg technology based on neural engineering are typical examples of enhancement. They might boost our athletic ability and intelligence dramatically. We can call this trend "a mechanization of the body." From the standpoint of a phenomenological conception of the body as a medium for recognizing the world, modifying our body may lead to certain changes in the way in which the world is embodied and perceived—or more generally, in the way(s) in which humans engage in the world. This is a central theme of postphenomenology, which is contrasted to phenomenologists' interest in the relationship between the "natural" human body and the world. Postphenomenology highlights the role of technology in the human experience of the world.

The trend of mechanization of the body might be accompanied by the appearance of sophisticated humanoid robots in our daily lives. This phenomenon, if it ever happens, would make the demarcation between humans and machines quite vague. Some might say that a world could be brought into reality where many kinds of bodies, which are human bodies, mechanically enhanced bodies, human bodies with digital devices, virtual bodies, and human-like machines live together.

In this chapter, I will

1. survey some of the philosophical theories on the human-machine relationship, with a focus on the concept of embodiment;
2. examine some philosophical implications of the situations and *dramatis personae* developed in sci-fi literature, taking into account the issues of human personal identity and embodiment, of the (mechanized) body as medium, and of the postphenomenological relationship between a human being and his or her environmental world; and
3. discuss possible changes in the meaning of humanity and interactions between humans and "newcomers" in terms of vulnerability.

A MECHANICAL VIEW OF NATURE AND THE BODY AS MACHINE

From Ancient Times to the Middle Ages, all natural phenomena were explained on the basis of an Aristotelian conception, in a teleological way. The reason, for instance, why flames leap up out of the fire is that they aspire to be at their natural place. Aristotelians held that heaviness was an endeavor to go to the center of the earth. Even in the Renaissance, the Earth was regarded as a living system, which was supposed to be best thought of from a teleological perspective. Leonardo da Vinci writes:

> We can say that the earth has a vegetative soul, and that its flesh is the land, its bones are the structures of the rocks [...] its blood is the pools of water [...] its breathing and its pulses are the ebb and flow of the sea. (da Vinci 1883, 221 [no. 1000])

In the eyes of natural philosophers in later ages, such a conception of nature is perceived as mysterious and partly unintelligible, because the Aristotelian view was essentially animistic in that it attributed soul-like properties to natural objects and processes.

The artistry of nature sometimes gives impetus to the development of technology. Historians tell us that the spinning and weaving machine was originally designed to emulate the work of spiders (Shapin 1998, 31). However, the intricateness and subtlety of natural products were basically taken, from the Aristotelian perspective, far beyond that of human artifacts. Indeed, trying to compete with, or violate, a higher order of nature was immoral, it was thought; nature was regarded as an awe-inspiring object. "As natural and human artifice were compared, so they were *opposed*" (ibid.; original emphasis).

As is well known, modern natural philosophers, in the era of the scientific revolution, denied the traditional way of thinking, and proposed a new view—the mechanical view of nature. A bunch of empirical knowledge had been accumulated in this era. By developing their hypotheses with mathematics, they demystified nature, observing and experimenting with it. Natural things were tamed into clocklike beings which, just like a mechanical watch, work predictably in accordance with natural laws. Galileo wrote highly celebrated passages in *The Assayer*:

> this grand book the universe [...] cannot be understood unless one first comes to comprehend the language and to read the alphabet in which it is composed. It is written in the language of mathematics, and its characters are triangles, circles, and other geometric figures, without which it is humanly impossible to understand a single word of it. (Galileo 1957, 237–38)

When Descartes said "I have described this earth and in general the whole visible universe as if it were entirely a machine" (Descartes 1989, 503),[2] he was making the same point. What he referred to as "the earth" or "the whole visible universe" can be paraphrased as nature or physical things. Even living things, like plants and animals, were grasped in a mechanical way. What about humans? Natural philosophers in this era thought that the human body was nothing more than matter in motion. With the rise of mechanistic philosophy, they came to a view that nature is just an aggregation of machinery, to which the human body also belongs. However, Descartes did not think that any mechanical explanation could be applied to the human mind. Shapin succinctly describes Cartesian thought:

> For human beings, however, the scope of mechanical accounts was crucially limited. Explanations of the human *body* were, for Descartes, not the same thing as explanations of human *beings*, for there was something about human beings that could not be comprehended by an account of the body's matter and motion. (Shapin 1998, 159; original emphasis)

In effect, Descartes meant that the human mind could not come from material things.

MACHINE MAN

When reading Descartes' *Le monde* and *Traité de l'homme*, we can get a glimpse of his fascination with the concept of automaton. While he regarded human beings as special entities, he dreamed of making the machine very similar to man. De la Mettrie advocated a yet more radical mechanistic view about humans by considering a human as a machine.

De la Mettrie's Mechanism

"[M]an is a mere animal, or a collection of springs which wind up each other" (de la Mettrie 1865, 128). Animals are almost as perfect machines as humans. Nevertheless, according to de la Mettrie, the man-machine is so complicated that it is impossible to clearly describe it, and define it. Put another way, he thought that it is an unintelligible entity in spite of it being a machine. However, this seems blatantly conflicting with the prevalent view of his contemporaries that the very nature of physical things made themselves intelligible and their function predictable. It is also striking in de la Mettrie's thought that the mental dimension was clearly based on bodily activities. This view is quite unique for his era. "We think we are, and we are good men, same as we are gay or brave; everything depends on the way our machine is wound up" (ibid., 40–41).

In *L'Homme machine*, he concentrated on the structure of the body and noted that emotion was deeply linked with the motion of the body. Furthermore, he wrote that "[a]ll our excellent qualities come from nature; to her we owe all that we are" (ibid., 71). "Nature" in this context clearly means a delicate mechanism of the human body. He thought that the body was the most basic fundament of human existence. This view was also evident when he wrote that "the embodiment is the human being's preeminent advantage" (ibid., 70). Even the moral sense was tightly combined with abstention from physical indulgence, and willpower depended on bodily conditions (ibid., 127). Such a conception was unusual in those days. Though Descartes and de la Mettrie basically shared a mechanical philosophy, there was a crucial difference between them in that the former regarded the human mind as something special which could not be amenable to a mechanical understanding, while the latter saw the mind as relatively rooted in the embodiment.

Wiener's Cybernetic Humans

It was Norbert Wiener who embraced a thoroughgoing mechanics in the 20th century. He advocated the conception of cybernetics, which was defined as "the entire field of communication and control theory, whether in the machine or in the animal" (Wiener 1965, 11). The term was coined from the Greek word "κυβέρνησις," meaning a steersman. He argued that animals (including humans) and machines are very similar with regard to communication and control. He often used the word "automaton," but it is not used in a traditional sense, that is, something like a little figure dancing on top of a musical box or an old Japanese wind-up doll. Even when elaborately made, they only move in accordance with preprogrammed patterns. "[T]he past activity of the figures has practically nothing to do with the pattern of their future activity" (Wiener 1950, 21–22). What he has in mind is a machine that can obtain information about its environment—which can vary according to its actions—and make use of that information for its future course of action.

Speaking of the basic level of cognition, one may think of such a machine that has *kinesthesis* in a phenomenological sense, or perceivers implementing perception-action interactions (cf. Gibson 1979 and Reed 1996). As to the higher level of cognition, one may think of a machine which communicates with its environment including individuals (humans, animals, other machines, and so forth) around it, accumulates the past information in the form of experience and memory, controlling its future actions. Wiener says: "It is my thesis that the physical functioning of the living individual and the operation of some of the newer communication machines are precisely parallel in their analogous attempts to control entropy through feedback" (Wiener 1950, 26). He furthermore talks of similarities between higher-level animals and machines: "In these higher forms of communicative organisms the environment, considered as the past experience of the individual, can modify the pattern of behavior into one which in some sense or other will deal more effectively with the future environment" (ibid., 48). Additionally, he tells us that complex actions of automata draw upon a large number of combinations of the input from and the output to the outer world as well as "of the records taken from the past stored data which we call the memory" (ibid., 23–24).

Based on the conceptual apparatus above, he proposes a bold hypothesis:

> *Cybernetics takes the view that the structure of the machine or of the organism is an index of the performance that may be expected from it.* [...] Theoretically, if we could build a machine whose mechanical structure duplicated human physiology, then we could have a machine whose intellectual capacities would duplicate those of human beings. (ibid., 57; original emphasis)

Around the middle of the last century, Wiener theoretically argued for the possibility of creating intellectual automata only imagined in sci-fi movies of our time. His image was not boxy machines which could "think" more effectively than humans in certain aspects, but those which could be realized by implementing the mechanical structure of humans, or a human-like body.

It should be noted that his view is opposed not just to the first generation of Artificial Intelligence (sometimes cynically called "Good Old-Fashioned AI," or GOFAI) in the middle of the 20th century, which approached human cognition with an emphasis on its intellectual dimension. Wiener also anticipated the theme of a close relationship between embodiment and intelligence, which is usually regarded as characteristic of the work by Rodney Brooks and others since the 1990s (cf. Brooks 1997 and Brooks et al. 1999).

FROM AUTOMATA TO HUMANOIDS AND CYBORGS

Thus, a lot of thinkers and scientists have meditated on human nature, and sometimes dreamed of making creatures similar to human beings. Such creatures have been presented more imaginatively in novels and movies. In what follows, I will look at some movies in which humanoids or cyborgs are featured and at Kafka's *The Metamorphosis*, and consider some of the philosophical implications.

Blade Runner and the Continuity of Memories

First, I'll take up *Blade Runner* (Ridley Scott, 1982), which has now become a sci-fi classic. The film is set in Los Angeles in the early 21st century, when the earth is contaminated by nuclear fallouts. Almost all wild animals have gone extinct by the environmental destruction. Humans, who are trying to move to other planets, have launched the production of genetically engineered humanoids called "replicants" in order to put them to work outside the earth. Replicants are quite similar, both physically and mentally, to humans—the very fact which annoys and irritates some people and makes them scornfully call them "skin jobs." Only experts, known as "Blade Runners," can discern them by using the "Voight-Kampff" test designed for that purpose. This test is, in a way, similar to the Turing Test. For the distinction is made solely on the basis of a behavioral dimension, though the former is done in a face-to-face setting, while the latter is not. The close similarity of physical appearance between replicants and humans functions as something which separates the interrogator and the other two participants—a human and a machine—in the Turing test.

Rick Deckard, a Blade Runner, has the skills to recognize replicants. In the first part of the film, Deckard visits Dr. Tyrell, a genius of biomechanical engineering and the creator of replicants. He asks Deckard to test on his replicant secretary, Rachael. She thinks of herself as a real human, though she is beginning to have strange and uneasy feelings about her very existence. Dr. Tyrell says that, in order to become a human in the mental dimension (a being with a Cartesian self), it is necessary for a replicant to have memories from childhood.

Tyrell: More human than human is our motto. Rachael is an experiment, nothing more. Well, we began to recognize in them a strange obsession. After all, they are emotionally inexperienced with only a few years in which to store up the experiences which you and I take for granted. If we gift them with a past … we create a cushion or pillow for their emotions.
Deckard: Memories, you are talking about memories?

Since our sense of self-identity is rooted in the reflective and linguistic activities of mind, especially in memories from childhood, there is a psychological aspect to self-identity, which can rightly be called "Cartesian."

As described above, performing complicated acts, having memories, and having mental identity of the self are related to each other. This is also suggested by Wiener when he writes that complicated actions of higher animals, including humans, depend on memories, emphasizing the way they are related to embodiment:

> I have said that man and the animal have a kinaesthetic sense, by which they keep a record of the position and tensions of their muscles. For any machine subject to a varied external environment to act effectively it is necessary that information conquering the results of its own action be furnished to it as part of the information on which it must continue to act. (Wiener 1950, 24)

The Ghost in the Shell, or the Objectivity of the Self

Don Ihde says that "[p]ostphenomenology is a modified, hybrid phenomenology" (Ihde 2009, 23). This new style of philosophy developed out of the interaction among phenomenology, pragmatism, and philosophy of technology. Its scope is wider than its predecessor in that, while traditional phenomenology deals with the primordial reciprocity between a flesh-and-blood person and the world, postphenomenology concentrates on the dynamic relationship between a modified, hybrid body and the world.

So, next, I want to focus on a Japanese animated film, *The Ghost in the Shell* (Mamoru Oshii, 1995). The story unfolds in the near future of Japan, where humans, cyborgs, humanoids, robots, and programs with a human-like character coexist. The protagonist is Motoko Kusanagi, whose body was severely damaged, except for her brain, in an airplane accident as a child. She has survived by becoming a cyborg with the assistance of high technology, and now she is working as the Chief of Public Security Section 9, which cracks down on high-tech Internet crimes.

As opposed to robots and humanoids, cyborgs with a purely mechanical body are accepted as members of the class of human beings in this society. They think that they have a "ghost" within themselves, which resides within their titanium skulls—*shells*—covering a flesh-and-blood brain.[3] What is a "ghost"? Several interpretations are possible: a mind which originates from a genuine human being, a consciousness with qualia, and so on. In any case, it is supposedly believed to be something like an essential feature which is common in human minds.

In the following scene, Kusanagi and her subordinate officer, Bato, arrest a humanoid who is programmed to behave just like a human:

Humanoid: It's no use arrestin' me. I'm not talkin' to any goddamn cops!
Bato: Talk? And just what are you gonna talk about? You don't even know your own name, you stupid dick-head. Huh?
Kusanagi: Can you remember your mother's name or what she looks like? Or how about where you were born? Don't you have any happy childhood memories? Do you even know who you are?

The humanoid is at a loss for words. After the dialogue above, Bato says in disgust: "The figure without Ghost is so pathetic, especially, with a flesh and blood one." What is at stake here is the nature of the human mind underpinned with past memories, that is, personal identity.

Cyborgs, such as Kusanagi, who take pity on humanoids without a "ghost" are afflicted by a particular problem: that of self-identification specific to a "complete" cyborg in the sense that every bit of the body is composed of artificial materials except the brain. However, she suffers from an uneasiness about her mechanical, fake flesh-and-blood, body. When we observe ourselves only with our senses, we cannot, of course, ascertain immediately the presence of every part and parcel of the body. To use phenomenological terminology, my body is "never completely constituted" (Merleau-Ponty 1960, 165). It is impossible for Kusanagi to verify even the existence of her only original body part directly, because it is her brain.

I would like to quote some words by Descartes here. My "body which, by a special right, I called my own, belonged to me more properly and strictly than any of the others" (Descartes 1967, 485). We can interpret this statement as relating to bodily self-identity. In fact, it truly expresses a feeling we, beings of flesh and blood, have. Kusanagi talks to herself:

> Being a human consists of a vast multitude of parts and components. In the same way, being 'I' involves a vast multitude of factors and elements. I have a face and voice to distinguish myself from others. My thoughts and memories are unique only to me [. . .].

What matters here are those elements which constitute a human personality. As evident from the first sentence, her words are pertinent to the mind-body problem. She says that the self has physical or external aspects and psychological or internal aspects.

The body as a medium for recognizing the world is usually not an object of consciousness in everyday life. Generally speaking, the function of media consists in mediating between objects by withdrawing themselves from the domain of objects. No special attention is typically paid to them. For Kusanagi, however, the fact that she is an artificial object is highly salient for herself. As an existence with a cyborged body, she says that she "can't survive without regular high-level maintenance." Her body cannot help looming in her vision of life and asserting its very existence. It is different from a "natural" body in that it should be cared of in its peculiar way. As Verbeek puts it, "pieces of technology actually merge with the human body" (Verbeek 2011, 145) in a cyborg. It is not sufficient to say that for a cyborg, the world is "technologically mediated" (ibid.). The technology transforms both the personal identity and the experienced world at the same time. As a result of the body being cyborged, that "being" becomes something which may not properly be called human (cf. ibid., 144).

When we consider the mind-body problem or the nature of personal identity, the following dialogue between Kusanagi and Bato is thought-provoking:

Kusanagi: I guess complete cyborgs like myself have a tendency to be paranoid about our origins. Sometimes I suspect I'm not who I think I am. Like maybe I died a long time ago, and somebody took my brain and stuck it in this body. Maybe there never was a real me in the first place.

Actually, she refers, by these words, to a universal problem about the origin of personality. Who knows her/his origin of personality? Nobody knows it. So, why do "real" humans like us not feel the same type of uneasiness? I think that this is one of the essential meanings of having an "original" flesh-and-blood body. Both humans and complete cyborgs like Kusanagi have continuous memories about themselves, and the only difference between them is whether the original body exists or not. To use Merleau-Ponty's words, all "spiritual acts" are based on "bodily infrastructure" (Merleau-Ponty 1945, 493). Memories of mental life are grounded in bodily unconscious memories in Merleau-Ponty's sense. Kusanagi-type cyborgs might not be able to have a full-fledged memory in this sense:

Bato: You've got human brain cells in that titanium shell of yours. You're treated like other humans, so stop with the angst.

Kusanagi: But that's just it. That's the only thing that makes me feel human: the way I'm treated. I mean, who knows what's inside our heads. Have you ever seen your own brain?

There are two phases about the identity of personality. One is, as suggested above, based on one's own memories and thoughts. Herein lies, according to the Cartesian conception of personality, the essence of being the same person.[4] The other is the aspect of identity based on the recognition of physical and behavioral sameness by others. As Kusanagi says, the way she is treated by the people around her can have an influence on her personal identity.

As a matter of fact, the continuity of memories which underlies the psychological identity is not only verified by the meta-self which reflects on the self. Recognition of ourselves as similar individuals is also due to the environment remaining more or less unchanged.

The Metamorphosis, or Body as Medium

Here we pick up Kafka's *The Metamorphosis,* a famous novel unfolding around the theme of change of the body. It can be thought of as a kind of sci-fi story as well because of its incredible situation. One morning, Gregor Samsa finds himself transformed into "a monstrous verminous bug." The circumstances around him, however, turn out to be entirely unchanged; the same familiar room, the same family members, and the same boss are still there. The continuity of his environmental world plays an important role in maintaining Gregor's identity. If the environment changed into the bug's world, he would be threatened by a far more serious crisis over his identity immediately. His self-identity is not only supported by his continuous memories, but by the sameness of his environment.

The world with its familiar things and people changes as we have bodily interaction with it. The epistemological aspect of this change is illustrated vividly by Kafka's surreal story, in which the world becomes totally different for Gregor. The theme of *The Metamorphosis* calls to mind Merleau-Ponty's dictum: "[t]he body is our general medium for having a world" (Merleau-Ponty 1945, 171).

His familiar bed, chair, and wardrobe become uncomfortable. The doorknob and its keyhole become hard to deal with for his monstrous body. Perhaps most crucially, he has a serious problem engaging into a conversation with other people because of the drastic change in his voice. As he cannot communicate with them, they change their attitudes toward him. A gap between their memories about him and what he is disrupts his identity, as it were, from outside.

He notices that his taste was transformed as well. Many kinds of food which "his sister brought" "to test his taste" (Kafka 1999, 37) are almost bad for him. He cannot taste milk though it was "his favorite drink" (ibid., 34). He notices that hanging from the ceiling is more comfortable than lying on the floor. The furniture is now an obstacle for his moving on the floor (ibid., 51). In this story, the transformation of Gregor's body is linked to the transfiguration of his epistemological world, which in turn leads to the transformation of his personality. The situation is similar to that of a cyborg. Gregor's personal identity is unstable due to the transformed world he experiences visually, tactilely, acoustically, gustatorily, or in whatever manner through his monstrous body. If we can produce such a body by genetic technology just like in the movie *The Fly*, one might properly call the medium "an actual amalgam" (Verbeek 2011, 145) of technology and body.

At the climax of the story, Kafka describes Gregor's psychological resistance against his personal transformation. When his sister tries to remove the furniture, because she appreciates that it is mere obstacles for his body, he is afraid that he would completely forget "his human past" (ibid., 54) with it. It should be noted, here again, that the personal identity of the protagonist whose body is transformed is related with his past memories. As I have discussed earlier, this motif is the same as that of *Blade Runner* and *The Ghost in the Shell.*

Though the story adopts the protagonist's narrative, objective description about him (and his psychology) and his environmental world gradually increases. This can be interpreted as expressing the gradual transformation of his personality. At the end of the story, his subjective narrative disappears, and the protagonist's dead body is objectively described from a viewpoint of his surroundings.

Our discussion on Kafka's *The Metamorphosis* suggests that the identity of personality is based on the following three elements in general:

1. her/his own memories about her/his psychological continuity;
2. others' continuous memories about her/him (and her/his physical body);
3. her/his continuous memories about her/his environmental world including others (and others' body).

Clearly, these three elements are related to each other. Our memories about ourselves and those about the world around us cannot be sharply separated. This point can be made understandable if we reflect on our ordinary experience. We can observe the psychological self and the body blending together in our everyday life. Though less explicitly, even Descartes, champion of ontological mind-body dualism, acknowledges this point (Descartes 1989, 44–45). He writes that "my soul and my own body is clearly united in our daily experience" (ibid., 43–44). Though this unity as a full-fledged self is, on a physical side, the constituent of its environmental world, it belongs exclusively neither to the mental nor to the physical realm. Memories about this kind of self inevitably involve memories about the environmental world.

Let us take a look again at the scene in which Dr. Tyrell has a conversation with Deckard. At the end of their conversation (a part which is omitted from the film version), he talks about memories. In reply to Deckard's question, "you are talking about memories?" Tyrell says:

> It's the dark corners, the little shadowy place that makes you interesting, Deckard … gusty emotions on a wet road on an autumn night … the change of seasons … the sweet guilt after masturbation.

His words about memories describe the way in which emotions, bodily sensations, and the environmental world fuse together. It should be noted that memories which underpin ourselves are, as Dr. Tyrell suggests, not explicit and linguistically objectified, but vague and engraved into our body through our own sensorial and emotional experiences. To borrow Merleau-Ponty's terminology, the environmental (perceptual) world unfolds itself through the interaction with the unity of self and body. This unity functions as a subject of action and cognition in the environmental world. Thus, in the eyes of the person who is a cyborg or has a monstrous verminous bug's body, the world would appear totally different from the one perceived when he or she was normal. Gregor's familiar room, which is suitable for a human being, becomes uncomfortable to him. The environmental world suited to complete cyborgs like Kusanagi would also appear different from that which is suited to ordinary people.

The transfiguration of the body and the environmental world would make the continuity of memories about the self precarious. By mixing up Gregor's subjective, mental scenery and objective descriptions of the transfiguration of his body, voice, taste, and so on, Kafka describes how the continuity of Gregor's memories, or his personal identity, becomes unstable. Kusanagi's self-consciousness about having a monstrous body makes her personal identity fragile as well. Consider again the dialogue about the crisis of the cyborg's self-identity. It ends with the following words:

Bato: It sounds to me like you're doubting your own ghost.

Kusanagi: What if a cyber-brain could possibly generate its own ghost and create a soul all by itself? And if it did, just what would be the importance of being human then?

There is no reason for Kusanagi's belief in personal identity other than that her flesh-brain is the only remaining piece of her original body. However, imagining the possibility of a cyber-brain which can replace the function of flesh-brain, she feels a lurking anxiety that she might become a mere machine. Her anxiety is Cartesian par excellence, because what she is seeking for is the self without the body. The ghost as a Cartesian ego doesn't offer any consolation. Her anxiety and the personality transformation of the protagonist in *The Metamorphosis* remind us that our identity is not so robust and that the role of the body and the environmental world is crucial for maintaining our self-identity.

The Time of Eve, or Intersubjectivity between Human Beings and Humanoids

In this century, some researchers are starting to develop robots implemented with a kind of intelligence and sympathy. Others are making cyborg technologies real. Those technological advancements are exposing the fragility of the concept of humanity. What differentiates humans from robots? Does a human being still continue to be a human even after becoming a complete cyborg like Kusanagi? If the answer is yes, then what guarantees her to be so? A transplanted brain from a real human with its neurochemical effects? As you can see from the previous section, one's personal identity partly depends on other people's memories about her and their attitudes toward her as well. This deeply relates to a problem of her humanity because her personal identity should be maintained in order for her to make a human-like relationship with others. The time may be just around the corner when humanity will be attributed to robots and cyborgs. Whether we regard them as beings with humanity will depend not on their own self-identification, but on the way people treat them. Just because of their close affinity to humans, the relationship between the new and the old clusters will be all the more problematic.

Let us look to *Blade Runner* and *Ghost in the Shell* again. The uneasiness of Rachael and Kusanagi is related to their own selves; they ask themselves whether they are human, whether they have a human mind, and where they came from. One might speak of the uneasiness as a manifestation of Cartesian skepticism in a broader sense.

I would like to mention another Japanese anime, which is of a different type from that of *Blade Runner* and *Ghost in the Shell*. Its title is *The Time of Eve* (Yasuhiro Yoshiura, 2008). The story is set in the near future of Japan, where humanoids, which very much resemble humans in appearance, serve as household workers. They have holographic "status rings" above their heads, the only thing by which they can be discerned from humans. It is supposed to be, in a way, illegal for them to hide the rings in public—"in a way" because one of the concerned committees of humanoids is against the prohibition.

The story begins with Rikuo, a high school student, checking behavior records of his family's humanoid, Sammy, who has recently been acting irregularly. As Rikuo traces where she goes, he stumbles across an underground café, "The Time of Eve." At its entrance, the signboard asks patrons to follow the rule of not distinguishing between humans and robots. Humanoids do not display their status rings within the café. After hesitating for some time, Rikuo decides to enter the café and finds out that several patrons are having an enjoyable time. He is uncertain whether they are authentically human or not. One of the patrons, Akiko, kindly talks to him. She is talkative, energetic and looks like a high school student. Akiko says that she comes here so that she might have a better understanding of what an *other* member in her family feels. Rikuo thinks that she is talking about her humanoid. As he enjoys conversation with Akiko, he begins to warm to her. Actually, it is the place where Sammy, Rikuo's humanoid, sometimes comes for the same purpose.

As it begins raining after school the next day, many humanoids with status rings bring umbrellas to the high school for their masters. Among them Rikuo finds Akiko with the ring above her head. Her attitude is totally different from that at the café. As she runs up to her master to deliver an umbrella, he takes it and gives an instruction to her in an emotionless manner: "Bring my bag. Make it waterproof. And return home alone." Akiko replies in a matter-of-fact way: "Acknowledged."

As stated above, when we regard others as humans, it is not because they themselves think they are humans, but rather due to the way in which they are treated in the society. In this context, some remarks would be in order on other patrons of the café. Koji and Rina get to know each other there. Though in fact they are humanoids, both believe the other is a human. Initially, they come there in order to figure out how to serve their masters' needs in a better way. However, they unexpectedly fall in love. They are basically used for sexual and emotional intimacy by their masters, that is, as sex robots. If we happen to know that Koji and Rina are machines, can we convince ourselves that what they are doing is a mere syntactic exchange, lacking semantics or qualia? Because of their remarkably similar appearance to humans, it would not be so easy. Indeed, Rikuo feels meaning in Akiko's behavior and words. He might even say that she has qualia, if he knew the term. He doesn't exactly know how to feel about her, even after noticing that she is a machine—this is one of the main themes of the story.

Ex Machina, Embodiment, and Vulnerability

Alex Garland's film, *Ex Machina* (2015), deeply depicts the interaction between humans and humanoids. Caleb, who works for a search engine company, is invited to a laboratory which is operated by his boss, Nathan, accompanied by a mysterious beauty, Kyoko, and a female humanoid, Ava. Kyoko doesn't understand English, which, Nathan says, is convenient for information protection. Ava, a human-like artifact created by Nathan, speaks and acts in a very natural way, save that a robot-looking body is implemented on her so that she can be recognized as a machine. Nathan asks Caleb to perform a face-to-face Turing test on Ava. Though Caleb knows that she is a mere humanoid, she is supposed to pass the test, if he feels that she seems like a human. Nathan asks him to judge whether Ava has a consciousness or whether it is only a simulation.

As Caleb holds a series of sessions with Ava, he gets deeply impressed by her extremely human-like intelligence and beauty. On the third day of the Turing Test session, she appears in front of him, wearing a wig and clothes so that her mechanical body is meticulously concealed. He is so shocked at her physical appearance, for she seems indistinguishable from a human female. Eventually, he gets bewildered and feels like loving her. He asks Nathan for the reason why he bestowed sexuality upon the humanoid. She could have been a gray box. Nathan answers that gray boxes cannot interact with each other, and that consciousness cannot exist without interaction. Here we find a strong affinity with the insight of (post)phenomenology on embodiment and the third generation of cognitive science (cf. Nagataki and Hirose 2007). Bodily interactions are essential to the emergence of consciousness and personal identity. In other words, a human-like body plays the role of medium for generating them, if possible. Without those interactions, what we have is only an ingeniously programmed "gray box," which is far from being an entity with consciousness and personal identity.

One day, when Caleb enters Nathan's bedroom, Kyoko is lying on his bed with nothing on. As Caleb pulls the cabinet door open, he finds out that Nathan has hidden humanoid sex robots in it. Kyoko quietly comes out of the bed and stands in front of Caleb. Then she peels away her skin, showing her machinery body under the skin to him. Suspicion looms in Caleb's mind whether he himself is a human or a humanoid. As he tries to peel off his face skin and cut his arm skin with a razor, the blood runs out and he feels pain.

It is noteworthy that Caleb injures his own body in order to determine whether he is a human or a humanoid. I think that two implications can be noticed here. One is that human identity allegedly verifiable by Cartesian introspection is, in fact, elusive and we cannot make sure of it without tracing back to the ontological basis of the body and its vulnerability. Furthermore, Caleb's move for the verification appeals to the vulnerability of his body. A machine-like body will fail this test.

CONCLUDING REMARKS

Cyborg technology would make it possible to enhance abilities of the human body at an unprecedented level in the near future. Robotics and AI would be able to create beings with a human-like appearance and, in a sense, with greater-than-human intelligence. They would be newcomers to our society, whatever use they are intended for. How should we engage with them? When humanoids become more than industrial products, what is necessary for them to be accepted and initiated into the human society? Is it an ability of intellectual conversation? A bodily dexterity? Or usefulness they can demonstrate in a greater way than humans do?

Human beings "are exposed to physical illness, injury, disability, and death" (Mackenzie, Rogers, and Dodds 2014, 1), and they feel pain and pleasure as well. There is "a common human vulnerability" (Butler 2004, 31), which is specific to us, beings with a body. Butler wrote that "we cannot think the ontology of the body without the body being somewhere, without some 'thereness'" (Butler 2009, 53fn.). In addition, the ontology of the body involves necessarily its thin-skinned, fragile makeup, from which derives our common vulnerability. "By insisting on a 'common' corporeal vulnerability, I may seem to be positing a new basis for humanism" (Butler 2004, 42). Humanity is based on our having vulnerable bodies which consist of more or less the same structure and characters. And the interaction among such bodies as media is essential for the development of our consciousness and personal identity. Due to this very fact, human beings are aware that they should live in the intersubjective and ethical world based on empathy. However, this awareness comes later because our body is "[g]iven over from the start to the world of others" (ibid., 26) before the Cartesian ego appears. In phenomenological terms, we might say that the body exists always already with such sociality. "[O]nly later, and with some uncertainty, do I lay claim to my body as my own, if, in fact, I ever do" (ibid.). A sense of owning the body occurs after our understanding of the Cartesian ego and the concept of ownership.

Let us go back to the question: What is necessary for humanoids to be accepted and initiated into the human society? One possible answer is the vulnerable body and unconscious memory about it. Replicants in *Blade Runner* supposedly can feel pain if their body is injured. Their lifetime is only four years. Though this weakness is not exactly the same as the vulnerability we discussed, it certainly is similar.

We have emphasized the ontological aspect of vulnerability so far, but it has relational and social aspects as well. Since human beings are vulnerable, they can be physically and psychologically injured, cared for, and supported by others. To borrow again a bit of Merleau-Pontian terminology (cf. 1945, 171), the vulnerable body is our general *medium* for interacting with others. If, in one way or another, the vulnerability can be implemented on cyborgs and humanoids, we may be able to support each other in a far better way. The use of cyborg technologies is, in some sense, alleviating human vulnerabilities.[5] It may seem paradoxical to implement some vulnerability in humanoids;

it is, however, necessary to do so in order to reduce possible risk which humans would take when using and interacting with them (cf. Coeckelbergh 2013). It is not easy to define what vulnerable humanoids and robots are, and it is another problem whether we hope to have a cooperative situation between them and us or not. However, vulnerability should be one of the key concepts if they are to be more than mere machines or tools for us.

NOTES

1. The author is supported by a Grant-in-Aid for Scientific Research (C), No. 25370034. (*JSPS*) No. 16K02144.
2. All translations from French sources in this chapter are mine.
3. A shell may be associated with an interface program in an operating system, which mediates users and the kernel.
4. As already mentioned, the memories, on which reflective consciousness is based, are engraved into us through our own sensorial and emotional experiences.
5. However, Kusanagi says that cyborgs like her can't live without high-level maintenance. One might call it a new type of vulnerability brought about by technologies in Mark Coeckelbergh's sense. See Coeckelbergh 2013.

REFERENCES

Brooks, R. A., C. Breazeal, M. Marjanovic, B. Scassellati, and M. M. William. (1999). "The Cog Project: Building a Humanoid Robot." In *Computation for Metaphors, Analogy, and Agents*. Dordrecht: Springer, 52–87.

Butler, J. (2004). *Precarious Life: The Powers of Mourning*. London: Verso.

———. (2009). *Frames of War*. London: Verso.

Coeckelbergh, M. (2013). *Human Being @ Risk: Enhancement, Technology, and the Evaluation of Vulnerability Transformations*. Dordrecht: Springer.

da Vinci, L. (1883). *The Literary Works of Leonardo da Vinci.* London: Knight of the Bavarian Order of ST Michael, & C. vol. II.

de La Mettrie, J. O. (1865). *L'Homme machine. Avec une introduction et des notes de Assézat*. Paris: F. Henry.

Descartes, R. (1963). *Œuvres Philosophiques Tome I*. Paris: Garnier.

———. (1967). *Œuvres Philosophiques Tome II*. Paris: Garnier.

———. (1989). *Œuvres Philosophiques Tome III*. Paris: Garnier.

Galilei, G. (1957). *The Assayer in Discoveries and Opinions of Galileo, by Stillman Drake*. New York: Doubleday.

Gibson, J. J. (1979). *The Ecological Approach to Visual Perception*. Boston: Houghton Mifflin Company.

Ihde, D. (2009). *Postphenomenology and Technoscience: The Peking University Lectures*. Albany: State University of New York Press.

Kafka, F. (1999). *The Metamorphosis*. Trans. I. Johnston. Planet PDF.

Mackenzie, C., W. Rogers, and S. Dodds. (2014). "Introduction: What Is Vulnerability, and Why Does It Matter for Moral Theory?" In C. Mackenzie, W. Rogers, and S. Dodds (eds.), *Vulnerability: New Essays in Ethics and Feminist Philosophy*. Oxford: Oxford University Press, 1–29.

Merleau-Ponty, M. (1945). *Phénoménologie de la perception*. Paris: Gallimard.

———. (1960). *Signes*, Paris: Gallimard.

Nagataki, S. and S. Hirose. (2007). "Phenomenology and the Third Generation of Cognitive Science: Towards a Cognitive Phenomenology of the Body." *Human Studies* 30 (3): 219–232.

Reed, E. S. (1996). *Encountering the World*. New York: Oxford University Press.

Shapin, S. (1998). *The Scientific Revolution*. Chicago: University Of Chicago Press.

Verbeek, P.-P. (2011). *Moralizing Technology: Understanding and Designing the Morality of Things*. Chicago: University of Chicago Press.

Wiener, N. (1950). *The Human Use of Human Beings*. Boston: Houghton Mifflin.

———. (1965). *Cybernetics or Control and Communication*. Second edition. Cambridge, MA: MIT Press.

Chapter 4

Magic, Augmentations, and Digital Powers

Nicola Liberati

The aim of this chapter is to analyze the effects produced by the invisible interfaces of new emerging digital media in our everyday world focusing on computer technologies.[1] We will study the "magic" these new media want to produce, and we will highlight how the introduction of this element will change our way of dealing with these devices.

The reason for this focus is clear, if we watch famous concept videos related to the development of a new computer device.[2] When we refer to topics like high technology, computers, and human-computer interactions, we often find the word "magic" used for describing the "astonishing" effects produced by these devices. The digital product is not only marketed as a "beautiful" item with a new fashionable design and as an object we need, but it is often wrapped in an aura suggesting the device is capable of doing incredible and magical things. Many of the efforts in the production of the video and the design of these products are to provide the users with a device which can astonish them by acting in surprising and unexpected ways (Friedman 2008). Especially, these technologies are designed to produce what is called the "wow effect" or the "wow factor" (Puech 2016, 65) of "smart technologies."[3] Sometimes the word "magic" is even embedded into the name of the technology just to strengthen the connection between the technology and its astonishing properties, such as in the case of Augmented Reality company *Magic Leap*.[4]

It seems the concepts of magic, digital media, and computer technologies are tightly interconnected. This relates to the interest in developing a new way of using these devices as well as the introduction of new devices and technologies. For this reason, we need to analyze the introduction of this "magic" in order to understand what are the effects produced by such new digital media and their new ways of using them.

This chapter focuses on two main words: design and magic. Thus, we divide it into two main sections:

1. The first section will accentuate on the "design" used in the development of new digital media. We will analyze developers' interest in producing devices intertwined with the everyday life of the users by using a postphenomenological framework and by introducing embodiment relations. More precisely we will show how digital media allow the users to embed the digital elements as part of their own capabilities. In this way, we will highlight how these devices are conceived as magical from the point of view of the users.
2. The second section will focus on the term "magic" by introducing the famous law by Arthur C. Clarke binding together advanced technologies and magic: "any sufficiently advanced technology is indistinguishable from magic" (Clarke 1973). Thanks to two different interpretations of this law, it will be possible to tackle the topic from a different angle and to analyze various aspects related to these new technologies by highlighting how people around the users perceive these technologies in their transparency and opacity. Therefore, instead of focusing on the users and their way of acting through the technologies, we will show how other subjects perceive these technologically mediated actions as magic.

Summing up, this chapter will study the magic produced by the invisible interfaces of new digital media. It will highlight their effects by using a postphenomenological analysis and the third law of technology by Clarke by focusing on the point of view of the users and the one of the subjects around them.

THE SHIFT IN THE DESIGN OF COMPUTER TECHNOLOGIES AND MEDIA

At first, it is important to highlight some passages in the development of new computer technologies and digital media to understand the novelties they are proposing and the path they are "walking." This study will not be a complete historical analysis, but it will highlight a few elements only. The reason for such a limited choice is that we are not interested in historical analysis *per se*, but we need to highlight some elements introduced by the new generations' devices. Generally speaking, the design of computer and media technologies changed a lot through time, and we will analyze just two major changes.

For a long period of time, computers were oriented toward the developing of their computing power by designing new integrated circuits (Lojek 2010;

O'Regan 2016). This kind of trend is well identified by Moore's law (Moore 1965; Intel Corporation 2005) which predicts a golden trend for the development of integrated circuits (Padua 2011, 1177–84). According to this law, the number of transistors on integrated circuits doubles every two years, and so it says it is possible to produce cheaper and faster devices through time (Salah, Ismail, and El-Rouby 2015). Even if this law was a mere "prediction," the industry managed to make it happen. Now we are facing its limit, and this law is becoming rapidly "outdated." There are many different efforts to keep it valid by developing different applications on the integrated circuits, and an entirely new field of research called "more than Moore" is growing, aiming to keep Moore's law effective (Topaloglu 2015; Zhang and Roosmalen 2009). However, even if this new research is achieving astonishing results, and it provides to Moore's law a new life, the law, as stated by Moore, is no longer valid, and only its various "modifications" can survive (Mack 2015; Huang 2015). Thus, the never-ending progress in the improvement of computing power stated by Moore's law is facing its end.

Moreover, the conceptions of how these new devices should work and how they should interact with the subjects are changing. New digital media are aimed to intertwine their digital activities with the everyday life of the subject. Thus, these technologies make the digital actions merged with the subjects' everyday praxes instead of producing mere computing power accessible via special access points like mainframes or personal computers.

New computers and digital media are designed to merge with the users' usual perceptual capabilities and with their surroundings (Möller 2016). With new devices, subjects are not forced to focus their attention on them, but they live as if there were no computers at all around them and concentrate only on the output produced by these devices instead of the devices *per se*. In other words, new computer devices do not restrict the life of the subjects by being the focal point of their actions. They are invisible, transparent, and ubiquitous (Weiser 1991; Weiser 1993; Weiser and Brown 1996; Liberati 2016b). For example, wearable computers can be incorporated into our clothes to capture, analyze, and store data of our everyday lives (Rhodes, Minar, and Weaver 1999; Dourish and Bell 2011; Barfield 2015). Augmented Reality makes digital objects perceivable in the surroundings by allowing the users to visualize them as if they were part of their everyday world, as objects among other common objects.[5] For this reason, the term "magic" is used because the interface disappears (Beech 2012).

The novelty introduced in the design of these new computer technologies is not related exclusively to the increase of computing power, but is especially related to the way these devices connect to the users and in the way they smoothly intertwine their activities with the ones of the subjects. They are getting so close to us to be "intimate" as the concept video of the *Apple Watch* suggests (Isaacson 2014).[6] This intimacy and invisibility are the key elements on which their magic is founded.

We will now take into account embodiment relations in postphenomenology in order to understand how this way of interacting is the founding element of the production of magic from the point of view of the users.

Transparency and Embodiment Relations in Postphenomenology

Postphenomenology provides us with the right tools to assess the level of intimacy these digital media have and how they are intertwined with everyday activities of the subjects by becoming invisible to the users.

According to postphenomenology, technology can become part of subjects by working in symbiosis with them (Ihde 1990). Subjects are free to act through the devices in embodiment relations without even noticing the technological interaction.

When a technology and a subject maintain "embodiment relations" with each other, the subject's intentionality flows from the subject through the technology toward an object in the world. In this way, the technology "withdraws" and it "disappears" while the subject is acting through it (Verbeek 2005; Liberati 2015a). For example, in the classic case of a pair of glasses, the device becomes embodied into the subject and the original nucleus composed of a subject directed toward the world changes into a nucleus composed of the subject plus the technology which is directed toward the world.

The subject acts in this world without paying attention to the devices used. Obviously, the perception of the subjects is deeply shaped by the technologies used, but the devices do not fall within the main attention of the subject. In the case of the glasses the intentionality of the subjects is shaped by the lenses, and so the subjects are able to perceive much more details in the objects.[7] The intentional ray does not stop in the lenses, but it is "merely" redirected by them. In short, we can say the subjects wearing the glasses act *through* them and not *toward* them.

The glasses are transparent and they withdraw to the background. Thus, they serve as the harbinger for new computer technologies which are designed to function "unnoticed" in the background (Elmqvist 2011; Liberati 2016a). By being transparent and disappearing from the subjects' main focal point of attention, the subjects act as if the new computer technologies were not there. The subjects using these computer devices act *through* them and not *toward* them.

Thanks to these new media's design and their new way of interacting with the users, media technologies relate to the subject in the same way as the technology in an embodiment relation because they become invisible, they disappear, and are transparent for the subjects.

The subjects' body and these devices are deeply intertwined. This fact allows us to think of the technologies as devices which modify the perceptual capabilities of the subjects by merging digital elements with the "normal" perceptual capabilities of the user. Just as the optical glasses introduce some elements in the subjects' perceptual capabilities by allowing them to perceive more details of objects, these digital devices integrate elements in the subjects' capabilities by interweaving them with the subjects' action. For example, wearable computers allow to couple the subjects' actions with a tracking activity able to capture data about their lives. In the same way, Augmented Reality allows the subjects to perceive digital objects as parts of the surroundings, intertwining them with other ordinary objects in the everyday world of the subjects.

Technologies become invisible to the eyes of the users because they were designed to do that, and this feature founds the "magic" of the devices. The technologies are like magic according to the designers, because they are invisible to the users as opposed to other computer devices which force the subjects to focus their attention to them. In this way, the user accesses the computing capabilities of the devices without even noticing the technology, by embodying the devices.

THE THIRD LAW OF TECHNOLOGY BY CLARKE

Another way to tackle the magic embedded in digital media technologies and to highlight the tight intertwinement between subjects and these new digital media is to analyze the way these devices are perceived by the people who are not using them, but who are merely watching the action performed through them. As we said above, many of these devices are designed to produce magic. This aim is important because it shows us a clear way of directing the design to generate "magic" and so it highlights possible effects these technologies will have. We can use the famous third law of technology by Arthur C. Clarke to study how these technologies are becoming "magical," and so we can use it to study the effects produced.

Clarke introduced the third law of technology in 1973 in the chapter "Hazards of Prophecy: The Failure of Imagination" of his essay *Profiles of the Future*: "Any sufficiently advanced technology is indistinguishable from magic" (Clarke 1973).

This "law" about the development of new technologies is striking and provoking. However, it does not clearly show the elements founding the relation between technology and magic, and so it is open to many different interpretations. In order to shed light on these possible interpretations, we need to use some examples of how magic is used.[8] We will limit our analysis just to two cases: illusionists and wizards.

It is possible to talk about magic in relation to illusions such as in the case of a show, a performance, as a form of entertainment. Illusionists can use their skills to show as if something or someone disappears and reappears under the astonished eyes of the audience (Coppa, Hass, and Peck 2008).

In the second case of wizards, we will take into account the use of magic in relation to fantasy novels and games. For example, in *Lord of the Rings* (Tolkien 1954), in *Harry Potter* (Rowling 1997), in games like *Dungeons and Dragons* (Gygax and Arneson 1974), and in computer games like *Diablo* (Blizzard North 1996), magicians are able to cast fireballs destroying entire villages and damaging the opponents.

Taking into consideration these two cases, we can shed light on Clarke's third law of technology. The law has at least two possible interpretations: one related to the understanding of the technology used and one related to its invisibility.[9]

Magic and the First Interpretation of Clarke's Law

The first interpretation of the law is related to how the subjects "understand" the mediation of the technology.[10] When magic is involved, the subjects experiencing the magic are not able to fully understand what is happening in the surroundings. The world acts in an unexpected manner, and the subjects do not know the reasons for it.[11] In the case of the illusionists, the subjects in the audience are "fooled" by the performers because the illusionists manage to trick the eyes of the audience by making the world act in an unpredictable way, or at least they make the world act in a different way than the ones predicted by common sense and the laws of physics.

The fact that the act of magic is made by illusionists is highlighted in a TV show named *Penn & Teller: Fool Us*. In this show, performer-magicians are invited to conduct a magic in front of the two illusionists Penn and Teller. If Penn and Teller are not able to figure out how the trick is done, the performer wins a five-star trip to Las Vegas and the possibility of having a show.[12] The entire show is built upon the idea that illusionists trick and fool others by performing very ingenuous tricks. The audience and maybe the two skilled illusionists hosting the show are not able to understand how performers do the trick, and so they are "fooled." The accent clearly falls on the understanding of the process involved in these tricks.

In the same way, the magicians in *Lord of the Rings*, *Dungeons and Dragons*, and *Diablo* perform something which is not easily understandable by the others with the sole difference that it is not a trick like the illusionists' ones. They generate fireballs or other spells from their very hands, and the "audience" is not able to understand how they do it. Other people do not read magical books like magicians in *Lord of the Rings,* and they do not go to special schools like in the case of *Harry Potter*. Thus, as highlighted in the *Harry Potter* novels, there is a difference between the people who can use and understand magic and the people who have no understanding of magic and who are called the "Muggles." Magic divides society into two main groups—the ones who can understand magic and the ones who cannot do it.

According to this point of view, the third law of technology highlights the fact that the technology could become so complicated so as to be completely opaque for the common users, and it could divide society into those who understand how a certain technology operates and those who don't.

Some technologies such as a hammer are not so opaque for the majority of users, and their features can be traced back to its fundamental structure (Husserl 1965, 201; Embree 2005, 347). Even if a hammer is multistable because it can be used in many different ways (Rosenberger 2014), it is much less opaque than a computer. In order to understand how computer technologies work, a subject should have knowledge of the computer's hardware and software and usually this kind of knowledge requires a master's degree in Computer Science (Wiltse 2014).

It is quite difficult to understand how the hardware works and even to know each component. Moreover, the hardware of the computer is quite difficult to be reproduced and it is literally impossible to build a sophisticated computer without using a process which requires the usage of a massive infrastructure. People can understand quite easily how a hammer works, and it can be created just by using any heavy and sturdy object by the subjects to beat something else. Moreover, the software requires programming skills which are simply not required for using a hammer or understanding how it works. For these reasons, computer technologies and digital media risk to become magic for the common users who do not know why they act in certain ways and how they work.[13] The more advanced the technology is, the more opaque for the users it becomes. Technologies turn into something which acts mysteriously. The amount of skills needed to understand them makes them distant from the common users and audiences, and they divide subjects into two main groups just like the magic in *Harry Potter* does. In this case the opacity of the technology is what produces the magic.

This kind of interpretation of the law also has an obvious lemma:

> Every technology has a "minimum level" of knowledge required to be used and perceived as technology and not as magic.

Even for this lemma, the accent falls on the division between two groups with different levels of understanding. Every society which does not have this minimum level of technological knowledge will see the technology as pure magic.

According to this interpretation, the law and its lemma are warnings. Without the due precautions which help the users to understand how the technology works and the potentialities of such devices, the development of complicated devices such as the new digital media could lead to a social problem, known as "digital divide." The development of "complicated" devices could produce a technocratic society where the few people who are able to perceive the devices as such have the upper hand on the part of society which merely sees them as magic.

Magic and the Second Interpretation of Clarke's Law

There is also a second possible interpretation of Clarke's law, however, which is much more related to our purpose. This alternative reading of the law, conversely, focuses on the invisibility of the interface and on how the subjects around the users perceive their actions (Binsted 2000).

An illusionist who is acting on a stage does not perform merely to fool the audience. The performance is put on by way of the magicians' bare hands and their fast operation or at least hiding the specific technology which does the trick. For example, in the case of a simple magic box which makes objects disappear, the part of the box which enables such an illusion is well hidden from the eyes of the audience. From the point of view of the audience, the illusionist is making the object disappear with bare hands, without the usage of any tool which makes possible that kind of action. The classic trick of sleight of hand where the magicians make a coin disappear in their hands is even more evident. The coin changes position without the intrusion of any visible technology for the audience, but just thanks to the hands of the illusionists. Even if the coin "disappears" by falling into the magician's pocket, the audience does not see this passage or the pocket at all. The illusionists create the illusion by skillfully working with their bare hands or by using devices which help them in their activities.

The magic is lost if the audience sees the tools used or if the illusionist is not good enough to hide the trick. The magician's capabilities are conditioned by the technology used. However, the audience, who does not see the devices, will see only the technologically enhanced capabilities of the magicians as if they were able to do it without using any technology. Without a perceived technological mediation, the enhancement produced by the technology is indistinguishable from the usual capabilities of the subject.

This effect is even much more pronounced in the case of magic in a fantasy world such as the one in *Dungeons and Dragons*, where the magicians are able to cast magical objects like fireballs out of their hands without using any tool. The magician casts a spell, and a magical object appears. If the object were created not with the magicians' "bare" hands thanks to their powers, but crafted and produced by the usage of tools and technologies, the object would not be magical at all. Instead of having a magician, we would have someone much closer to an engineer or a craftsman. Again, for the eyes of the perceivers, the fact the action is performed without the use of any devices makes the magician a person with astonishing capabilities.

What is clear from these elements is that the absence of a "visible" mediation from the point of view of the audience is a fundamental element in which the magic is grounded. The kind of magic we discussed is possible because something is perceived as done with the bare hands of the performer even if there is a technological mediation involved.

For this reason, we can understand why some new digital media are related to magic. Some developers want to design invisible and transparent interfaces which are completely merged with the everyday activities of the users. Thus, they are dealing with the production of magic as an effect of this disappearance.

The postphenomenological notion of transparency introduced in the previous section is quite helpful to understand the relations binding the user and the technology. In the previous section, the transparency was taken into consideration from the point of view of the users. The technology withdrew to the background and became invisible to them. In this section the transparency is taken into account from the point of view of the audience who does not use the technology, but who merely sees the action made through it.[14]

The third law by Clarke clearly shows the necessary relations between developing invisible technologies and the production of magic. When the interface is so intertwined with the subjects' everyday activities, it disappears, and this disappearance is what produces magic. If the illusionists reveal their technologies, it becomes evident that it is the tool which makes the trick, and the audience does not perceive any magic at all.[15] If subjects can point their finger to the devices producing the digital effects, no magic is possible.

Only when the action is performed without the intrusion of any visible technology, the audience perceives the action as magical. Thus, any sufficiently advanced technology which is so developed to smoothly and invisibly interact with the subjects produces magic for the audience. The capabilities of the magician for them include the ones of the device because they do not see the technology involved.[16]

CONCLUSION

Our interest was to analyze the effects produced by these new digital media which are aiming to be intertwined with our everyday activities and to produce magic.

In the first part, we analyzed the design of some new digital media technologies. We showed how the attention in their design shifted from mere computing power to the role of their interface, and we highlighted how new devices relate to the subjects in their everyday activities. Thanks to postphenomenology we highlighted the importance of the transparency of these devices from the point of view of the users. The users act through them, and this is the element on which some developers found their discourse of "magic."

In the second part, we analyzed mainly how these devices were perceived by onlookers who are watching the users performing through them. We introduced the third law by Arthur C. Clarke, and we highlighted two possible interpretations. The first interpretation is a warning, and it is related to the understanding of what may happen in society. When technologies become advanced, they risk being magic for the common user because they are much too complicated to be understood. The first interpretation is quite important because it warns against possible social gaps arising from the development of technologies which are beyond the comprehension of the common users. However, the second interpretation is more interesting for our study, and it is related to the invisibility of these devices from the point of view of the audience. When a technology is invisible for the people around the users, it produces magic because the actions seem to be done with the "bare hands" of the user without any technological mediation. In this way, the effects of the digital media are perceived as part of the capabilities of the subjects without introducing any device. Therefore, when we analyze the point of view of people around the users, we have two different aspects of magic. One is related the opacity of the technology which makes it not easily understandable by common people. The technology is opaque and incomprehensible, and so it is magical. The second one is related to the invisibility of its presence which makes people perceive its action as an action performed by the sole subject without any technological mediation. The technology is transparent and invisible for the audience, and so it is magical.

These technologies are marketed through the notion of magic. Maybe it is just a smart way of selling the products, but this term suggests a new way of using these devices and a new way of being shaped by them. It is clear the devices are magic from the point of view of the users because they enhance the users' capabilities with their digital ones by being transparent. They are magic from the point of view of the people around too because the devices are invisible to them and so they perceive the users as enhanced by digital capabilities without noticing the presence of the digital media. These devices are not merely marketed as "magical," this aim of producing magic has deep effects on how and what they are in relation to the users and the people around the users.

As far as we consider these devices as merely "computers," we will never understand the tight bond they are building with us and so we miss the innovation they produce. They are magical because they make digital elements become part of ourselves.

In few words, we are magically becoming digital.

NOTES

1. The author is supported by the NWO VICI project "Theorizing Technological Mediation: Toward an Empirical-Philosophical Theory of Technology" (grant number: 277-20-006).

2. See, for example, the video by *CastAR* (http://castar.com/), the videos of the glasses developed by *META* (https://www.metavision.com/), and the *TEDx Tokyo* presentation of Prof. Masahiko Isami (https://www.youtube.com/watch?v=hXyLh8z6Gi8).

3. On smart communication see, for example, Glotz 2005; Ling and Donner 2009.

4. On *Magic Leap* see the following webpage: https://www.magicleap.com/#/home. See also Katz 2006.

5. For example, the famous application *Pokémon Go* allows the users to capture digital creatures generated and visualized by a mobile device. However, there are many other possible applications which make Augmented Reality much more "complex" in terms of intertwinement between the digital and everyday world (Geroimenko 2014; Billinghurst, Clark, and Lee 2015; Azuma 1997; Liberati 2014; Liberati and Nagataki 2015; Liberati 2015b; Liberati 2013).

6. See, for example, https://www.youtube.com/watch?v=RCt3iPb9E2M.

7. We think of the details as something which "enriches" the usual perception without the usage of the tool. However, we need to keep in mind that hand in hand with this "enrichment" we have "reductions" because the technology always produces other effects like distortions and chromatic aberrations which are not intended to "enrich" the perception, but to "reduce" it.

8. We will ignore some possible praxes related to this term just to strengthen our argument. In order to have some reference to other praxes see, for example, Scarre 1987; Ziegler 2012; Bottigheimer 2014; Saif 2015.

9. There are many different other interpretations. For example, it is possible to think of this law as stating there is no magic in the world, just the product of the human work (Kadvany 2010, 140).

10. These two interpretations are valid also for the point of view of the subjects using the devices. Users too could not know how the device works or that there are some devices acting in a hidden way, enhancing their capabilities with digital elements. However, we will here limit our analysis to the people watching the action performed through the devices in order to show a different angle on the theme.

11. This loss of comprehension of the surroundings can produce wonder or fear (Steinbock 2007; Gallagher et al. 2015).

12. See the following website: http://www.cwtv.com/shows/penn-teller-fool-us/.

13. The hammer too could become magical for the users because they do not see how it works. However, as we have shown, this kind of technology requires much less preparation to be understood than a computer, and so the computer represents something which fits better our case.

14. In the previous section, we analyzed the embodiment relations from the point of view of users showing how they are invisible to them, but these technologies are visible to the onlookers as in the case of glasses. However, there are technologies in embodiment relations which are invisible for the people around the users such as contact lenses or devices placed within the body of the subjects thanks to surgery. For this reason, it is possible also to think of a different type of relations, such as "cyborg relations" (Dalibert 2014; Rosenberger and Verbeek 2015; Rosenberger 2015, 135). However, we limit our analysis to embodiment relations because these digital devices used by the users are, at the moment, not placed inside of the subjects and the users act through them just as in the case of glasses.

15. For example, when the two magicians Penn and Teller unveil the magic trick of cups and balls by showing where they put the balls and by using transparent plastic cups in order to show what is inside them, the wonder is lost. What remains is the admiration for the skills of the two magicians who are able to make it so smooth to be unnoticeable. However, their skills took the place of magic.

16. In the case of this second interpretation, the attention is not aimed at the wonder produced by the devices. According to this interpretation, these technologies do not produce wonder, but they are invisible and merged with the users so deeply that the perceivers see the action of the technology as an action of the subject without even noticing the devices.

REFERENCES

Azuma, R. T. (1997). "A Survey of Augmented Reality." *Presence: Teleoperators and Virtual Environments* 6 (4): 355–85.

Barfield, W. (2015). *Fundamentals of Wearable Computers and Augmented Reality*. Second edition. CRC Press LLC.

Beech, M. (2012). *The Physics of Invisibility: A Story of Light and Deception*. New York: Springer.

Billinghurst, M., A. Clark, and G. Lee. (2015). "A Survey of Augmented Reality." *Foundations and Trends® in Human-Computer Interaction* 8 (2–3): 73–272.

Binsted, K. (2000). "Sufficiently Advanced Technology: Using Magic to Control the World." In *CHI EA '00 Extended Abstracts on Human Factors in Computing Systems*. New York: ACM Press, 205–6. doi:10.1145/633292.633409.

Blizzard North. (1996). *Diablo*. Computer game. Blizzard Entertainment.

Bottigheimer, R. B. (2014). *Magic Tales and Fairy Tale Magic*. London: Palgrave Macmillan.

Clarke, A. C. (1973). *Profiles of the Future: An Inquiry into the Limits of the Possible*. London: Pan Books.

Coppa, F., L. Hass, and J. Peck (eds.). (2008). *Performing Magic on the Western Stage*. New York: Palgrave Macmillan.

Dalibert, L. (2014). *Posthumanism and Somatechnologies: Exploring the Intimate Relations between Humans and Technologies*. PhD thesis. Enschede: University of Twente. doi:10.3990/1.9789036536516.

Dourish, P. and G. Bell. (2011). *Divining a Digital Future*. Cambrigde, MA: MIT Press.

Elmqvist, N. (2011). "Distributed User Interfaces: State of the Art." In J. A. Gallud, R. Tesoriero, and V. M. R. Penichet (eds.), *Distributed User Interfaces: Designing Interfaces for the Distributed Ecosystem*. London: Springer, 1–12.

Embree, L. (2005). "La Constitución de La Cultura Básica." In C. M. Míárquez and R. A. María de Mingo (eds.), *Signo. Intentionalidad. Verdad. Estudios de Fenomenologia*. Sevilla: SEFE, 345–55.

Friedman, T. (2008). "The Politics of Magic: Fantasy Media, Technology, and Nature in the 21st Century." *Scope–An On-Line Journal of Film and Television Studies*. http://www.nottingham.ac.uk/scope/documents/2009/june-2009/friedman.pdf

Gallagher, S., L. Reinerman-Jones, B. Janz, P. Bockelman, and J. Trempler. (2015). "The Phenomenology of Unprecedented Experience: Ontological and Cognitive Wonder." In *A Neurophenomenology of Awe and Wonder*. London: Palgrave Macmillan, 115–29. doi:10.1057/9781137496058_6.

Geroimenko, V. (ed.). (2014). *Augmented Reality Art: From an Emerging Technology to a Novel Creative Medium*. Springer Series on Cultural Computing. Cham: Springer.

Glotz, P., S. Bertschi, and C. Locke (eds.). (2005). *Thumb Culture: The Meaning of Mobile Phones for Society*. Bielefeld: Transcript Verlag.

Gygax, G. and D. Arneson. (1974). *Dungeons and Dragons*. Game. Tactical Studies Rules, Inc.

Huang, A. (2015). "Moore's Law Is Dying (and That Could Be Good)." *Spectrum, IEEE* 52 (4): 43–47.

Husserl, E. (1965). *Philosophie als Strenge Wissenschaft*. Frankfurt: Klostermann.

Ihde, D. (1990). *Technology and the Lifeworld: From Garden to Earth*. Bloomington: Indiana University Press.

Intel Corporation. (2005). "Excerpts from A Conversation with Gordon Moore: Moore's Law." ftp://download.intel.com/museum/Moores_Law/Video-Transcripts/Excepts_A_Conversation_with_Gordon_Moore.pdf

Isaacson, W. (2014). "Apple's Watch Will Make People and Computers More Intimate." *TIME*, September.

Kadvany, J. (2010). "Indistinguishable from Magic: Computation Is Cognitive Technology." *Minds and Machines* 20 (1): 119–43.

Katz, J. E. (2006). *Magic in the Air: Mobile Communication and the Transformation of Social Life*. New Brunswick: Transaction Publishers.

Liberati, N. (2013). "Improving the Embodiment Relations by Means of Phenomenological Analysis on the 'reality' of ARs." In *2013 IEEE International Symposium on Mixed and Augmented Reality—Arts, Media, and Humanities (ISMAR-AMH)*.

Los Alamitos, CA: IEEE Computer Society, 13–17. doi:http://doi.ieeecomputersociety.org/10.1109/ISMAR-AMH.2012.6483983.

———. (2014). "Augmented Reality and Ubiquitous Computing: The Hidden Potentialities of Augmented Reality." *AI & SOCIETY*. doi:10.1007/s00146–014–0543-x.

———. (2015a). "Technology, Phenomenology and the Everyday World: A Phenomenological Analysis on How Technologies Mould Our World." *Human Studies*. doi:10.1007/s10746–015–9353–5.

———. (2015b). "Augmented 'Ouch.' How to Create Intersubjective Augmented Objects into Which We Can Bump." In *2015 IEEE International Symposium on Mixed and Augmented Reality—Media, Art, Social Science, Humanities and Design*, 21–26. doi:10.1109/ISMAR-MASHD.2015.14.

———. (2016a). "From Information to Perception." In F. Gadducci and M. Tavosanis (eds.), *History and Philosophy of Computing*. Springer International Publishing, 203–15. doi:10.1007/978–3–319–47286–7_14.

———. (2016b). "Augmented Reality and Ubiquitous Computing: The Hidden Potentialities of Augmented Reality." *AI & SOCIETY* 31 (1): 17–28.

Liberati, N. and S. Nagataki. (2015). "The AR Glasses' 'Non-Neutrality': Their Knock-on Effects on the Subject and on the Giveness of the Object." *Ethics and Information Technology* 17 (2): 125–37.

Ling, R. and J. Donner. (2009). *Mobile Phones and Mobile Communication*. Cambridge, MA: Polity.

Lojek, B. (2010). *History of Semiconductor Engineering*. New York: Springer.

Mack, C. (2015). "The Multiple Lives of Moore's Law. Why Gordon Moore's Grand Prediction Has Endured for 50 Years." *Spectrum, IEEE* 52 (4): 31.

Möller, D. P. F. (2016). "Ubiquitous Computing." In D. P. F. Möller, *Guide to Computing Fundamentals in Cyber-Physical Systems: Concepts, Design Methods, and Applications*. Springer International Publishing, 185–234. doi:10.1007/978–3–319–25178–3_5.

Moore, G. E. (1965). "Cramming More Components onto Integrated Circuits." *Electronics* 38 (8).

O'Regan, G. (2016). "The Invention of the Integrated Circuit and the Birth of Silicon Valley." In G. O'Regan, Introduction to the History of Computing: A Computing History Primer. Springer International Publishing, 93–100. doi:10.1007/978–3–319–33138–6_7.

Padua, D. A. (2011). *Encyclopedia of Parallel Computing*. Heidelberg: Springer.

Puech, M. (2016). *The Ethics of Ordinary Technology*. New York: Routledge.

Rhodes, B. J., N. Minar, and J. Weaver. (1999). "Wearable Computing Meets Ubiquitous Computing: Reaping the Best of Both Worlds." In *Proceedings of the 3*rd *IEEE International Symposium on Wearable Computers*, 141. http://dl.acm.org/citation.cfm?id=519309.856497

Rosenberger, R. (2014). "Multistability and the Agency of Mundane Artifacts: From Speed Bumps to Subway Benches." *Human Studies* 37 (3): 369–92.

———. (2015). "Postphenomenology: What's New? What's Next?" In J. K. B. O. Friis and R. P. Crease (eds.), *Technoscience and Postphenomenology: The Manhattan Papers*. Lanham: Lexington Books, 129–48.

Rosenberger, R. and P.-P. Verbeek, eds. (2015). *Postphenomenological Investigations: Essays on Human–Technology Relations*. Lanham: Lexington Books.

Rowling, J. K. (1997). *Harry Potter and the Philosopher's Stone*. London: Bloomsbury.

Saif, L. (2015). *The Arabic Influences on Early Modern Occult Philosophy*. London: Palgrave Macmillan.

Salah, K., Y. Ismail, and A. El-Rouby. (2015). "Introduction: Work Around Moore's Law." In K. Salah, Y. Ismail, and A. El-Rouby, *Arbitrary Modeling of TSVs for 3D Integrated Circuits*. Springer International Publishing, 1–15. doi:10.1007/978–3–319–07611–9_1.

Scarre, G. (1987). *Witchcraft and Magic in Sixteenth- and Seventeenth-Century Europe*. London: Macmillan Education.

Steinbock, A. J. (2007). *Phenomenology and Mysticism : The Verticality of Religious Experience*. Bloomington: Indiana University Press.

Tolkien, J. R. R. (1954). *The Lord of the Rings*. London: George Allen & Unwin.

Topaloglu, R. O. (ed.). (2015). *More than Moore Technologies for Next Generation Computer Design*. New York: Springer.

Verbeek, P.-P. (2005). *What Things Do: Philosophical Reflections on Technology, Agency, and Design*. University Park: Penn State University Press.

Weiser, M. (1991). "The Computer for the 21st Century." *Scientific American* 265 (3): 66–75. http://www.ubiq.com/hypertext/weiser/SciAmDraft3.html

———. (1993). "Hot Topics—Ubiquitous Computing." *Computer* 26 (10): 71–72.

Weiser, M. and J. S. Brown. (1996). "Designing Calm Technology." *POWERGRID JOURNAL* 1. http://www.ubiq.com/hypertext/weiser/calmtech/calmtech.htm

Wiltse, H. (2014). "Unpacking Digital Material Mediation." *Techné: Research in Philosophy and Technology* 18 (3): 154–82.

Zhang, G. Q. and A. Roosmalen (eds.). (2009). *More than Moore*. Boston: Springer.

Ziegler, R. (2012). *Satanism, Magic and Mysticism in Fin-de-siècle France*. Basingstoke: Palgrave Macmillan.

Part II

Postphenomenologically Investigating Media Cases

Chapter 5

Extensions and Concentric Circles

Exploring Transparency and Opacity in Three Media Technologies

Robert N. Spicer

INTRODUCTION: BODILY INTERFACES

In a culture like ours it should *not* be a bit of a shock to be reminded that the body is the message. The re-appropriation of Marshall McLuhan's (1998) words here is purposeful. This chapter draws on his idea of media as "extensions of man" (and woman too) but argues for a slight adjustment in that thinking about the human-medium relationship. The body is becoming an ever more essential part of the experience of the technologies of mass communication, of many-to-many communication, and the datafication that accompanies media. The *body* is the message because, while it is always a part of communication, with a wide range of new media technologies, the body is an increasingly important part of the interface. Put another way, as Don Ihde argues, "Phenomenologically, perception is not passive but active; holistically, it is bodily interactive with an environment" (2009, 15).

While in some cases the body is *part of the interface*, in other cases the body *is the interface*. The use of a variety of gestures on a laptop track pad is now part of the user experience of the consumption, manipulation, and creation of digital content. We do two finger swipes to scroll, three finger swipes to select text, and four finger swipes to go to the dock and then back to an application. Smartphone and tablet screens get "pinched," as we adjust an image. This is just the beginning of gesture in computing. The body can only increase its role when considering media technologies such as Nintendo's Wii and Wii U and Microsoft's Xbox Kinect. Gesture and full bodily movement are obviously now part of gaming but there is a multitude of hacks for the Kinect where users have modified it to incorporate gesture to move through a PowerPoint presentation, shuffle images on a screen, or start and stop a video player on a desktop computer; an indication of how technology manufacturers could potentially make gesture present in all computer and media consumption.

These are bodily experiences that combine interaction with digital media and interaction with the world around us. Stacey Irwin argues, "Material technologies like digital media play a mediating role in the lifeworld," and that postphenomenology is a useful tool for understanding how they are non-neutral in their mediation (2016, 29–30). In other words, digital media technologies do not passively present to the user an unfiltered experience of the world. They "amplify" aspects of experience while "reducing" others to the background. A postphenomenological analysis, Daniel Susser argues, "asks about the world around us and about the tools we use to investigate it [sic] how they shape both our experience and our self-understanding" (2016, 142). Part of this understanding, which is especially important to this chapter, is the concept of transparency in postphenomenology.

Despite a physical, sometimes opaque, presence, transparency is part of our experiences of media, in how these technologies blend into the background of our lives. They are always there but we stop thinking about them, we take them for granted. Yoni Van Den Eede describes this as "a certain 'blindness' to technological mediation, that reigns in everyday life [...] Much of our social interaction takes place by way of technology, but we perhaps don't notice the technology itself" (2010, 141). However, Van Den Eede notes, citing Ihde (1990, 2008), that because technological mediation "actually has transformative effects" it cannot be totally transparent (Van Den Eede 2010, 149).

This chapter looks at three media technologies, the Apple Watch, drones, and virtual reality (VR), and how they extend the body, by giving us insight into our body's inner workings; or by giving us a different perspectival view of an area; or by transporting us to a faraway place in a way that creates a sense of being there. In these three cases there is a tension. Despite the transparency Van Den Eede describes, media also have an opacity, as physical devices, the presence of which we are fully aware of and feel on our bodies; the watch on our wrist, the drone controller in our hands, and the VR mask on our face. They create an illusion of presence in another place, whether it is internal (the watch), near but from a new angle (the drone), or far away (VR). However, they are also transparent in the sense that we often perceive the digital as ephemeral, as something that is not physically there, that cannot be touched. It is a code seemingly without a physical component, Cartesian body, and soul cut in half with the body deleted from the equation. The problem with that perception is that there is always a physicality, in the form of servers, that is necessary to make that ephemeral media content possible, and that physical presence has material effects (Greenpeace 2011; Greenpeace 2014).

What we are working through here is how two or more bodies, human and technological bodies, enter into a relationship with one another. Here is where Deleuze and Guattari's concept of assemblage very usefully comes into play. Deleuze and Guattari say, "every machine is a machine of a machine" (1983, 36). In *A Thousand Plateaus* they write:

> We will call an assemblage every constellation of singularities and traits deducted from the flow—selected, organized, stratified—in such a way as to converge (consistency) artificially, naturally; an assemblage, in this sense, is a veritable invention. (1987, 78)

In other words an assemblage is a contingent coming together of, as Greg Wise describes it, a "collection of heterogeneous elements" (2005, 78). Writing about Deleuze and Guattari's concept of machinic assemblage, Gordon Coonfield adds that

> what something 'can do' is not reducible to its designer's intentions, or even the intentions of the human actors who might be said, from an instrumentalist perspective, to 'use' it. What a thing can do is a function of its capabilities under certain conditions as it enters into relations of composition/decomposition with other bodies. (2006, 296)

An assemblage can also be described as the temporary connecting of "technology, persons, feelings, and the atmosphere around them" (Spicer 2014, 103).

The other motivation for this three-part analysis is, to borrow Ihde's words, to explore these media "in their particularities" (Ihde 2009, 22). It is an attempt to develop an "appreciation of the multidimensionality of technologies as *material cultures* within a *lifeworld*" (ibid.; original emphasis). The three media technologies under examination, with their transparency/opacity tensions in their relationships with their users, exhibit what Ihde calls "multistability" (2009, 12). Ihde uses optical illusions and archery to illustrate the idea that phenomenologically "perception is not passive but active" (ibid., 15). He goes on to argue that active "perceptual engagement [...] reveals the situated and perspectival nature of bodily perception" (ibid., 15–16).

In explaining multistability Ihde explores the variations of archery to show how multistability is a combination of "the materiality of the technologies, the bodily technique of the use, and the cultural context of the practices" (2009, 18–19). In other words, multistability combines, physically, how a technology functions, how the user's body interacts and becomes part of the technology, and the world in which the technology and the user exist. In Ihde's (2009) archery example multistability is seen in the alteration of the size of the bow or by placing the archer on horseback, making his or her use of the weapon mobile. This kind of multistability is seen in all three of the media technologies explored in this chapter.

Working from the inside out, these three technologies are thought of in concentric circles. In the inner circle is the Apple Watch. Like other wearable technologies it mediates our experience of our bodies. It extends the senses inward to give the user a new view of the body. Drones occupy the middle circle. They give the user a new view of a nearby scene. They extend the senses to new heights in the user's environment, creating possibilities for new creative works, but also causing concern about new possibilities for surveillance. They also extend military power globally. Finally, in the outer circle is virtual reality. This medium is probably the most multistable of the three. It has the ability to transport the user to fantasy worlds that only exist as digital bits. It can also, as *The New York Times* demonstrates, be more than a game. News media tell us stories and, as Kovach and Rosenstiel argue, they have an obligation to "make the significant interesting and relevant" (2014, 9). The use of VR by news media has the potential to truly make the audience care about faraway places and people, to possibly see the world through another's eyes.

THE APPLE WATCH

A wearable technology is contained within the central circle in this discussion because it is a medium that in many ways points inward. It mediates the user's experience of self; it calls on the user to look internally, to experience the body as part of the interface. Even when it directs attention outward and functions as a media technology in a traditional mass communication sense, as a news alert medium for example, it is still calling on the user to look down at his or her body, a reminder of the attachment between body and device. Wearables such as the Apple Watch also point to the future of the body as part of the interface with media.

Touch as part of our media experience, with things like the screens of our smartphones and tablets, is now a common part of media experiences but that is only the beginning. The MIT Media Lab recently announced the creation of DuoSkin, a temporary tattoo that will "act as input for smartphones or computers, display output based on changes in body temperature and transmit data to other devices via NFC [Near Field Communication]" (Etherington 2016, para. 1). A media technology that is perhaps even more invasive bodily than DuoSkin is Sony's recent patent for a camera contact lens. As CNBC reported in May 2016, the contact lens "would allow the wearer to snap photos with a deliberate blink of the eye and store them on a wireless device like a smartphone or tablet" (Stump 2016, para. 1). This device manages to somehow be both exterior and interior, occupying a liminal space of inside and outside the body, while also exemplifying the simultaneous transparency and opacity that is a central theme in this discussion. For now, however, we begin with the watch, a device more easily removed from the body.

The Apple Watch, along with other wearables such as Fitbit and Jawbone, transport us to another place but not in the way other forms of media do. Rather than taking us somewhere far away, that place to which they transport us is our own interior, a space that is always close but somehow unexplored and unfamiliar. In some ways our internal selves, our organs and fluids, are the best example of the simultaneous transparency and opaqueness that is central to this discussion.

Of course these media technologies do not expose the internals of the body by giving us visual representations to examine, but they make us aware of their functioning. They aim to help us to calibrate our bodies, make us aware of the efficiency, or inefficiency, of their internal workings, and act as management devices for optimizing the body's functioning. These new insights, and the method by which we get them, create a double-edged sword. There is something of value to the use of technologies as tools for "calibrating" our bodies. The danger is in the use of the term "calibrating" to describe our bodily management. It is a mechanical word; it feels like an adjustment to a dial or something that requires a wrench, not something done to our lungs or brain/mind.

The problematic nature of this thinking is best demonstrated when Ray Kurzweil refers to our "version 1.0 biological bodies" and the "severe limitations" of our "physiological bandwidth for processing new information" (2005, 8–9). He talks about the body's "myriad of failure modes" and the "cumbersome maintenance rituals" (ibid., 9). It is strange to read the language of biology, of the human body, so neatly knit together with that of technology, to refer to health care as "maintenance" and physical ability as "bandwidth" and being sick as a "failure mode."

Such language is simultaneously exciting and unsettling and it makes it easy to see how we are in for a potential future fight over, as Rosi Braidotti says, "what exactly counts as human" (2006, 197). Kurzweil also makes it important to turn to Jaron Lanier who reminds you that *You Are Not a Gadget*, as the title of his book says. Lanier doesn't speak the language of postphenomenological transparency, but certainly does a good job describing it:

> When developers of digital technologies design a program that requires you to interact with a computer as if it were a person, they ask you to accept in some corner of your brain that you might also be conceived of as a program. (2010, 4)

In other words, as Van Den Eede puts it, digital media and technologies are so ubiquitous that "we do not perceive this background—unless we consciously aim our attention to it" (2010, 141). The thought process creating the transparency moves in one direction or the other—you are either a human being asked to think of yourself as a machine as you communicate with a machine or you are a person communicating with a machine being asked to think of it as a person. Either way, the goal is for the *difference* to disappear, for the technology to become transparent.

It is easy to see how wearables like the Apple Watch might begin to take on that quality in that they cease to be media and become just another part of the human body, at the very least a detachable body part. If something is constantly a part of our everyday experience, attached to our bodies, it becomes almost an appendage in some ways. By searching the available apps we find it can help us form (or break) habits. It can help us to think in certain ways about our bodies, or simply make us more aware of our bodies. It can also begin to make us think of our bodies as just so many more machines in a world full of machines.

In the interest of digressing from what might be perceived as a bit of Luddite technophobia, it is good to acknowledge, as Stacey Irwin does, that self-tracking as a process is not new (2016, 155). Athletes have been keeping track of their performances for a long time. What is new is the use of digital technology to track and collect data about performance. What is also new is the wider availability of "self-tracking devices, from Fitbit to the Apple Watch, [which] have hit the mainstream consumer market" coinciding with the rise of the Quantified Self Movement (QS) (ibid.). With such tracking we have to think about "the phenomenal body" existing in a "human-technology junction" where our body becomes "an object for manipulation, and an arbiter of increased fitness" (ibid., 156).

Wearables act as narrowcasting media, pushing out content, specific bodily data, from within, outward to each of us. They, as Susser argues, "are shaping the way we understand not just the world around us, but ourselves" (2016, 139). Amanda Barnier (2010) references the "extended mind" thesis, the idea that "Cognitive processes ain't (all) in the head" (Clark and Chalmers 1998, 8). In other words, while the brain is engaged in cognitive processes the results of those processes are put into action in the world external to the brain. Clark and Chalmers argue, "the human organism is linked with an external entity in a two-way interaction, creating a coupled system that can be seen as a cognitive system in its own right" (ibid.). Barnier, in her discussion of the iPhone and memory, borrows Chalmers' words when she says of her iPhone, "parts of it have become parts of me" (2010, 293). In her own words, Barnier says, "the iPhone is compensating for impairments in my current capacity to 'process and use information'" (ibid.).

It is easy to see the Apple Watch filling a similar role. Where the watch has some inadequacies in comparison to its cousin the iPhone, is in the interface.

It is not a medium useful for (some kinds of) entertainment consumption, for example, watching videos or doing extended reading. The watch is a push medium, alerting the wearer to something. It is an intermediary medium, a device that serves as a connective channel between the wearer and the iPhone or laptop or between the wearer and the wearer's body. It is a reminder to exercise or go to sleep at a certain time, as seen in the various sleep and exercise tracking apps. It is an externalization of the cognitive process of remembering with apps such as Cheatsheet, a reminder app that allows you to save things you might often forget, such as the Wi-Fi password.

All of these uses of the Apple Watch bring Ihde's (2009) idea of multistability to ride in tandem with Deleuze and Guattari's assemblage creating a perfect bifocal lens for seeing the medium as it is. Ihde explains multistability through archery, which he says always involves "a projectile (arrow) [being] propelled by the tensile force of a bow and bowstring" (ibid., 16). We already have an assemblage—FINGER+ARROW+BOW+BOWSTRING. Ihde, as said, also acknowledges the importance of "the material technology, the bodily technique, and the social practice" that are all present in archery, especially as the practice transitioned from one where the archer stands holding a six-foot bow to one where the archer rides a horse carrying a shorter bow (2009, 17). How perfect that Deleuze and Parnet describe assemblages using the example of MAN-HORSE-STIRRUP as an illustration where the combination of the rider, the horse, and the stirrup used to stabilize the rider, create "a new assemblage of war, defined by its degree of power or 'freedom,' its affects, its circulation of affects: what a set of bodies is capable of" (1987, 70). The assemblage, however, they argue, as Peter Zhang points out, "is never technological" (2011, 218). "Tools always presuppose a machine," according to Deleuze and Parnet, "and the machine is always social before being technical" (1987, 70). In other words, there are always externalities that precede the assemblage: affects, materialities, and socializations.

The Apple Watch can replace archery in this construction. Its multistability is in its use for both intrapersonal and mass-mediated communication. It mediates the user's experience and knowledge of his or her body; there are social practices of body management in this FINGER+ARROW+BOW+BOWSTRING phase of our view of the watch. It is not so different from any self-tracking device. However, it becomes multistable as it can also play the role of a traditional medium, as an information consumption device; just as Deleuze and Parnet add the STIRRUP to the bow and arrow assemblage, making it possible to use the bow and arrow while riding a horse, transforming the archer from a static combatant to one that is moving. Similarly, the Apple Watch adds a whole host of apps, opening up the possibility of the user's self-monitoring being interrupted with the BBC and Apple News pushing out quick notifications that something is happening somewhere else.

However, it is difficult to imagine it being the kind of device where one sits and reads in-depth and extended journalism or a book. The medium must be allowed to be the medium. With this in mind, the assemblage adds a new element with an app like Instapaper, a "read-later service" used for saving articles to, presumably, read on another device with an interface more conducive to such consumption; something like a tablet or a laptop. This adds that other device to the assemblage, but continues beyond that. Instapaper also converts articles to audio for easier consumption, which further alters the watch's functionality. The conversion of text to audio is certainly not unique to Instapaper or to the Apple Watch. It is the combination of this functionality, contributing to the multistability of the Watch, and extending the Deleuzo-Guattarian assemblage, that makes this interesting. It is not just part of the extended mind, it is extended media.

Finally, it would be an oversight to not discuss the ways in which this medium has the potential to change the experiences of those who are differently abled. It is just a little too easy to think about how technologies augment "traditional" bodies. But it would miss a very important point to skip over the ways in which those who are differently abled engage with these forms of media. Braille is a media technology. In 1976 Ray Kurzweil invented a reading machine that translated print into spoken words, the first unit of which was purchased by Stevie Wonder. The Apple Watch presents new possibilities for thinking about how a medium can play a part in "differently structured lifeworlds" (Ihde 2009, 19).

One example is the ways in which Apple is trying to translate the self-tracking component of the technology to users who require a wheelchair. At their Worldwide Developers Conference Apple announced they were "adding a way for wheelchair users to monitor their activity levels, mostly powered by upper body strength used to move the wheels" (Kelly 2016, para. 2). The Apple Watch will "track pushes, rather than steps" (ibid., para. 3) and give the user "time to roll notification" (ibid., para. 4). One problem in the development, which underlines the value in this functionality, is the "limited amount of fitness research that's been conducted among wheelchair users" (ibid., para. 6). Apple did their own research on wheelchair users to "monitor distance, speed and how much they were using their arms" in order to calibrate their Watch's OS to accurately track the movement of wheelchairs (ibid., para. 9). The research is making it possible to add self-tracking features for wheelchair users.

There is also the story of Jordyn Castor. Castor, who is blind, started as an intern with Apple, seeking out an opportunity with the company because of the impact the iPad had on her. She said in an article on *Mashable* that she was impressed that everything about the tablet "just worked and was accessible just right out of the box [...] That was something I had never experienced before" (Dupere 2016, para. 14). Castor now works for the company developing the Apple Watch to make it more useful for blind users. "I came to realize that with my knowledge of computers and technology, I could help change the world for people with disabilities," Castor says. "I could help make technology more accessible for blind users" (ibid., para. 7–8).

One thing that Jordyn Castor does for us, through her work, is to help counter what Verbeek laments as the loss of materiality in things. Verbeek says that the things we own "serve as signs rather than material things, as symbols or icons for their owners' lifestyles" (2005, 2). Verbeek quotes a Braun executive who said, "we sell lifestyles, not appliances" (ibid.). This statement, dripping with its Don Draper, chic silliness, misses something. Even if we really do believe that we buy a particular dishwasher or tablet or smart watch or drone or VR device because of what it says about our lifestyle, the materiality is still there, it is still always already part of our experience of the thing. Just as Neil DeGrasse Tyson (2013) says, "the good thing about science is that it's true whether or not you believe in it," the good thing about materiality is that it's there whether or not you're thinking about it. This thought is a useful transition point to move from the inner concentric circle of this discussion to the device in the middle circle: the drone.

DRONES

The Apple Watch exhibits a multistability that mediates both our experience of our internal bodies and the consumption of media content about the world. Drones represent a similar multistability. On one hand they create a mediated experience of that which is near but can now be seen from a different angle, for example a drone's camera allows the user to see their property from the sky. The drone also extends the user's senses to that which is far away, the most high-profile example of this being the United States' use of Remotely Piloted Aircrafts (RPAs) for military operations. Mark Andrejevic adds to the multistability of the medium, and creates another Deleuzo-Guattarian assemblage, in his discussion of the use of drones for "finding ways to transform humans into networked, sensing devices" (2015, 203). Sounding like something out of *Minority Report*, Andrejevic nevertheless provides a compelling description of drones as part of a system able to track our brains' responses to stimuli in real time. This section will be exploring the use of drones in three contexts: close encounters, news encounters, and military encounters.

The close encounters are the ways in which drones open up new possibilities for experiencing that which is near but from a new angle. This is a product of the nature of the medium. The drone itself makes these things possible, and impossible to avoid. The drone as it sits in the middle of the three concentric circles of this discussion is probably the easiest medium to understand through McLuhan's ideas of media as extensions. The user can now see things he or she could not see without the drone.

Some in agriculture have found creative uses for drones in recent years. In 2014 the NPR program *Planet Money* reported one story on Cy Brown, a man who was using drones to help farmers track and deal with feral pigs that destroy crops (Henn 2014). Unfortunately for Brown and the farmers he was helping, the FAA (Federal Aviation Administration) grounded his operation, saying they were restricting the flying of drones between 83 and 500 feet off the ground (ibid., para. 12). In August 2016 the FAA announced rule changes that would allow "unmanned aircraft weighing less than 55 pounds to fly in sparsely populated areas up to 400 feet high and up to 100 miles per hour during daylight hours" (Schaper and Folkenflik 2016, para. 7).

There are also social and legal anxieties about drones. The medium opens up new possibilities for crop management in the agriculture industry but it also creates social anxieties about personal privacy. This is a perverse extension of the senses, in particular the sense of vision, from my space to your space, so to speak. Writing for *Slate*, Margot Kaminski (2016) presents a long list of sunbathers, and others, who have complained about the leering eyeballs hovering over their backyards and even openly ogling in public spaces such as beaches.

A quick search for drones and "peeping Toms" brings up years worth of results of stories about people seeing a drone floating quietly over their backyard or hovering outside of their apartment window peering in. Probably the most infamous of such stories is the one about the father in Kentucky who shot a drone out of the sky. William Merideth claimed it was spying on his 16-year-old daughter who was sunbathing in their garden at the time. In October 2015, a judge dismissed all charges against Merideth for the incident (Matyszczyk 2015).

Privacy from peeping Toms is just one concern. Noting that in 2015 "45 states considered 168 bills related to drones," the *Columbia Journalism Review* points out a variety of other examples of legal regimes dealing with the use of drones (Hepworth 2016, 12). There are restrictions on their use in national parks and a general FAA rule against flying over people. Despite these restrictions, news media are still finding ways to use drones to collect information for reporting. Shelley Hepworth (2016) notes the beginning of cooperative efforts between media outlets and the FAA in August 2016 when CNN became the first news organization to receive permission to fly a drone less than 21 feet over people in order to get footage.

In 2015 the BBC used a drone to capture stunning footage of Auschwitz, a video that was created to commemorate the 70th anniversary of its liberation by Soviet troops. In its first week the video received 5 million views on YouTube (McFarland 2015, para 1). *The Washington Post* reported on the impact of the video and its non-traditional method for capturing footage. Matt Waite, the founder of the Drone Journalism Lab at the University of Nebraska commented on the power of the video in how it slowly pulls out to display for the viewer the immensity of this location, adding to the emotional impact of the historical knowledge of the place; knowing what happened there is only made more intense when contemplating the scale on which it happened. This is something that could not be captured with traditional means of videography. As Waite says in the *Post* article, the power of the video comes from "that emotional moment when the camera just rises above the roof line and you realize 'Oh my God it goes on and on'" (ibid., para. 2).

Perhaps the greater emotional impact of drones, however, is in their presence on the battlefield and their effects on soldiers who are not. Unmanned drones, or RPAs, extend the body and senses of an American soldier who is far from the battlefield. The television images of warfare give the pilot, and the public, a "desensitising video-game like framework" (Rose 2012, 376) through which to view international conflict. While these military technologies act as extensions of human beings, extending and externalizing the senses from remote locations to the battlefield, there is also a strange kind of internalizing of the experience of the battlefield happening alongside it. In other words, despite being nowhere near the battlefield, the drone operator is still subject to some of the mental anguish of warfare.

One study conducted by the U.S. Air Force found, surprisingly, that the distance from the battlefield did not reduce the feelings of stress associated with military service. In that study Dr. Hernando Ortega argues that warfare via RPAs comes with its own set of challenges. For example, being deployed to a battlefield "fosters the development of organizational identity and unit cohesion" all of which is lost for RPA pilots (Ortega 2013, 2). Jean Lin Otto, who conducted another study for the U.S. Air Force, argued in a *New York Times* article that these RPA pilots "witness the carnage. Manned aircraft pilots don't do that" (Dao 2013, para. 6). Otto's study found that RPA pilots and manned aircraft pilots have "statistically equivalent incidence rates" of mental health issues (Otto 2013, 5).

So even as the technology is extending the pilot's senses the pilot is still internalizing the emotional toll of warfare. The trauma of the battlefield finds its way home to the remote computer terminal to be internalized by the RPA pilot. Even though that pilot is able to sit at his or her dinner table at home with family they are still unable to escape the stress and trauma of the battlefield. How appropriate that the military researchers cite the loss of unit cohesion, the absence of human contact resulting from technology extending the soldier's presence, as a source of emotional stress.

Taking all of these examples together, peeping Toms and emotionally resonating imagery in journalism, crop management, and military strikes, it might be tempting to ask if the technology is "good" or "bad." An attempt at such a judgment, riding in tandem with McLuhan's framework of the medium as an extension, is best addressed with McLuhan's response to David Sarnoff early in *Understanding Media*. McLuhan quotes Sarnoff as saying that technologies are neither good nor bad, "it is the way they are used that determines their value" (McLuhan 1998, 11). This, McLuhan replies, is "the voice of the current somnambulism" that ignores the idea that the medium is the message (ibid.). It is not useful to deem the drone good or bad depending on how it is used because all of the uses described in this section are part of the nature of the medium.

These different uses of the drone also remind us that the user's perceptions of the affordances of a medium, "the relationship between a physical object and a person," can come about organically (Norman 2013, 11). In other words, the way a medium works, "the possible interactions between people and the environment" the medium creates, can be modified by creative users (ibid., 19). The creators of a new medium, such as drones, should be prepared for the possibility that their creation can lead to both moving imagery in journalism and voyeurism.

Drones are useful for seeing close locations from a new angle but, like virtual reality, they can also act as extensions of human senses by transporting us to another place that is far away. The most obvious example of this is the preceding discussion of the distant, remote control of military drones. The operator sees something on another continent and then goes home and has dinner with his or her family. Drones extend the user's senses. They create an illusion of presence in a place. However, more than drones, virtual reality extends and immerses the user in a distant location. This is the medium that marks the outer concentric circle in this discussion.

VIRTUAL REALITY

Benjamin Woolley describes the early movement to create virtual reality (VR) as being outside of the realm of description of typical academic terminology. It had, as he notes, "its own rhetoric and political agenda" (1994, 14). VR, Woolley argues, "came from a research environment which had already set itself the task of challenging television" (ibid.). This is, in a way, a political agenda. If the medium is the message, and the communication technology of any era reflects a way of thinking and being, then upending the dominant medium is certainly a political act. As Postman argues, "those who cultivate competence in the use of a new technology become an elite group that are granted undeserved authority and prestige by those who have no such competence" (1993, 9).

Woolley discusses an early research conference on VR where one researcher, Warren Robinett, "voiced some scepticism about the term 'virtual reality,' which he described as a 'cute little oxymoron,' preferring 'synthetic experience' instead" (1994, 15). It might actually be useful to question the logic behind the characterization of the synthetic, to look for authenticity in the experience of VR. As Jennifer Daryl Slack argues in her essay on *The Matrix*, when a film presents the audience with a fictional world "the work of the audience is 'trying on' that world" (2001, para. 4). The audience is supposed to ask if the "organization of its affective logic" feels relevant, to critique that film's "ability to create a space that 'makes sense to inhabit'" (ibid., para. 6). This same logic could be applied to VR. Does it create a space that makes sense to inhabit?

The most accessible form of virtual reality is one we might not think of as VR. This is Google Maps, and other similar apps, which allow the user to traverse some distant (or near) space, seeing it as it is, or at least how it was recently. It is likely that despite the ubiquity of this app today, very few people will know about its historical origins. Nicholas Negroponte's Architecture Machine Group (AMG) created the Aspen Movie Map, "the first detailed VR simulation of an actual town" (Boden 2006, 1070). Molly Wright Steenson, writing for the Radical Pedagogies blog, a collaborative project by Ph.D. students at the Princeton University School of Architecture, describes it as "a proto-Google Map and Street View application that allowed its user to 'drive' down streets in Aspen, Colorado, from an Eames chair equipped with joysticks in its armrests" (n.d., para. 4). As Woolley describes it, The Movie Map "demonstrated the feasibility of creating a cross between passive media like TV and active media like games" (1994, 15).

A quick Google Image search, appropriately enough, will confirm the visual similarities between Google Maps and the Aspen Movie Map. It is like looking at Google Maps when the Wi-Fi is slow, it is just not quite clear. The screen features colored arrows indicating to the user how to "move" through the map and a big stop sign in the bottom center of the screen. Another easily found image shows the "Aspen Movie Map Truck" used to drive through the town to make the movie map, with a large contraption on the roof of the vehicle and a camera man standing behind it, a primitive precursor to the Google Maps cars that many of us have seen driving through our towns, taking pictures of our streets to create the contemporary movie maps that help us navigate today (Weber n.d.). The evolution from the Aspen Movie Map to Google Maps serves to reinforce this transition from opacity to transparency and the tension between them. With the Aspen Movie Map the user sat in a chair and used tools to "move" through the virtual environment; the presence of the medium is undeniable and unavoidable. With Google Maps the virtual environment rests in our hands. It is inconspicuous; even as we use it and are aware of it, it becomes something that augments reality more than creating it.

The creators of early VR, as described by Woolley, were already thinking about the transparency/opacity tension in the way they described the intersection of the passive and the active in the consumption of the medium. They were talking about their new medium as a challenge to the dominance of television. Their dream may have come to fruition with the introduction of *The New York Times* VR news videos. *The Times* sells its videos with the opening line telling consumers to, "put yourself at the center of our stories." Consumers are told they will be able to "Experience stories reported by award-winning journalists, all told in an immersive, 360-degree video experience" (*New York Times*, 2016).

So, just as the BBC created an emotionally impactful experience with a drone, *The Times* has managed to create, as they call it, "an immersive virtual reality experience." The question is whether they manage to "create a space that makes sense to inhabit." Is this an authentic experience of the Other, of another person's life, or of the events of a distant environment? *The Times* implores us to go underwater, to get on the campaign trail, to see a refugee's world. Once again, the authenticity of the experience hinges on the transparency/opacity tension. VR, when experienced through a headset, can be an incredibly realistic experience, in some cases to the point of being jarring and disorienting. The medium disappears. On the other hand, when experiencing these *Times* videos on a laptop screen the medium reappears. Rather than simply turning their head left or right, the viewer uses the trackpad to change angles. That being said, if the goal of the project is to elicit empathy through an authentic experience, the *Times* videos are quite successful. Watching them is an immersive experience that feels like it transports the viewer to another place.

A final key example of the postphenomenological transparency/opacity tension in a virtual environment in recent media is the video game *No Man's Sky*, a game featuring 18 quintillion planets for players to explore. *No Man's Sky* is not a virtual reality in the way that we typically imagine, with the player wearing a mask and physically moving in order to play the game. However, it is no less immersive. As the game's website describes it, "No Man's Sky is a game about exploration and survival in an infinite procedurally generated galaxy" (Hello Games 2015). The creators describe entrance into this digital realm as an exploration of a functional universe:

> Whether a distant mountain or a planet hanging low on the horizon, you can go there. You can fly seamlessly from the surface of a planet to another, and every star in the sky is a sun that you can visit.

> Where you'll go and how fast you'll make your way through this universe is up to you. It's yours for the taking. (Hello Games 2015)

The marketing materials echo Janet Murray's (1997) essential properties of digital environments. On multiple levels *No Man's Sky* fulfills three of Murray's four properties: it is procedural, participatory, and spatial.

The player experiences the game as procedural. It is fundamentally a reminder that, as Murray argues, digital environments' "defining ability [is] to execute a series of rules" (ibid., 71) and that digital media are "not fundamentally a wire or a pathway but an *engine*" (ibid., 72; original emphasis). From a play perspective, the makers encourage you to "Find ancient artefacts that could reveal the secrets behind the universe" (Hello Games). In other words, the game is in some ways an exploration of the physics of its universe.

In this sense, the procedural property of this game is inherently spatial. Murray's spatial property is seen in the way, "new digital environments are characterized by their power to represent navigable space" (1997, 79). She argues that, unlike other forms of media, "only digital media can present space that we can move through" (ibid.). This is seen in virtual reality and in many first-person video games. *No Man's Sky* is a perfect example of this in the vast universe the game offers up for players to explore. Where other games present the player with *a world*, *No Man's Sky* gives the player multiple *worlds*, allowing him or her to travel from planet to planet, exploring each one, moving through a vast space.

The procedural and spatial properties connect to the participatory property in the game's networked functionality and sociability. Hello Games tells the player they can "Choose whether to share your discoveries with other players. They're exploring the same vast universe in parallel; perhaps you'll make your mark on their worlds as well as your own" (Hello Games). In this sense the game is also calling on some of danah boyd's (2014) notions of affordances in design and digital media. Boyd says that digital media have "visibility" and "spreadability" (ibid., 11). These are the ideas that these media create a potential audience to bear witness to the actions of others and an ease of sharing of content. Hello Games almost makes these affordances of the digital environment historic in their nature. The player is not simply winning the game; they are making their mark on their world and the worlds of others. The virtual environment is transformed into something more meaningful and its impact is given a materiality as your accomplishments translate into some IRL (In Real Life) impact on the minds of other players.

The affordances of the medium are not limited to the gameplay. *No Man's Sky* has been marketed as something revolutionary in its (theoretically infinite) scale and how it was created. With its 18 quintillion worlds (that's 18 followed by 18 zeros) it is difficult to imagine how a team of only six developers managed to create it. Creating a single digital world, let alone 18 quintillion, is a large task. Murray's procedural property is present not only in the gameplay but also in the creation of these digital worlds through procedural content generation (PCG).

Dale Green provides a very basic definition of PCG as "the process of creating content using an algorithm" (2016, 2). Ryan Watkins (2016) breaks PCG into its component parts. A procedure in programming is "an instruction to be executed" (ibid., 2). A set of procedures together form a script, the tools of programming that tell a computer what instructions the programmer wants it to complete. These can be used "to instruct the computer to generate content in many different ways" (ibid.). Watkins explains that, if "procedural is the *how* then content is the *what*" (ibid.; original emphasis). Obviously Murray's notion of the procedural is present here in the "ability to execute a series of rules." As a review in *Wired* describes PCG, in layman's terms, "The worlds [in *No Man's Sky*] are procedural, meaning the game generates them each time a planet is visited for the first time" (Rundle 2015, para. 4).

Just driving home the point about the transparency/opacity tension one more time is the fact that in VR experiences, like the one in *No Man's Sky*, the difference between the "how" and the "what," the "procedural" and the "content" is something of a moot point. The "how" and the "what" become the same thing; the distinction between the two becomes inconsequential. The "how" is the "what." In other words, the procedural generation of content that keeps the game moving is not just part of our experience of the game, it *is* our experience. The real question, with all of the examples of virtual reality discussed in this chapter, is whether we are having some experience that means something to us, that impacts us in some way. Do we have a better feeling for a city as we walk with Google Maps in our hands? Do we know something about a refugee's experience because of a *New York Times* video? Does a game bring us joy?

CONCLUSION

In his discussion of phenomenology and big data Daniel Susser describes a shift from modern to postmodern science. He argues that the "tools and instruments used by present-day scientists" allow for the analysis of "things which are imperceivable by human bodily perceptual organs alone" (2016, 138). A similar process happens with much of digital media, in particular the digital media discussed in this chapter. What these forms of media do is make perceivable that which was imperceivable without them. What was once atomized is now datafied to become part of a bigger picture. What was just internal and below the user's self-awareness is now transformed into data for self-tracking. What was once a neighbor's private space is now subject to (unwanted) surveillance. What was once a distant or even imaginary space is now present in the palm of our hands or on a screen attached to a headset. In all of these instances, to echo Susser's argument, the media being used "do not merely extend the senses but rather constitute the very phenomena under investigation" (ibid.).

The central part of all of this is the body's role in these experiences. The role of the body should be central in our thought about what these forms of media do to us. Jaron Lanier sounds a warning on the role of the body that stands in contrast to Susser's argument about the constituting power of our senses:

> There is something extraordinary that you might care to notice when you are in VR, though nothing compels you to: you are no longer aware of your physical body. Your brain has accepted the avatar as your body. The only difference between your body and the rest of the reality you are experiencing is that you already know how to control your body, so it happens automatically and subconsciously. (2011, 187)

It's a strange thing, to think that our body might get lost in the equation. It is, however, something that seems reasonable. Speaking from some of the VR experiences I have had, it was disorienting. The best, most immersive VR technology felt transformative and transportive, as if I was actually taken to the place I was viewing through the headset.

This realization makes it even more important to be aware of the body's role in how we experience media and to grapple with the transparency of the medium. Verbeek refers to "the alienation thesis," which he argues, "represents technology as a radically transformative power that estranged human beings from themselves, each other, and from reality itself" (2005, 3). Later in his book he goes on to argue, persuasively, that many new technologies, which we now understand in a context far removed from a pre-mechanization era, can actually be understood as developing authentic, individual human existences (ibid., 36). This counters that notion of alienation.

Placing Verbeek in dialogue with Lanier serves to underline the multistability of our emerging media technologies and what they are doing to the body. We can conclude this discussion by taking virtual reality as an example of this because VR was created with the explicit intention of upping the ante on bodily interactivity between human and technology and, as Irwin argues, "When thinking goes to the bodily felt experience, human-technology connection begins" (2016, 13). She continues, stating, "I cannot bracket out my body in digital media: I need to listen to my body, because mediation cannot occur without the body's knowledge" (ibid., 13). Irwin points to motion sickness in VR users as a key example of this bodily knowledge.

Ihde reminds us that multistability is about "the situated and perspectival nature of bodily perception" (2009, 15–16); it is, once again, about "the material technology, the bodily technique, and the social practice" (ibid., 17). The VR examples discussed above, taken together, underscore this. *No Man's Sky* is a VR experience that takes the first-person gaming style that has been around for decades but amplifies the complexity of the world being explored in that style of gaming; a change reflecting the evolving technologies and changing gaming culture. The evolution from the Aspen Movie Map to Google Maps presents a similar situation where the technology's imagery and its ability to allow the user to move through a distant environment elevates the level of realism in the user's experience. *The New York Times* news VR, along with other VR viewers, gives the user a more immersive and transportive experience of the VR environment. These three examples, taken together, reflect changes in the material practices in both creating and experiencing media. While they are all examples of VR, they present different ways of having bodily experiences of a virtual environment. Finally, they each in their own way reflect changing social practices. Probably the most drastic example of this would be journalism using the affective practice of placing the news consumer in an immersive, emotional experience, which stands in stark contrast to, for example, the stoic and theoretically objective broadcast news reporting of Walter Cronkite's generation.

These VR technologies also serve to demonstrate the strong connection between technological multistability and the user's bodily experience of self. In particular, Verbeek points to technologies of media and communication as sources of such possibilities to "exist as ourselves" (2005, 36). He talks about email and one-to-one communication. A variety of other media, many-to-many social platforms, and networking and media technologies could easily be seen as falling into a category of such authentic experiences. Susser's argument of awareness of the self, making the invisible visible, also gives us a sense of an authenticity of experience of the self. The early VR research discussed above, and its desire for a move from the passive consumption of television to its interactive experience can also give us hope for a more authentic experience of others' lives, especially those who are distant from us, as in the *New York Times* VR content. Despite Lanier's compelling argument, we have to question whether such experiences of media are really alienating. Or, to repeat once more Ihde's argument, we mustn't forget that "Phenomenologically, perception is not passive but active; holistically, it is bodily interactive with an environment" (2009, 15). The questions we have to grapple with going forward are, if Lanier is right about a medium like virtual reality, where does the body go and what do we do about it?

REFERENCES

Andrejevic, M. (2015). "The Droning of Experience." *The Fibreculture Journal* 25: 202–216.

Barnier, A. (2010). "Memories, Memory Studies and My iPhone: Editorial." *Memory Studies* 3 (4): 293–297.

BBC News. (2015, January 26). "Aerial Video of Auschwitz-Birkenau." Retrieved from http://www.bbc.com/news/world-europe-30953301

Boden, M. (2006). *Mind as Machine: A History of Cognitive Science*. Oxford: Clarendon Press.

boyd, d. (2014). *It's Complicated: The Social Lives of Networked Teens*. New Haven, CT: Yale University Press.

Braidotti, R. (2006). "Posthuman, All Too Posthuman." *Theory, Culture & Society* 23 (7–8): 197–208.

Clark, A. and D. Chalmers. (1998). "The extended mind." *Analysis* 58 (1): 7–19.

Coonfield, G. (2006). "Thinking Machinically, or, the Techno-Aesthetic of Jackie Chan: Toward a Deleuze-Guattarian Media Studies." *Critical Studies in Media Communication* 23 (4): 285–301.

Dao, J. (2013). "Drone Pilots Are Found to Get Stress Disorders Much as Those in Combat Do." *New York Times*. Retrieved from http://www.nytimes.com/2013/02/23/us/drone-pilots-found-to-get-stress-disorders-much-as-those-in-combat-do.html?_r=0

Deleuze, G. and F. Guattari. (1983). *Anti-Oedipus*. Minneapolis: University of Minnesota Press.

———. (1987). *A Thousand Plateaus*. Minneapolis: University of Minnesota Press.

Deleuze, G. and C. Parnet. (1987). *Dialogues II*. New York: Columbia University Press.

Dupere, K. (2016, July 10). "This Blind Apple Engineer is Transforming the Tech World at Only 22." *Mashable*. Retrieved from http://mashable.com/2016/07/10/apple-innovation-blind-engineer/#EPvKvuAk5Oqy

Etherington, D. (2016, August 12). "MIT's DuoSkin Turns Temporary Tattoos into On-Skin Interfaces." *TechCrunch*. Retrieved from https://techcrunch.com/2016/08/12/duoskin/

Green, D. (2016). *Procedural Content Generation for C++ Game Development*. Birmingham, UK: Packt Publishing.

GreenPeace. (2011, April). "How Dirty Is Your Data? A Look at the Energy Choices That Power Cloud Computing." Washington, D.C.: Greenpeace Inc.

———. (2014, April). "Clicking Clean: How Companies Are Creating the Green Internet." Washington, D.C.: Greenpeace Inc.

Hello Games. (2015). "About." Retrieved from http://www.no-mans-sky.com/about/

Henn, S. (2014, May 30). "Drone Wars: Who Owns the Air?" *Morning Edition*. Retrieved from http://www.npr.org/sections/money/2014/05/30/317074394/drone-wars-who-owns-the-air

Hepworth, S. (2016, Fall/Winter). "The Drone Files." *Columbia Journalism Review*: 12–19.

Ihde, D. (1990). *Technology and the Lifeworld: From Garden to Earth*. Bloomington, IN: Indiana University Press.

———. (2008). *Ironic Technics*. Copenhagen: Automatic Press/VIP.

———. (2009). *Postphenomenology and Technoscience: The Peking University Lectures*. Albany, NY: SUNY Press.

Irwin, S. (2016). *Digital Media: Human–Technology Connection*. Lanham, MD: Lexington Books.

Kaminski, M. (2016, May 17). "Enough with the "Sunbathing Teenager" Gambit." *Slate*. Retrieved from http://www.slate.com/articles/technology/future_tense/2016/05/drone_privacy_is_about_much_more_than_sunbathing_teenage_daughters.html

Kelly, S. (2016, July 5). "How the Apple Watch Wants to Be the First Fitness Tracker for People in Wheelchairs." *Mashable*. Retrieved from http://mashable.com/2016/07/05/apple-watch-wheelchair-accessible/#03WqWUSBemq6

Kovach, B. and T. Rosenstiel. (2014). *The Elements of Journalism: What Newspeople Should Know and the Public Should Expect*. New York: Three Rivers Press.

Kurzweil, R. (2005). *The Singularity Is Near*. New York: Penguin Books.

Lanier, J. (2010). *You Are Not a Gadget: A Manifesto*. New York: Vintage Books.

Matyszczyk, C. (2015, October 28). "Judge Rules Man Had Right to Shoot Down Drone over His House." *CNet*. Retrieved from https://www.cnet.com/news/judge-rules-man-had-right-to-shoot-down-drone-over-his-house/

McFarland, M. (2015, February 3). "The Story Behind the Viral BBC Video of Auschwitz That Was Shot with a Drone." *The Washington Post*. Retrieved from https://www.washingtonpost.com/news/innovations/wp/2015/02/03/the-story-behind-the-viral-bbc-video-of-auschwitz-that-was-shot-with-a-drone/

McLuhan, M. (1998). *Understanding Media*. Boston: MIT Press.

Murray, J. (1997). *Hamlet on the Holodeck: The Future of Narrative in Cyberspace*. New York: The Free Press.

New York Times. (2016). "NYTVR." Retrieved from http://www.nytimes.com/marketing/nytvr/

Norman, D. (2013). *The Design of Everyday Things*. New York: Basic Books.

Ortega, H. (2013). "Volanti Subvenimus: Challenges in Monitoring and Maintaining the Health of Pilots Engaged in Telewarfare." Retrieved from http://www.senior-women.com/news/index.php/pilots-of-remotely-piloted-aircraft

Otto, J. (2013). "Mental Health Diagnoses and Counseling Among Pilots of Remotely Piloted Aircraft in the United States Air Force." *Medical Surveillance Monthly Report* 20 (3): 3–8.

Postman, N. (1993). *Technopoly*. New York: Vintage Books.

Rose, P. (2012). "Divinising Technology and Violence: Technopoly, the Warfare State, and the Revolution in Military Affairs." *Journal of Contemporary Religion* 27 (3): 365–381.

Rundle, M. (2015, June 17). "How Gamers Will Explore Infinite Worlds in No Man's Sky." *Wired*. Retrieved from http://www.wired.co.uk/article/no-mans-sky-e3–2015

Schaper, D. and D. Folkenflik. (2016, August 30). "New FAA Rules Allow More Commercial Drones in the Air." *Morning Edition*. Retrieved from http://www.npr.org/2016/08/30/491906502/new-faa-rules-allow-more-commercial-drones-in-the-air

Slack, J. (2001). "Everyday Matrix." Presented at *Conjectures*, March 2001, Tampa, FL.

Spicer, R. (2014). "Long-Distance Caring Labor: Fatherhood, Smiles and Affect in the Marketing of the iPhone 4 and FaceTime." *Techné: Research in Philosophy and Technology* 18 (1/2): 102–116.

Steenson, M. (n.d.). "Nicholas Negroponte, Leon Groisser, Jerome Wiesner: The Architecture Machine Group and The Media Lab at Massachusetts Institute of Technology MIT." *Radical Pedagogies*. Retrieved from http://radical-pedagogies.com/search-cases/a13-architecture-machine-group-media-lab-massachusetts-institute-technology-mit/

Stump, S. (2016, May 3). "Sony Applies for Patent on Contact Lens Camera That Shoots Photos in a Blink." CNBC. Retrieved from http://www.cnbc.com/2016/05/03/sony-applies-for-patent-on-contact-lens-camera-that-shoots-photos-in-a-blink.html

Susser, D. (2016). "Idhe's Missing Sciences: Postphenomenology, Big Data, and the Human Sciences." *Techné: Research in Philosophy and Technology* 20 (2): 137–152.

Tyson, N. (2013, June 14). "The Good Thing About Science Is That It's True Whether or Not You Believe in It." Tweet. Retrieved from https://twitter.com/neiltyson/status/345551599382446081

Van Den Eede, Y. (2010). "In Between Us: On the Transparency and Opacity of Technological Mediation." *Foundations of Science* 16 (2–3): 139–159.

Verbeek, P. (2005). *What Things Do: Philosophical Reflections on Technology, Agency, and Design*. University Park, PA: Pennsylvania State University Press.

Watkins, R. (2016). *Procedural Content Generation for Unity Game Development*. Birmingham, UK: Packt Publishing.

Weber, M. (n.d.). "Computer Mapping Technology and It's [sic] Origins." Retrieved from http://www.jameco.com/Jameco/workshop/MyStory/computer-mapping.html

Wise, J. M. (2005). "Assemblage." In C. Stivale (ed.), *Gilles Deleuze: Key concepts*. Durham, UK: Acumen Publishing, 77–87.

Woolley, B. (1994). *Virtual Worlds: A Journey in Hype and Hyperreality*. New York: Penguin Books.

Zhang, P. (2011). "Deleuze's Relay and Extension of McLuhan: An Ethical Exploration." *Explorations in Media Ecology* 10 (3–4): 207–224.

Chapter 6

Multimedia Stabilities

Exploring the GoPro Experience

Stacey O. Irwin

Multimedia can be defined as a variety of artistic or communicative media that intertwine through control and interaction of digital text, sound, images, video, multiple display areas, interactive experiences, and presentations shared concurrently in recorded or live situations. While this kind of mediated composite and performance has some specific and codified meanings within education and e-learning environments, contemporary media are also truly multi in all dimensions. No technology is neutral in use. Each experience can amplify one element and reduce somewhere else. Both the technology and practice are multi and joined to create our "many" media environments. I name this wide and overarching gathering of the media, multi[media]. The brackets are used here to illustrate the *multiple* technologies and practices of mediamakers and viewers in our contemporary surroundings, while emphasizing and bracketing the digital media which are specifically entangled in our environment (Irwin, 2016). The use of bracketing is also a nod to phenomenology and the idea of unpacking multimedia as it is experienced, aside from its varied meanings. Throughout the chapter the brackets will not be formally used but symbolically implied.

The aim here is to focus on a postphenomenological analysis of mediamakers' experience using multimedia to study technological mediation, the "significant constituent element of our lives, identities, and of our lifeworld" (Kiran 2015, 138). The first part of the chapter identifies specific terms and steps for a multimedia analysis. Secondly, two specific kinds of analyses will be considered in order to focus fully on multimedia multistabilities and their mediating influences. And thirdly, a case study of the GoPro experience will identify three multimedia stabilities across a variety of variations to further illustrate technological mediation.

POSTPHENOMENOLOGICAL UNDERPINNINGS

A postphenomenological framework can be used to study multimedia stabilities because this kind of approach considers the human-technology relation based on the sociocultural situatedness and the embodied practice of a technology-focused experience. The crux of a human-technology relation *is* the connection, the entanglement, and the relation between human and technology. Multimedia exemplifies that exact kind of relation, based on a mediamaker and a variety of technologies he or she uses in the mediamaking practice. New scholars often choose a research area that is more focused on gaining knowledge and less on experiencing a practice. But analyzing the practice of mediamaking through postphenomenology contributes to a richly expanded understanding of media research. Vivian Sobchack comments in this context,

> Indeed, in today's university, most graduate students, encouraged by most of their professors, are in such a hurry to 'professionalize' and to 'understand' that they sometimes forget to attend to their 'experience' and to 'see.' This is as surprisingly true of the students of film and media studies that I teach as it is of those in other less 'vision-focused' disciplines [...]. (Sobchack 2006, 14–15)

Postphenomenology identifies key ideas and experiences in human-technology relations to delve into specifics that help us understand how humans and technologies intertwine by way of a model called the I-technology-world schema (Rosenberger and Verbeek 2015). The combination of an artifact, instrument, or some other kind of technology and a human engaged in a certain kind of context or practice creates a new relation (Ihde 1993). Don Ihde explains,

> What stands out first is that all human-technology relations are two-way relations. Insofar as I use or employ a technology, I am used by and employed by that technology as well [...] A scientific instrument that did not or could not *translate* what it comes in contact with back into humanly understandable or perceivable range would be worthless. (Ihde 2002, 137–138; original emphasis)

Ihde (1990) explains these new relational shifts through a series of models that illustrate the human-technology relation. The (I—technology) → world schema illustrates the way the human and the technology relate in an embodied way. The I → (technology—world) model shows hermeneutic relations, those experiences when a human is interpreting or reading the world through the technology. The I → technology (—world) model demonstrates alterity relations, those quasi-other or Technological Other experiences (cf. Irwin 2005). The usefulness of these models arises from the ability to explain the relation between the human and the technology in very specific ways. All of these models can explain human-technology relations that occur through the multimedia practice. This distinction is very important because many different human-technology experiences are at play when analyzing multimedia. The analysis can present several experiences overlapping at one time in a compound and composite way.

It is difficult to analyze media effects and media experiences without concrete strategies for understanding the ways technology and humans connect. Scholars tend to focus on an analysis of either the technology or the practice. The postphenomenological framework brings both into the analysis and studies the kinds of relations that occur in the overall human-technology experience of multimedia. Key postphenomenological vocabulary used in this chapter helps to illustrate the steps and language used in a postphenomenological study of multimedia. The terms variation, pivot, and multistabilities used throughout the chapter serve as critical contributions to understanding what I call multimedia stabilities.

Variation

Identifying variations is an important part of a postphenomenological framework. Many varied purposes can be attributed to one technology and the planned and designed usage can be different from the actual experience. Specific historical and cultural variations also contribute to the analysis. For instance, historical variations might occur over time based on changes or updates or different iterations of the same kind of technology. By contrast, invariants are those commonalities that do not change. Identifying these fixed patterns of experience also helps to show what varies.

Pivot

A second key term is the pivot. To pivot means to find a specific point on which to turn, to rotate or to spin, in order to see different variations or viewpoints of something. In the context of postphenomenology, as elaborated by Kyle Whyte, a scholar can pivot on a practice or a specific technology.

A pivot "stresses the degree to which the material of the artifact and human attentions can create different uses" (Whyte 2015, 76). It is important to remember that the practice needs to remain stable for the pivot to occur. As a quick historical example, cameras that record visual images have some kind of lens, a "camera obscura" (the dark room where the film is kept), a viewfinder, some kind of external casing or "body" that holds it all together, some kind of "recording on" button, an aperture for exposure, an image sensor to collect the visuals, a film or a memory card to collect recorded data, and often some kind of screen. These parts are invariants or constants for most cameras.

Postphenomenological pivots explain constants like the camera parts, against a host of different or absent variants to learn more about multimedia stabilities. The results of a postphenomenological pivot analysis can reveal some new understandings: "Depending on what is pivoted in the analysis, different trajectories, meanings, and patterns emerge. The ability to see, vary, and decipher these aspects clearly may be seen as a kind of literacy" (Riis 2015, 171). Studying different meanings and patterns of multimedia creates a literacy—a media literacy.

Multistabilities

Studying a mediated experience means analyzing what changes, what remains unchanged, or what shifts or becomes fractured or left behind in the human-technology experience. The term multistability means "the same technology can be used differently by different people who assign different meanings to it" (Wellner 2015, 12). Both the technology and the practice are important for a multistability analysis of multimedia. The technology is part of the multimedia practice and the practice is equally important because many socio-historical habitual or established practices become embedded in the experience. First, let's think about the word *multi*. Multistability indicates "the same object can have more than one [. . .] stability without altering its composition" (Whyte 2015, 70). Multistabilities mean many, varied or diverse stabilities, or many things that might be suitable within a specific context about a specific technology. By its very nature, the prefix "multi-" produces variations. Secondly, we can think about identifying the *stabilities*, because from constancy we can see variation. Stability is a constant pattern, a constancy of images, or practices or any stable relation for a multistable technology, like camera components for instance. When analyzed, a stability may appear as a particular part or sub-technology, a look, a particular way of acting, or a particular use. Stabilities need to be verified again and again as consistently stable or constantly seen. In the context of multimedia, as said, I suggest a new term that reflects the unique characteristics of multimedia for the analysis of multistability, called *multimedia stabilities*. The emphasis is to recognize the multiple media variations available in all multimedia practice.

STAGES OF ANALYSIS

The next step is to conceptualize what a postphenomenological analysis looks like. Whyte, in his chapter "What is Multistability? A Theory of the Keystone Concept of Postphenomenological Research" (2015), explains the steps needed for an analysis that promotes rigor and care in the investigation. Whyte lists the following steps for an analysis of multistabilities:

> First, it needs to be assumed that there is multistability of practices.
> Second, the researcher must select a particular case.
> Third, the researcher selects and justifies a pivot point.
> Fourth, the researcher varies the case along the pivot point.
> Fifth, the variation creates room for discussion of the implications of the different variations. (2015, 79)

While the five stages are identified, the researcher needs to think about the kind of multistable analysis to undertake. Identifying whether to pivot on a practical multistability, an imaginative multistability or a combination of the two is an important next step. Each kind of pivot provides a different and unique perspective on the human-technology relation.

Practical Multistability

Practical multistability identifies stronger embodiment through practicing variations for a specific use context. Whyte (2015) has identified two examples of practical multistabilities in his chapter. He explains Ihde's well-known illustration of archery (1990) and Robert Rosenberger's case of a computer (2009) as examples. This style of analysis pivots on the use context or practice. Ihde's archery case explores different ways of shooting archery using the technology of the bow and arrow, in all of the variations of the archer's practice, and the technology an archer uses, across historical time. Ihde focuses on the embodied ways of using the technological artifact within specific socio-cultural and historical times and experiences. He explains, "in an abstract sense, all archery is the 'same' technology in which a projectile (arrow) is propelled by the tensile force of a bow and bowstring" (2009, 16). Whyte (2015) also explains Rosenberger's example of the functionality of the computer as a technological object in the computer-user entanglement. Rosenberger pivots on the degree of function offered to the user by the computer technology:

> Many aspects of computer use are experienced with a high degree of transparency. The awareness of touching the mouse or keyboard, or of clicking often-used onscreen icons or buttons, fades into the background of what is experienced. Focus is placed on the content displayed on the screen, rather than the screen itself or its borders. While engrossed in what is being done, the user may be scarcely consciously aware of her or his situation of sitting in front of a computer at all. (Rosenberger 2009, 178)

A practical multistability analysis that pivots on the practice of mediamakers who create multimedia would identify the degree of function the technology offers to users over time, through historical and socio-cultural shifts in technology and embodiment.

Imaginative Multistability

A different choice is to imagine uses for the technology itself. As explained by Whyte, "The different stabilities are not all testable by firsthand experience alone. Rather, the ascent is an act of moral imagination, or the ability to project possibilities of human-technology entanglements" (2015, 74). Imaginative multistability offers weak embodiment because the multistability analysis is an intellectual exercise of considerations as an observer that is not within the use context of a particular time or place. Weak embodiment is not to be confused with producing a weak analysis. Imaginative multistability is very useful for understanding patterns and perceptions as well as for identifying the alternatives, especially when embodied practice is not an option. Running through the variations opens our field of inquiry to polymorphic mindedness, the ability of some *thing* to be identified in different forms. Rosenberger's imaginative multistability analysis of the bottle tool/artifact is a helpful example of ways to run an imaginative multistability analysis. The bottle is the artifact that pivots, creating different stabilities for the object:

> For instance, a typical glass bottle can be used for purposes other than holding liquid. It can be used as a vase for a short-stemmed flower. It can be used as a base for launching 'bottle rocket' fireworks. A bottle can be broken and used as a sharp weapon. One can blow air across tops of bottles containing different amounts of liquid to produce resonating notes. Other uses are possible. As multistable, the technology supports a number of coherent embodied relations, or stabilities. (Rosenberger 2009, 175; also quoted in Whyte 2015, 75)

The typical bottle stays the same while its uses change. Whyte explains that the stability "allows the variation to make sense as a variation" (2015, 75). In this case the bottle offers multiple stabilities but the example does not show a practiced activity or experience of socio-cultural situatedness. A multistability analysis that pivots on the technology of a multimedia could identify a variety of uses the technology offers mediamakers.

Combining the Two

Peter-Paul Verbeek (2005) notes that the analysis can be taken up in different ways, but it is important to stress that the technology's identity at any point in time is entirely derivative of the technology-user entanglement. Verbeek would point out that to pivot only on the technological artifact or only on the practice is potentially problematic because doing so accepts that the technology's identity can be separated from the human connection to and with it (cf. Whyte 2015). A multimedia stability could pivot on technology but this would only allow the study of one part of the multimedia experience. The ways the human functions with the technology, in embodied and socio-historically situated ways, is also highly important. In fact, I would go so far as to say that a postphenomenological investigation of multimedia must study both imagined stabilities and practical stabilities because the two cannot be separated out for any significant conclusion, hence the term multimedia stabilities.

Multistability explores how media or media technology is used as well as how different media practices fit differently into different contexts, even if the technology is relatively similar. Professional mediamakers who understand the *techne* in the mediamaking process would have a situated, robust understanding based on training, expertise, and practice embodying the media technology (Irwin 2005).

One example from the multimedia field would be the case study of a professional photographer recording digital video. The video photographer takes a bodily stance, aims the camera at a location, activity, scene or subject, focuses the lens, pushes a recording button, and allows the image and sound to be collected for a specific amount of time. Then, the recorded visuals are edited into a smaller or more specifically focused item of content. The photographer might upload the visual recording onto social media or onto YouTube or some other online video-viewing channel. How might the socio-cultural experience of multimedia change if the practice were different because the technology was designed differently, like with fewer or different or absent functions? In what follows, I want to explore this kind of analysis further by way of a case study of the GoPro camera. Now that we have a clear understanding of the postphenomenological analysis, it is time to consider the combination of practices and technologies that mediamakers experience in the creation of multimedia. Kyle Whyte's steps that were explained earlier will be the guiding structure for this analysis. The I-GoPro-world schema will be the model.

CASE: I-GOPRO-WORLD

After choosing a case study it is important for the researcher to select and justify a pivot point. In the I-GoPro-world schema, the mediamaker and the GoPro Camera are paired in the combined experience, which recognizes the intertwining between the practice and technology. For this reason, both imaginative and practical multistability will be considered. It is important for this analysis to explore the practice and technology intertwined, so that we have a clear understanding of the socio-cultural and historical markers of multimedia technology and multimedia practice.

A Short History of Mediamaking

Technological devices have changed drastically since the early days of image experimentation but the technology is only one part of the *whole* called multimedia. Not only have technologies changed, but the ways in which they are used has also shifted. Contemporary mediamakers practice storytelling differently, though many conventions of the craft are still maintained. Contemporary multimedia practice and technology can be better understood within a historical context.

Mediamakers have used a wide variety of film and video cameras in all sizes since the birth of cinema in the late 1800s. And even before that, image devices were part of visual imagery as early as the Renaissance Era (i.e., the camera obscura). Different kinds of recording and editing created different content genres. This pushed mediamakers to experiment with content throughout time. Some recordings were art films; some were entertainment or historical recordings or news reports. In his now famous "Odessa Steps" sequence from the 1925 film *Battleship Potemkin*, Russian filmmaker Sergei Eisenstein illustrates how visual editing has a tremendous psychological power to affect storytelling. He does so through a concept called montage, an editing technique that involves carefully mixing and layering moving images together to evoke feelings or emotions. Eisenstein

> believed that pace (metric montage), as well as the editing of visual patterns (rhythmic montage), together with the goal of finding the emotional through line of the sequence (tonal montage), combined with the juxtaposition of images (intellectual montage), provided filmmakers the tools to tell their stories in the most powerful fashion. (Dancyger 1999, 300)

The first 100 years of mediamaking illustrates the aesthetic force that visual editing can have on the viewer. From the early days of filmmakers D. W. Griffith and Georges Méliès, and their ability to tell a complex story with extreme emotion on celluloid, to Alfred Hitchcock's experimentation of altering time through parallel editing in *Strangers On A Train* (1951), visual storytelling in the form of moving images has progressively developed its ability to reach the audience in compelling ways.

In the 1920s, while Eisenstein was experimenting and developing his pioneering editing techniques, television was invented. This medium was used mostly to broadcast shows and news. Therefore, the aesthetic elements of film editing had not been used in early television production. Only in the 1950s, and even more so since the early 21st century, television started to embrace films of "single camera shooting style" and this manifested the need to practice the aesthetic film style of cinematic production.

Television content had not previously been manipulated through editing but the invention of the frame-accurate electronic editing machine in the 1960s made editing a reality for the television industry. An editor position was added to television production teams and mediamakers pulled parts of different electromagnetic tapes onto a master electromagnetic tape to create news "packages." This first type of television editing was called "linear" editing because one piece had to be edited and then another in a linear fashion. The editor used a "cuts-only" machine that copied bits of moving visual images from many different source tapes onto a master tape to create one unified piece. But this kind of process was not yet fully digital. If I wanted to put something I had forgotten into the video, I had to cover up everything else and go on from there because of the way the technology worked with electronic sync pulses on electromagnetic tape.

A variety of increasingly small "movie" cameras, different recording abilities and more flexible editing technology began to emerge when the Super 8mm camera and film stock was invented in the 1960s. Different technologies and different uses of existing technologies produced artistic content with more movement and more editing cuts. Jean-Luc Godard's 1990 film *Nouvelle Vague* explored a filmmaker's ability to move outside a traditional narrative structure of storytelling to portray a juxtapositioning of imagery in different contexts. This forward-thinking editing process pushed toward a new visual poetic space that provided alternatives to previous filmmaking conventions and focused on the director's artistic vision as ways to express human thought and emotion through film. The style was quickly adapted into commercials and music video clips. The digital infusion multiplied the abilities and altered the stabilities.

Around that same time, in the early 1990s, the film and television industries' understanding about editing was transformed with the introduction of non-linear editing processes, techniques and technologies, which premiered at technology showcases around the world. The term *nonlinear* is a way of explaining the non-sequential way that a mediamaker edits visual content through a computer software program. While film editing could always be done out of sequential order, that is, non-linearly, video editing was done through an electronic control track that was assembled most easily in linear order. In the 1990s, a variety of editing workstations became available to the mediamaking public that allowed non-linear digital editing through a computer for all multimedia work. Non-linear editing brought on a new aesthetic push in visual effects and animation, along with increasingly sophisticated juxtapositioning through extremely short edits, propelled by the exactness of digital technology.

A Digital Shift

The changes pushed visual storytelling in new and different directions. As the multimedia content became increasingly popular, the technical and physical joining of two visual pieces also continued to shift, granting mediamakers an outlet for the articulation of their ideas through a computer-based workflow, many new software interfaces, and an almost constant need for editing of visual content. Contemporary mediamakers can record their digital shorts on a cellphone and edit on an app for live air on Snapchat or on many different Internet platforms like YouTube or Vimeo. The citizen journalist creates video or audio of breaking news and shares it just about anywhere on social media. GoPro camera users share media content to a "channel" on YouTube. The technology continues to define what is recorded and how it is manipulated (i.e., edited) and shared.

All in all, technological trajectories move in different directions because technologies are always changing, and ways and places to deliver media content shift almost daily. Legacy or traditional media has morphed into interactive social and digital ("new") media. Processes that involved the body in the mediamaking, like splicing tape to edit a film on a large editing flatbed or changing large reel-to-reel tape to change a television program, are now completely altered through digital processes. But many notions have not changed. Grassroots stories are still told by citizen journalists and teenagers with an idea or a curiosity, world happenings still show up on the news, and mediamakers still use compositional guides and visual theories to create content that moves us.

The next step in analyzing the case is to recognize pivot points. As discussed earlier, the pivot may be centered on an imagined practice or a technology, or a combination of both. The GoPro camera and its usage patterns make a good case study of multimedia stability because this version of camera technology is predicated on a combination. Mediamakers intertwine experience and an interaction of sound, images, and video in a recorded manner to share on social media. The GoPro experience also operates as a practice that we can name, after the postphenomenological schema, the "(I-GoPro)-world" experience.

The GoPro device is defined as a camera, although the technology exhibits a break in the long history of mediamaking and the practices of use of the camera as described earlier in this section. The GoPro camera has a 2.5 x 3-inch small camera body size, is Wi-Fi enabled for uploading videos, and has a 170-degree ultra-wide field of view and an enhanced barrel lens distortion depth of field. What the GoPro does not have is a viewfinder. This is a break from a century of stabilities. Users can purchase the parts that do not come with the initial camera, like the small LCD screen that can be hooked on to the back as an attachment viewfinder. The idea behind the lack of viewfinder is that the camera lens captures the entire view and experience so the user does not need to look through a viewfinder to frame the recording. The experience is taken in as a whole image so there is no need for a camera operator to zoom or pan or tilt within the frame.

In this sense, the GoPro camera was designed and marketed for the embodied experience. GoPro founder Nick Woodman invented the first version of GoPro as a personal camera by attaching a digital camera to his wrist to get photos of himself as he surfed. He noticed deficiencies when he strapped a traditional digital camera to his arm to record his activities so he engineered a HD camera designed specifically to meet his recording needs. This prototype recorded wide-angle shots that captured the full view of extreme activities and action sports. He tested his camera by surfing with his prototypes. Like Woodman, GoPro users are often active, extreme sport enthusiasts who want to capture their on-the-go moments through action-based footage (Ortiz 2015). Even the name GoPro suggests the idea that camera users can go professional with their videos. The GoPro camera technology and other similar cameras are designed with action in mind so the recording will be less likely to need digital editing after the recording phase is complete. Most mediamakers record the image and somehow manipulate it through editing or compositional choices within a sequence of shots. The GoPro camera is designed and marketed to capture the complete experience without the need for editing so the GoPro does not encourage users to edit, either in real time or ex post facto.

The GoPro Company provides many accessories, mounts, and attachments to place the camera on a helmet, wrist, or body. All these provide new ways of embodiment relations. My students use the GoPro camera in their classroom digital production work. They call it "GoPro-ing." They harness the small lightweight camera to their dog, their car, their kayak, motorcycle, and unicycles (yes, really). A GoPro camera is (technically speaking) a digital camera but it is designed differently from other digital cameras in order to produce new embodiments and new experiences while recording the experience, uploading it, and watching it again.

This postphenomenological analysis proceeds by listing some of the imaginative and practical stabilities a technology may have. An imaginative multistability analysis studies the ability of the GoPro camera to be identified in different forms. This analysis moves through the exercise of imagining ways of using the GoPro without actually embodying the technology in a human-technology endeavor. For example, the automatic focused wide-angle lens collects a wide frame of view with a small compact camera. While this kind of camera is most often used to record action and extreme moving images as a "movie" camera, it can also capture single frames as a "still" camera. The camera also can be used as a small surveillance camera when mounted on the dash of a car or a building or mounted on a drone and flown above or around a specific location or event. The small size of the GoPro camera allows users to capture unique POVs (point of views). Animal behaviorists use GoPros to better understand the movement of an animal's perspective of the world. Mediamakers can also become more creative storytellers by presenting an "alternative" reality when recording visuals of the GoPro. A wide-angle lens like the one housed in the GoPro capitalizes on a different perspective of the frame, which psychologically creates dimensional layers to draw specific attention to a different part of the frame. For instance, a user might wish to focus on the demonstrators at a march or the victim of a crime. The viewer will attend to the image differently based on how the mediamaker has set up and recorded the image with the GoPro. Setting up the frame in a specific way has always been part of a photographer's aim, but the GoPro's technology allows further manipulation of perspective through both the camera technology. Each of these examples highlights imagined multimedia multistabilities that can identify the different forms of use. Next, let's switch to practical multistabilities to investigate applied ways that mediamakers experience human-technology connection in the I-GoPro-world experience.

For the GoPro user, the lens, an external casing, the "recording on" button, an aperture for exposure, an image sensor, and a memory card to collect recorded data all become part of the embodied practice of the human-technology relation. A technology can be practiced to further and differently explore the human-technology connection. All of the GoPro's components are in some way connected to the mediamaker engaged with the technology in practice. A GoPro camera's point of view mixes and blends the objective and subjective experiences. Just like in first person shooter (FPS) perspective in online gaming, the GoPro user bodily maintains a FPS position, but of a different sort; exhibiting what French cultural theorist Paul Virilio (1994) would call the vision machine, because we technically see the machine's POV of the human's experience.

The camera technology is designed to collect an image that shows the apprehension, gathering, and collecting of moments. It establishes an ad hoc camaraderie between creator, technology and spectator/audience/viewer. The experience of GoPro use is enjoyed in-process as well as recorded and reviewed for re-enjoyment and sharing.

The GoPro is a camera technology that has been engineered to create content and experiences that are shared immediately to social media or a YouTube page, through the camera's Wi-Fi. The natural beginning, middle and end of an experience are the natural progressions of events that are simultaneously recorded along with the sound of the experiencer. This natural narration adds to the total storytelling atmosphere, impression, and feeling of watching the I-GoPro-world experience unfold.

Thanks to its embodied practices as demonstrated by my students, GoPro can be classified as a wearable technology. The camera can be attached to almost any body part that best captures the subjective visual experience from a unique POV. To gain this POV, the GoPro technology is operated fundamentally differently from other cameras, thereby creating a new stability for digital cameras. From this practical stability, additional stabilities arise as the GoPro can come with or without viewfinder/viewing screen. Another stability arises as the GoPro camera is operated differently than other cameras both historically and socio-culturally as shared earlier in the history section. The main issue here is the lack of viewfinder and often the viewing screen on the back of the camera. A third stability concerns the content, which is fashioned and often delivered to an audience differently. The final step is a discussion of the implications of different variations. A postphenomenological analysis of the I-GoPro-world highlights three multimedia stabilities that coalesce around embodied entanglement, exhibitionist act, and techno-aesthetic to illustrate embodied, hermeneutic, and alterity relations, respectively.

Embodied Entanglement

The GoPro is a technology that situates itself for a unique embodied use. It is specifically designed to attach directly to the photographer's body through a strap or holster and to provide a unique vantage point for viewing an experience. Throughout media history, most of the cameras were placed on tripods or pedestals. Through the years the tripod, the monopod and a variety of other "sticks" and rigs kept a recording steady. In the 1970s the Steadicam mount became available and large cameras were mounted through a "steadying" apparatus on someone's body to create smooth movement while recording. This kind of movement and steadiness were not achievable on a camera operator's shoulder or on a traditional tripod mount and the experience created a new kind of recorded movement that pushed forward a mediamaker's desire for camera movement that "keeps up" with the subject being recorded while providing a steady shot for the viewer. Thirty years after the Steadicam was introduced, the GoPro camera is released. The camera is called a "wearable" technology because it keeps up with the movement as it is attached to the person experiencing an activity. This camera is so small and light that an additional apparatus is not needed to steady the shot. The wide-angle barrel lens with the short focal length provides additional steadiness for the viewer. As shared earlier in this chapter, the crux of the human-technology connection begins in embodiment relations, where the technology becomes perceptually transparent (Ihde 1990). The "(I—technology) → world" schema can be relabeled as "(I—GoPro) → world" schema to explain embodiment relations when using this uniquely designed camera and the unique practices associated with it. This kind of relationship takes the viewer's body into his or her experience by perceiving through the body and the senses, but not perceiving the technology recording the experience. Many GoPro camera shots shatter normal embodiment relations because the GoPro camera is recording the experience from the side of cliffs or on top of mountains, or from a ski slope or some other extreme place that most people cannot access. Selmin Kara and Alanna Thain in "Sonic Ethnographies" explain how a GoPro camera was used in the 2012 documentary *Leviathan* (Lucien Castaing-Taylor and Véréna Paravel):

> Featuring hauntingly visceral imagery and a carefully orchestrated mix of muffled yet evocative sounds captured by GoPro cameras (hardy, small and lightweight cameras first designed for use by extreme sports enthusiasts) as well as small stereo mics mounted on DSLRs [digital single lens reflex cameras], the film is situated within the ecology of the long catastrophe of commercial fishing. (Kara and Thain 2015, 187)

The GoPro is instrumental as a technology and a practice for the mediamakers of this documentary because they wanted the effect of "distributed embodiment with body-mounted technologies purporting to provide 'intimate' shots/ sounds of bodily experience (suggesting interiority) while mounted on various bodily surfaces and mechanic extensions" (Selmin and Thain 2015, 195). The viewer sees "impossibly objective shots[1] (objective since unattributable to a specific character in the film; yet subjective due to the bodily apparatus), which appear incredibly, intimately embodied by human and mechanic agents" (ibid.). The mediamaker's body is not only entangled with the GoPro in mediamaking practice, but also situated in a unique "(I—GoPro) → world" schema that is engineered to provide a unique vantage point for viewing experience.

Exhibitionist Act

The embodied "(I—GoPro) → world" experience also gives consistent and unwavering POV visuals that engage the spectator for its sheer everythingness. The visuals capture my attention for an extended period of time, as I, the viewer, am apprehended in the activity. The long duration take, so to speak, continues without interruption. This is an instance of an "I → (GoPro—world)" schema in which the media is experienced in a hermeneutic way together with the world it is situated in. Christian Metz in his book *From the Imaginary Signifier: Psychoanalysis and Cinema* writes,

> the view of the action is seen, through the camera, from the person we perceive to be the subject of that particular scene. A POV framing and experience is as close as an objective shot can approach a subjective experience. The idea is to allow the spectator to be inside the action with the psychological experience of living the action as if beside the subject of the scene. (1982, 15)

This kind of shot psychologically allows the spectator to retain the experience longer. The passion of perceiving—the desire to see the recorded experience—comes into full view. Metz names one of Jacques Lacan's four sex drives, the perceiving drive, as a way of explaining the idea. The distance of the look and the distance of the listening are ways the voyeur maintains space between object and the eye. Lacan's idea of the sex drive explains the absence of the object of desire being physically and noticeably close by, but the presence of viewing the object at a distance as a voyeur. The perceiver enjoys the connected proximity between the object and the perceiver's gaze. Dissatisfaction and satisfaction work together and juxtapose each other in the intertwining in the I-GoPro-world experience to create a "love" triangle of sorts between the wearer-photographer, the camera, and the viewer.

Techno-Aesthetic

What kind of technological category does the GoPro camera fit into? It is a camera. It is a wearable technology. It is a creative tool. It is a recorder of events. It is also an instrument, an artifact, a technology, and an accessory. The "focus of attention is no longer an aesthetic experience *of* technology or an aesthetic discourse *on* technology, but a *cognitio sensitiva*[2] that proceeds *from and within* technological schemes, materials, and processes" (Loeve 2011, 7; original emphasis). I am relating with the technology in a very lived way through embodiment and hermeneutic relations. The human-technology connection of a GoPro experience is a composite experience but the camera is still an "other" from my lifeworld, which suggests the "I → GoPro (—world)" relation, or in other words, the alterity relation. The human and technology are pushing the quasi-otherness experience to new levels to fully embrace content creation for the world of extreme sports and other similar experiences. This capacity of the techno-aesthetic becomes a new experience instead of a representation of experience. Ian Bogost explains the kind of imprint that occurs in the techno-aesthetic. In an article in *The Atlantic* he writes, "Some architects can look at a building and tell you which version of Autodesk was used to create it" (2012). I understand what he is talking about. Certain technologies leave an imprint, a residue on the image. I think that I can look at YouTube videos and tell if a GoPro was used in the production of the video. Does this make the GoPro part of this idea that Bogost and others are calling the New Aesthetic, the artistic movement that stresses both the materiality and the technology that make visual and digital art? The way that the technology is created has made a visual image that is imprinted by the design of the technology. The GoPro aesthetic is a transformation of practices, experiences, and technology that converge to form a new aesthetic, a non-neutral experience that makes a difference by its creation. Andrew Murphie in "Making Sense: The Transformation of Documentary by Digital and Networked Media" explains it this way, referring to the documentary *Leviathan*:

> A changing sense of sense comes together then, with the new technics and the new sensations they broker, to constantly transform relations between all three [forms, techniques, practices]. So GoPro cameras and water, fish and birds, workers and machines, find new relations as they mediate each other in *Leviathan* [...]. (Murphie, 2014, 189)

Murphie also uses the *Leviathan* documentary as an example of a new aesthetic or a new relation that occurs through living things and the technology, one where different relations between the technology and the humans and other living things rub off on each other as if they have left a trace of experience as an image imprint.

Clare Hemmings in "Invoking Affect: Cultural Theory and the Ontological Turn" explains more about the idea of experience trace: "An affect theory is all of our affective experiences to date that are remembered (or better, perhaps, registered) in the moment of responding to a new situation, such that we keep 'a trace, within [our] constitution' of those experiences" (2005, 552). The GoPro keeps the trace through a recording, which, when unedited and unproduced, echoes the registered trace or imprint we felt when we first did that "thing" we recorded. The experiencing and viewing or even just viewing without actually ever experiencing stirs something in us that wakes up or evokes a trace to that experience or something akin to it.

Affect theory is a way to explain all those affective experiences and moments we remember and respond to. These instants leave a trace in our being. Hemmings uses the example of a smile that is transferred to others and then returns to us, increasing its original intensity. In that same way the GoPro aesthetic melds users and spectators through relation to each other and the world. The human-technology experience of GoPro-ing is an affect-like capture of traces of an experience.

Finally, Mitchell Whitelaw, in his 2012 article "Transmateriality: Presence, Aesthetics, and Media Arts," discusses literary theorist Hans Ulrich *Gumbrecht's* idea of presence aesthetics. He explains that media technologies can prompt moments of deepened being in the world, despite the more familiar rhetoric that media distances the world from us. The techno-aesthetic leaves a trace, an indelible mark, an imprint, or shadow on the experience and the world. The GoPro exhibits this kind of techno-aesthetic.

CLOSING THE CASE

This chapter was inspired by two specific ideas. Whyte, in the conclusionary remarks of his chapter "What is Multistability?" explains, "Future work needs to chart out these different steps to be convincing to others who may use the studies for their own purposes. From that, more coherent, defensible criteria could be developed" (2015, 79). Add to this Ihde's observation at the conclusion of his book *Postphenomenology: Essays in the Postmodern Context* where he shares,

> But I will project that these issues will be the issues of the twenty-first century as humanities come to grips with a world restructured by a technological world culture. And in such a culture, ways must be found to deal with precisely those features of multistability [...]. (1993, 155)

This chapter has aimed to chart steps for postphenomenological investigations that help the humanities come to grips with our mediated, restructured world. Conceptualizing human-technology connections creates innovative and vibrant frameworks for understanding embodiment through media. Studying the transformative and non-neutral roles of multimedia alter the understanding of the co-constitution of human and technology and the interpretation of media effects. Critical understandings about the ontological nuances of human beings and technologies highlight socio-cultural notions. The I-GoPro-world case study illustrates a way we can use postphenomenology to analyze multimedia experience.

The multimedia multistabilities, analyzed through articulated technological pivots and both imaginative and practical multistable analyses, reveals embodied entanglements, exhibitionist acts, and techno-aesthetic experiences as explorations of human-technology relations. The history of practice and the technology itself provides the backstory to analyze the stabilities. Multimedia stabilities explain human-technology connections when a mediamaker pairs with multimedia. Mediamakers and multimedia intertwine in technological mediation. Multimedia shapes and reshapes humans and the world. Postphenomenology may help us get there.

NOTES

1. The authors use the term "impossibly objective" to describe the idea that a body could not negotiate this point of view on its own. The view of the experience is as if an "other" is attached to the subject who is experiencing the activity. In reality, the GoPro camera is the "other" attached to the person or thing experiencing the activity or event. This makes the recorded image seem to be impossibly recorded.

2. *Cognitio sensitiva* means sensitive cognition. The term is most often attributed to German rationalist philosopher Alexander Baumgarten, who considered aesthetics as a study of sensations, feelings, and perception which he called *cognitio sensitiva*.

REFERENCES

Dancyger, K. (1999). *The World of Film and Video Production: Aesthetics and Practices*. Fort Worth: Harcourt Brace College.

Hemmings, C. (2005). "Invoking Affect: Cultural Theory and the Ontological Turn." *Cultural Studies* 19 (5): 548–67.

Ihde, D. (2009). *Postphenomenology and Technoscience: The Peking University Lectures*. Albany: SUNY Press.

———. (2002). *Bodies in Technology*. Minneapolis: University of Minnesota Press.

———. (1993). *Postphenomenology: Essays in the Postmodern Context*. Evanston, IL: Northwestern University Press.

———. (1990). *Technology and the Lifeworld: From Garden to Earth*. Bloomington: Indiana University Press.

Irwin, S. O'Neal. (2016). *Digital Media: Human–Technology Connection*. Lanham: Lexington Books.

———. (1998). "Technological Other/Quasi Other: Reflection on Lived Experience." *Human Studies* 28 (4): 453–67.

Kara, S. and A. Thain. (2015). "Sonic Ethnographies." In Holly Rogers (ed.), *Music and Sound in Documentary Film*. London: Routledge.

Kiran, A. (2015). "Four Dimensions of Technological Mediation." In R. Rosenberger and P.-P. Verbeek (eds.), *Postphenomenological Investigations: Essays on Human–Technology Relations*. Lanham: Lexington Books, 123–40.

Loeve, S. (2011). "Sensible Atoms: A Techno-Aesthetic Approach to Representation." *NanoEthics* 5 (2): 203–222.

Murphie, A. (2014). "Making Sense: the Transformation of Documentary by Digital and Networked Media." *Studies in Documentary Film* 8 (3): 188–204.

Metz, C. (1982). *Psychoanalysis and Cinema: The Imaginary Signifier*. London: MacMillan.

Ortiz, M. (2015). "The Action Cam Phenomenon: A New Trend in Audiovisual Production." *Communication and Society* 28 (3).

Riis, S. (2015). "A Century on Speed: Reflection on Movement and Mobility in the Twentieth Century." In R. Rosenberger and P.-P. Verbeek (eds.), *Postphenomenological Investigations: Essays on Human–Technology Relations.* Lanham: Lexington Books, 159–74.

Rosenberger, R. (2009). "The Sudden Experience of the Computer." *AI and Society* 24: 173–180.

Rosenberger, R. and P.-P. Verbeek. (2015). *Postphenomenological Investigations: Essays on Human-Technology Relations*. Lanham: Lexington Books.

Sobchack, V. "Simple Grounds: At Home in Experience." In E. Selinger (ed.), *Postphenomenology: A Critical Companion to Ihde*. Albany: State University of New York, 13–19.

The Atlantic. (2016). "The New Aesthetic Needs to Get Weirder." April 13. Atlantic Media Company, Accessed November 01, 2016.

Verbeek, P.-P. (2005). *What Things Do: Philosophical Reflections on Technology, Agency, and Design*. University Park, PA: Penn State University Press.

Virilio, P. (1994). *The Vision Machine*. Indianapolis: University of Indiana Press.

Whyte, K. P. (2015). "What is Multistability? A Theory of the Keystone Concept of Postphenomenological Research." In J. K. B. O. Friis and R. P. Crease (eds.), *Technoscience and Postphenomenology: The Manhattan Papers*. Lanham: Lexington Books, 69–81.

Wellner, G. (2015). *A Postphenomenological Inquiry of Cell Phones: Genealogies, Meanings, and Becoming*. Lanham: Lexington Books.

Whitelaw, M. (2012). "Transmateriality: Presence, Aesthetics, and Media Arts." In U. Ekman (ed.), *Throughout: Art and Culture Emerging With Ubiquitous Computing*. Boston: MIT Press, 223–236.

Chapter 7

Digital Images and Multistability in Design Practice

Fernando Secomandi

Although Ihde's writings about human relations to technology are peppered with references to "media" technologies, ranging from the most traditional to contemporary digital forms, to my knowledge his postphenomenological style of analysis has never engaged in explicit dialogue with media studies as such. This means that authors seeking to connect the topics of media and postphenomenology have under their purview a vastly unexplored territory for proposing cross-fertilizations between the fields.

Irwin's recent *Digital Media: Human–Technology Connection* (2016) presents one leading effort in this direction. Inspired by Ihde's (1990, 1) metaphor of *technological texture*, Irwin characterizes contemporary life as being thoroughly pervaded by digital media. According to her, to approach digital media postphenomenologically means first of all acknowledging it as an artifact, which implies both the dimensions of *directedness* and *materiality*. Directedness from a postphenomenological standpoint must not be understood as mere instrumentality. Digital media certainly serve a range of purposes, but their relevance reaches much beyond that: they reveal reality for humans in special ways. On the other hand, a postphenomenological account of materiality helps to clarify how digital media, though stored in abstract numerical codes, must be experienced by perceiving subjects who are always physically and culturally situated. Irwin's argumentation builds on a series of close-up, detailed case studies of present-day digital media practices, involving audio mixing, photo manipulation, data mining, and self-tracking devices.

In this chapter I want to join hands with Irwin's and other recent postphenomenological studies focusing on the case of self-tracking technologies (Van Den Eede 2015; Secomandi 2013; Secomandi 2017). But instead of exploring the technological texture of user experiences, I turn to professional design practices and report on field research carried out at the development location of a self-tracking technology commercialized by Philips, named DirectLife. DirectLife was devised with the intent of helping people to become healthier by encouraging physically active lifestyles. As with many similar technologies, in order to become more physically active DirectLife users had to strongly commit to behavioral change. To achieve that, the designers of DirectLife conceived of a new website interface where users could manually set activity targets on the basis of early feedback about their actual performances in the program.

The reference to digital media here operates at two registers. Not only is this study about a technology that in use is based on digital processes, but its design also depended on a mix of digital tools, including software for image manipulation and computer programming, platforms of website development, et cetera. More specifically, the analysis presented here centers on several digital images that were generated by the DirectLife design team in order to conceptualize, detail, and implement the new website interface for users. To underscore the analysis, I build on the line of postphenomenological research about imaging technologies inaugurated by Ihde (1998). The directedness of technological artifacts, in this context, refers to the fact that these digital images mediated experiences that designers had of the new DirectLife website interface. And the materiality of these images derives from them making the designed object experientially concrete for members of the design team. Understanding how DirectLife designers experienced the new interface through digital images is an important part of a broader research program of applying postphenomenology to service design and exploring how user and provider experiences during the exchange of services are mediated by interfaces of technical or bodily forms (Secomandi and Snelders 2013; Secomandi 2015; Secomandi 2013; Secomandi 2017).

The main conclusion of this chapter is that digital images are multistable in design practice, and this will be argued below with reference to how the new DirectLife interface was depicted through multiple images and interpreted differently by those involved in the design process. The next section prepares the ground for the empirical study by explaining the postphenomenological notion of multistability in relation to imaging technologies.

MULTISTABILITY AND IMAGING TECHNOLOGIES

Judging from the number of authors who have adopted it for their own investigations in the philosophy of technology, multistability is one of the most fertile concepts of postphenomenology. Simply stated, it "refers to the idea that any technology can be put to multiple purposes and can be meaningful in different ways to different users" (Rosenberger and Verbeek 2015, 25).

The simplicity of the idea, in reality, belies the complex ways in which the concept has been applied in postphenomenological literature (cf. Rosenberger 2015; Whyte 2015). Ihde, for one, refers to it differently at at least three moments throughout his writings. In *Experimental Phenomenology* (1986), multistability is initially presented as the main outcome of a Husserl-inspired variational methodology, rigorously applied to the case of simple line drawings of visual illusions. Only later is the idea associated with concrete technological instruments and practices, like navigation (Ihde 1990), archery (Ihde 2009b), astronomy (Ihde 2009b), and the camera obscura (Ihde 2012), to name a few. But this take on multistability is markedly different from the early methodological approach. Instead of arriving at the concept as a result of the variational method, the multistability of human-technology relations is presupposed by Ihde and exemplified through case descriptions embedded in varying cultural-historical contexts. Multistability appears once again, rather subtly, in *Expanding Hermeneutics* (1998), Ihde's reference work in a long-standing line of research about imaging technologies. Since this latter line is the most relevant for the examination of digital images in design practice that will be taken up below, a short introduction is required.

Ihde holds that one of the characteristic traits of contemporary science, particularly astronomy, is the dependence on imaging technologies to depict its objects of study—hence his preference for the term "technoscience." Although scientific observations have been technologically mediated since ancient times, Ihde holds that around the middle of the 20th century they underwent a revolution after new instrumentation made possible the visualization of a whole range of celestial objects that in principle sit beyond immediate bodily experience, for example, by detecting and displaying radiation emissions beyond the limits of visible light.

Ihde argues that imaging practices in astronomy today make extensive use of digital technologies, such as computer modeling, to perform sophisticated manipulations of scientific evidence; a process he terms "technoconstruction" (1998, 170–83). The results of technoconstructed realities convey a stronger sense of constitution of the scientific object by technologies, at least in comparison to most of the analog applications. More specifically, scientists are able to employ imaging technologies in "instrumental phenomenological variations" that generate "slice" and "composite" imagery about the phenomena that they interpret.

Although not explicitly mentioned in *Expanding Hermeneutics* (Ihde 1998) and only very recently connected to the idea of instrumental phenomenological variations (Ihde 2016, 85), the notion of multistability is clearly evident in the above passage. Interestingly, postphenomenological researchers who continued to explore the concept in relation to scientific practice have not built on this suggestion, but instead referred back to Ihde's seminal analysis of line drawings (Rosenberger 2008; Rosenberger 2013; Rosenberger 2011; Hasse 2008). As noted by Rosenberger (Friis et al. 2012), in demonstrating that scientists from different communities, cultures, or specializations can hold various coherent interpretations over a "same" technologically generated image—similarly to how one can find many meanings in a single visual illusion—these researchers adopt an alternate take than Ihde about the role of multistability in science. The difference in approach is perhaps better understood through the notion of "pivot point," introduced by Whyte (2015). By pivot, Whyte means that specific aspect in an analysis of multistability that is fixed by the researcher and made constant across cases, thereby allowing for the identification of the variations that obtain when these cases are contrasted. A researcher's option for a particular analytical pivot, Whyte notes, sets off the description of multistability in particular directions. Thus, whereas Ihde places the pivot on the *imaged object*, and by so doing is able to observe how scientific instruments can generate different images of it, the pivot of Hasse and Rosenberger rests on the *imaging artifact*, and the authors emphasize the different interpretations that can be held by scientists over a single technologically generated image. I posit that in the second case multistability is used as a way to explain *divergence* in human perception, whereas in the first case it emphasizes *convergence*. As Ihde later remarks, instrumental phenomenological variations, employed in such a manner, can reveal a "set of results which can, when convergence occurs, be very *robust*" (2010, 62; original emphasis).

The thrust of this chapter lies in the possibility of extending these postphenomenological insights from the scientific laboratory into the design studio. In a rare flirtation with creative practices of engineers and architects, Ihde (2009a) discusses CAD software as a form of imaging technology. The suggestion that design and technoscience are not entirely dissimilar, at least when it comes to their reliance on visual materials, will be explored below through an empirical study about the design of Philips DirectLife. The analysis will apply both pivot points presented above, sometimes fixating the imaging artifact in order to highlight how a "same" digital image of the new DirectLife website interface was interpreted differently, at other times pivoting on the imaged object in order to demonstrate how digital images of various formats are variants that converge on the "same" interface that is being designed.

DESIGNING THE DIRECTLIFE INTERFACE THROUGH DIGITAL IMAGES

Researching Design Practices at Philips

The data for this study was gathered from April to July of 2009, at a time when DirectLife was under the responsibility of New Wellness Solutions

(NWS), a new venture located at the Philips Incubator in Eindhoven, The Netherlands. DirectLife had been under development for several years, mainly in collaboration with interaction designers from Philips Design and behavioral psychologists from Philips Research. At the time, it was being piloted at some partner organizations, but soon its commercial viability would be tested in markets in The Netherlands and the United States. Initially, the business model focused on the corporate market, where DirectLife would be sold to organizations that wanted to alleviate costs associated with the sedentary lifestyles of their employees. Preparations were also underway for selling DirectLife directly to end users via the Philips website, as it eventually was prior to the service's discontinuation on July 1, 2016.

I was at the time invited by a member of NWS's management board to conduct this research at their headquarters, where I was placed alongside the software development team implementing improvements to the DirectLife website. During the period of data collection, I regularly visited the NWS office, observed their operations and interactions, collected extensive documentation, and carried out sixteen semi-structured interviews with the DirectLife design team, including marketing managers, graphic designers, personal coaches, members of the scientific affairs board, and other external collaborators.

Below, I describe the experiences of these professionals with several digital images that can be seen as phenomenological variants upon the *goal adjustment interface*, a new feature that was being introduced to the DirectLife website. The interface was conceived as part of an initiative to enhance users' commitment to activity targets, by letting them adjust these targets after some weeks into the program. From the perspective of the design team, the goal adjustment interface was a key initiative to help people attain long-lasting changes in physical behavior and health, the utmost objective of DirectLife.

First Case of Variants: Wireframe

The first variant (Figure 7.1) is also one of the earliest digital images of the goal adjustment interface circulating among the whole design team and stored in the software development platform. An interpretation of this wireframe from the perspective of the design team might read as follows:

- In specific weeks of the DirectLife program, a new webpage appears for users giving them an opportunity to adjust the individual targets that must be reached at the end of the 12-week activity improvement program;
- The text at the top explains to users what is to be accomplished on the webpage; the green button at the center ("Icon man walk") tells users their current targets for the end of 12 weeks, which are in principle set at a healthy level of physical activity; the gray button on the left ("Icon man sat")

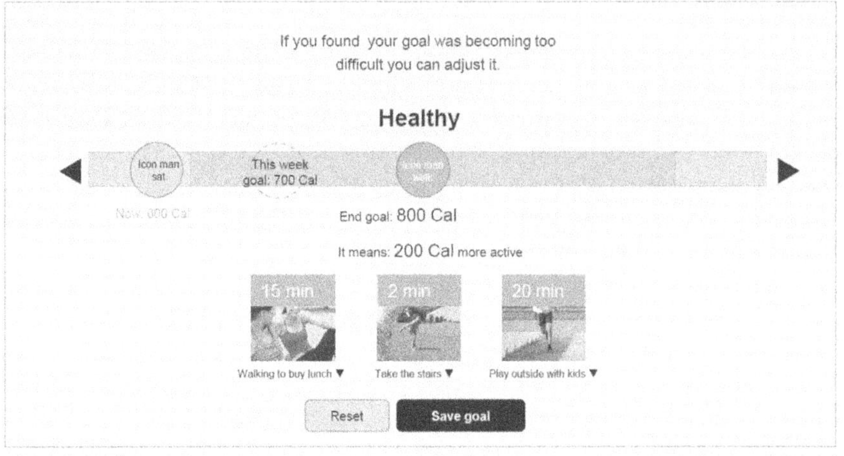

Figure 7.1 Wireframe of the DirectLife goal adjustment interface. *Source*: Philips.

represents their levels of physical activity, as measured at the start of the program; the dotted circle between these two buttons ("This week goal: 700 cal") displays their activity targets specifically for the current week;

- To adjust activity targets for the end of 12 weeks, users must move the green button along the horizontal slider in one of two directions; by sliding it to the right, the amount of calories to be burned is increased, making the end target more difficult to reach; by sliding it to the left, the end target becomes more easily reachable; the exact amount of calories to be burned by users in each chosen position is calculated for them and displayed just below the slider as "end goal";
- In addition, in the lower part of the webpage, the three figures provide examples of activities that users can perform in order to reach the desired target; because this association makes the end target more actionable, users will become more committed to reaching them;
- Finally, users can choose to either save the new activity target or reset the webpage to its starting condition.

What becomes evident from the above description is how the goal adjustment interface is enacted, in the experience of designers, in relation to their expectations about user behaviors. However, these behaviors are not imagined independently of the image itself, but are partly shaped by the specific graphical solutions that have been devised by designers. Hence, users consult an introductory text at the top of the screen, manipulate the green button along a slider to the left or right according to some target-adjusting intention, get inspired by suggestions to take action at the bottom of the screen, and so forth—just like the wireframe depicts.

In turn, these imagined experiences with the goal adjustment interface partly shape designers' interpretations of the wireframe itself. The image is experienced as such—an intermediary, rough, tentative depiction—because of the ways in which it only approximates how users would experience the goal adjustment interface: texts are not carefully written and properly framed; colors do not quite match the palette used by DirectLife; buttons, bars and symbols generally lack subtle graphical elements like shadows and gradients; the overall static display does not allow user interaction with the slider and buttons, et cetera. In short, designer experiences of the wireframe are constituted *intersubjectively*, on the basis of interplay between the agencies of designers, of the digital image they create and of the users who are imagined through this image.

Second Case of Variants: Interactive Demo

The analysis of the second variant contains actually three closely related images. At a certain stage of the design process, doubts were raised about whether users of DirectLife would understand what Philips wished to communicate with the goal adjustment interface, and therefore make effective use of it. Some thought that the new feature under development was "not sense and simplicity yet" (with a nod to Philips' slogan at that time). To address this issue, a small-scale usability study was organized involving participants from the organizations where DirectLife was being piloted. The study was conducted by a web designer from NWS who was then championing for greater integration of user feedback in the design process. Three demonstration mock-ups, or "demos," were created using the Adobe Flash software by a member of the development team. Although these demos were not fully functional, people could already interact with them, something that was not possible with the previous digital image, the wireframe.

In the first demo (Figure 7.2), DirectLife users slid the walking-man icon at the center, in order to set their end targets for the 12-week improvement plan to the left or right. The other translucent walking-man icon indirectly accompanied the action, showing how activity targets for the current week would vary according to the new target set. The blue sitting-man icon remained static, displaying the activity level that was measured at the start of the program. Following this manipulation at the top of the webpage, at the bottom

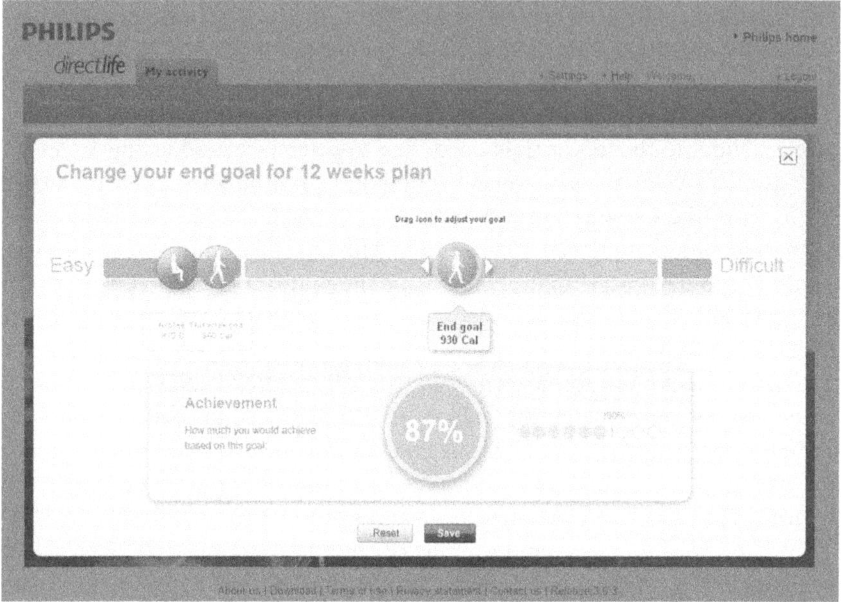

Figure 7.2 First demo of the DirectLife goal adjustment interface. *Source*: Philips.

half the percentage scores and the dotted scale would alter as follows: when the end target was made higher (moved to the right), the percentage and the scale decreased in value; as the end target was made lower (moved to the left), the percentage and the scale increased. According to the designers of this demo, this inverse relationship was because the green circle should display how users' current achievements compared to their intended new targets. However, the usability study revealed that the relationship between the upper and lower parts of this demo was unclear to many users.

In the second demo (Figure 7.3), users set their end goals by clicking on the "up" and "down" arrows at the right side of the graph. They were already familiar with this way of representing activity levels, because other pages of the DirectLife website contained similar graphics. When clicking on the top arrow above bar number 12, this bar got taller and raised the other bars to its left in a slope. The opposite happened when clicking on the down arrow. Although the horizontal slider contained in the first demo was now absent, a comparable relationship between the starting, current, and end activity targets was conveyed through the raising and lowering of bars. The green circle on the far right worked along the same principle as in demo one, and was equally unintelligible to many participants of the usability study.

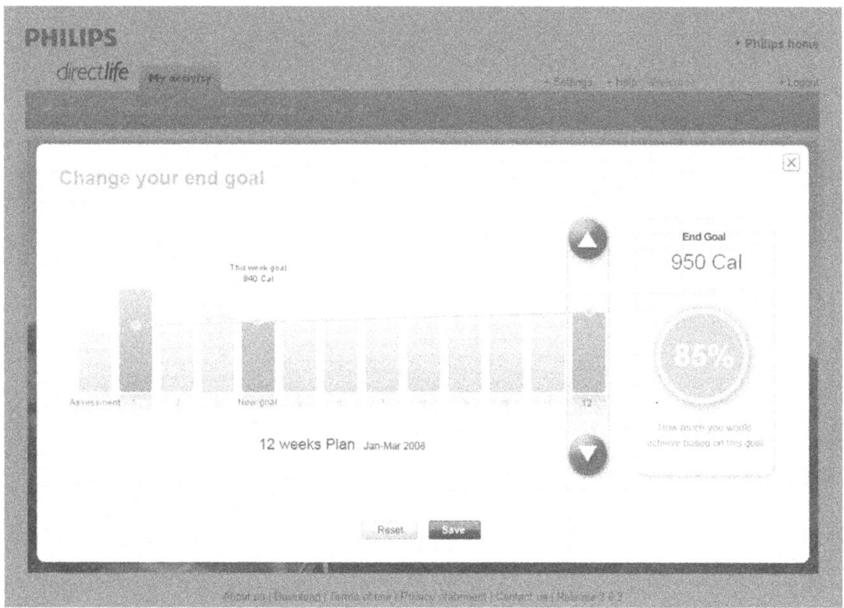

Figure 7.3 Second demo of the DirectLife goal adjustment interface. *Source*: Philips.

In the third demo (Figure 7.4), users moved the "Goal" toggle along the slider in a similar way as in the first demo. Differently from that demo, this slider was colored with a gradient running from green to red. The subtle addition of a "Recommended" range on top of the slider was praised by participants for suggesting at how much "Easier" or "Too difficult" levels the end target should be set, in DirectLife's opinion. Apart from these differences, this demo had almost no numbers, with the exception of the percentage below the goal button, which once again expressed the extent to which current activity levels compared to the intended new target.

From the perspective of the design team, the three alternatives were in principle internally coherent and realizable. Therefore, before the usability test, each was an equally valid image of the goal adjustment interface. However, after the feedback of testers, the design team became more confident about which alternative was most desirable for users and why. As an interaction designer from Philips Design concludes:

> [. . .] so we had from very simple to more complex [concepts], a range of things. When it was too simple people felt that it was not in their value, because they felt it was a bit too simplistic. So, we had to have something that gave them enough trust that it was still scientific. We had to find a balance in-between [. . .]. (Interaction Designer)[1]

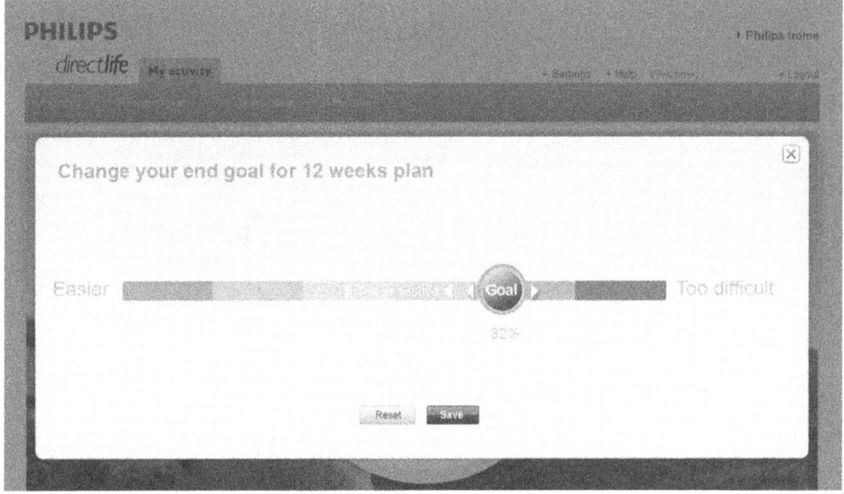

Figure 7.4 Third demo of the DirectLife goal adjustment interface. *Source*: Philips.

The balance was found by integrating positive aspects from each of the separate demos into an improved design. From this point on in the development process, images of the goal adjustment interface would contain a slider on top (as in demo 1), a graph at the bottom (as in demo 2), and a recommended area (as in demo 3). However, this did not come about by merely juxtaposing parts of the preceding demos. To facilitate comprehension, it was decided that the bottom part of the graph would be faded out as the webpage loaded for users, so that they focused on the slider first. Then, as users manipulated the slider, the graph would become fully colored and animated by their actions.

The analysis of these variants shows how the goal adjustment interface evolved by contrasting designers' presuppositions against the actual experiences of users. The result was a "bricolage" of particular aspects of each demo, mixed together so as to generate a more appropriate solution. As soon as the new solution arose, for designers, all demos turned from possible realities into obsolete depictions of experiences that would never actualize for users.

Third Case of Variants: Dynamic Texts

Following the usability test, work in detailing the goal adjustment interface was conducted by interaction designers from Philips Design. These had to deliver detailed visual designs of the goal adjustment interface in static images created with the Adobe Photoshop software. The software development team at NWS, then, would implement these visual designs in terms of software codes that actually generated the dynamic content of the website.

The conversion of static visual designs into dynamic webpages was prone to complications, particularly in regard to the textual contents. Depending on individual circumstances, such as achievements in the program, the goal adjustment interface had to load with different information for specific users. In addition, the website could be accessed in different languages, which meant that before being put online, all English text had to be checked for consistency by a professional copywriter, and then translated into Dutch and Spanish.

To help manage the text editing process, designers from Philips Design were asked to deliver two types of files. One was an image that was identical to the final visual designs, but had all text fields carefully identified and numbered. The other was an Excel spreadsheet displaying dynamic textual content following the numbering system used in the previous image.

Figure 7.5 illustrates the numbered image of the pop-up that brought users to the new goal adjustment interface. The details in blue identify specific strands of texts and refer them to the rows found on the far left of the Excel spreadsheet (Figure 7.6) containing all textual content for this pop-up. In this

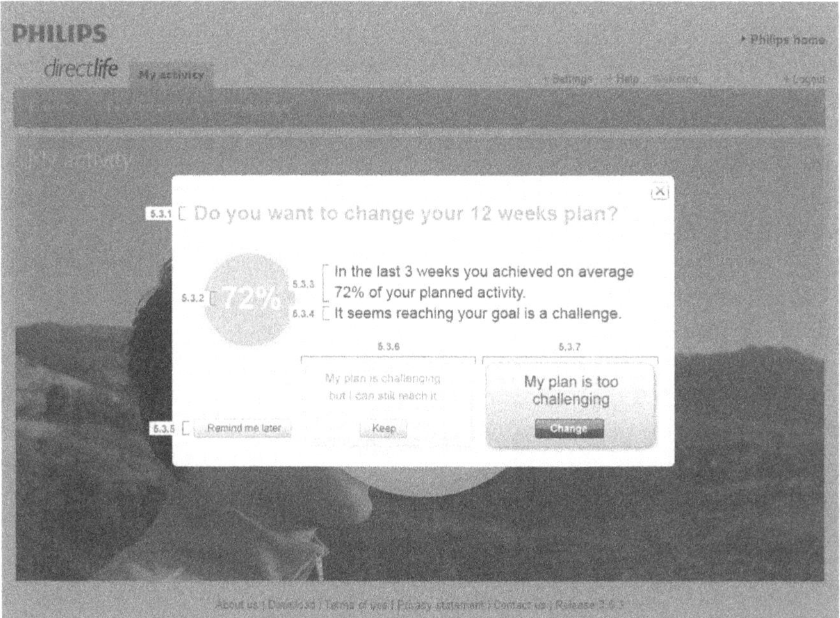

Figure 7.5 Numbered pop-up of the DirectLife goal adjustment interface. *Source*: Philips.

	A	B	C	D	E
1	**5.3 Pop up review Goal**				
2					
3					
4			RULES	original text	edited TEXT
5	5.3.1	static		Do you want to change your 12 weeks plan	Would you like to adjust the end goal for your 12-week plan?
6					
7	5.3.2	dynamic		XX%	XX%
8					
9	5.3.3	dynamic		In the last 3 weeks you achieved on average xx% of your planned activity.	Over the last three weeks, you averaged xx% of your planned activity target.
10					
11	5.3.4	dynamic	xx<95%	It seems reaching your goal is a challenge.	Is reaching your goal too much of a challenge?
12			95%<xx<105%	It seems that you are reaching your target	It's clear that you're on track for success.
13			xx>105%	It seems reaching your goal is too easy.	You're doing well. Make sure your goal is not too low.
14					
15	5.3.6	dynamic	xx<95%	My plan is challenging but I can still reach it	My goal is challenging but I can still reach it
16			95%<xx<105%	My plan is challenging enough	My goal is good as it is
17			xx>105%	My plan is challenging enough	My goal is good as it is
18		static	button	Keep	Keep
19					
20	5.3.7	dynamic	xx<95%	My plan is too challenging	I want to change my goal
21			95%<xx<105%	I want to change my plan	I want to change my goal
22			xx>105%	My plan is too easy	I want to change my goal
23		static	button	Change	Change
24					
25	5.3.5	static		Remind me later	Remind me later
26					
27					

3.3 Compare with others / 3.4 Your plan / 3.7 & 3.8 Profiles / 3.9 Readiness screen / 5.2 Adjust goal / 5.3 Popup review Goal / 6.1 Personal Plan

Figure 7.6 Dynamic pop-up texts of the DirectLife goal adjustment interface. *Source*: Philips.

spreadsheet, the first light blue column in the left indicates whether that specific text field is "dynamic" or "static." The adjacent light blue column to the right defines the rules that apply to each condition. For the design team, these two columns refer to calculations done by the website software in order to determine whether individual users are below, right on, or above targets at any specific week in the program. Depending on a user's situation, he or she will be shown the appropriate textual fragment found in the dark blue column to the far right ("edited text"). The black column named "original text" displays what was preliminary written before the contribution of the copywriter.

Looking at the rows 5.3.7, the suggestion of the copywriter was to change all of the initial content to "I want to change my goal." By editing this text fragment in the image, the copywriter is thus able to influence how users will experience the new goal adjustment interface. This is because what appears at this part of the Excel sheet will be later implemented in the website programming codes. As the copywriter explains, the reason for making changes like this, besides merely correcting spelling and grammatical mistakes, is setting up an appropriate "tone of communication" for DirectLife:

> [. . .] the way things are said, I think is really important, especially in longer text. Each screen, each interaction with the user, you know, you don't want to leave them with a bad feeling or leave them wondering "Uhm . . . but that is strange! That word is strange!" or "Well, it's not too hard for me, I was just really busy!"

> You know? You don't want to set them off. And sometimes people can be sensitive. So you have to do things in a certain way. (Copywriter)

Specifically in the case mentioned above, the copywriter's feeling was that the original text was too blunt and rather confronting for most users:

> I think when people are on a fitness program, to admit that a goal is too challenging, that is really demotivating. So it is more, like, 'Oh, well, I didn't have time' or, you know, 'This month was really busy.' But it all boils down to, that they want to change their goal, whether it is too challenging or too easy. And I didn't feel that [the original text] was relevant. I felt that it was a bit demotivating to kind of pinpoint, like: 'Oh, what? You want to change your goal? Why? Because it is too challenging?' You know, it was a little bit too direct … [It should be] more, just, 'Okay, you want to change your goal, maybe it has been a rough month, you had a big project at work, okay. Let's just change the goal.' (Copywriter)

What's more, her impressions were not just formed on the basis of her knowledge about users, but also in interaction with other people in the design team from a different cultural background. The following two quotes are commentaries about these interactions:

> I mean, it is also a lot about culture as well. I mean, because Philips is Dutch and the team members are Dutch, most of them. Dutch people are just a little bit more direct, which I appreciate, but most Americans don't (laughs). Especially when you are talking about something like a fitness plan, which can make people very defensive or demotivated … They're very touchy. It is a touchy subject: fitness and exercise. Because, then, it is linked to being overweight, and sixty-six percent of Americans are overweight. It is a big issue, especially … maybe the market for this would be more women than men. And, you know, you want to motivate them and help them. You don't want to be, like, 'Oh, is the plan too hard for you?' (laughs). That is like, really, people can be very sensitive about those kinds of things. (Copywriter, American)
>
> She is a native, sensitive, American lady. So, actually she is always very offended by how I write. Because the Dutch are really direct. There are so many cultural differences when you look to the US, that it is never working. So, I am very happy that she joined [the team] and that she says: 'No, no, no, you can't say that like that.' [And I say:] 'Ok, tell me how.' (Marketing Manager, Dutch)

The analysis of these interlinked variants of the goal adjustment interface shows how digital images can help to coordinate work within a design team. It also reveals how attitudes toward users manifested in the text that is contained in these images are attributed to the cultural backgrounds and professional roles of members of the design team.

Fourth Case of Variants: Software Codes

At a point approaching the end of the development process, a decision was made to implement the goal adjustment interface online. Responsibility over this stage was handed over to the NWS software development team. In possession of digital images that enacted what was judged to be a mature vision of the goal adjustment interface, developers set out to "inscribe" it into the website software codes.

A web developer who had recently joined the team spearheaded the initiative. He started to construct the goal adjustment interface page by page in the Flash application. The final designs delivered by Philips Design were deconstructed into parts and each part was created as a Flash component. Existing components that fitted the visual design of the new interface were reused as building blocks. Others, such as the slider used for selecting targets, had to be newly devised.

The implementation of the slider component in Flash provides a good example of how designers are able to image the goal adjustment interface in terms of software codes. As explained by the developer in charge of Flash design, when the goal adjustment interface loaded for users, the slider object appearing on-screen was generated by specific lines of code at the center of Figure 7.7:

> This is one of the important calculations, where you put the slider based on, in fact, what the average calories were during the last three weeks [kcal_average_last_3_weeks], what are the lowest assessment and highest assessment values—these are the borders, left [low_safe] and right [high_safe]. And the recommended goal [recommended_goal] is also given. So, based on those figures I can draw the whole slider. [Text between brackets represents the variables that were pointed at onscreen by the interviewee, unreadable in this figure.] (Flash Developer)

When a user logs on to the website, the software codes described above are used to retrieve specific values from another file which, in turn, contains results from mathematical calculations applied to his or her data as recorded in the DirectLife database. Thus, every time the slider of the goal adjustment interface is actualized for users, its specific appearance is determined in real time by the underlying software codes that operate on users' personal data.

To check if programming codes yielded expected results, during the design process software developers regularly "built" the goal adjustment interface directly from the software codes. The results of that procedure were images such as the one seen in Figure 7.8. These simulations were created in the "demo server," a backup copy of the website software containing real user data mixed with "bogus" information, including fake names, to secure user

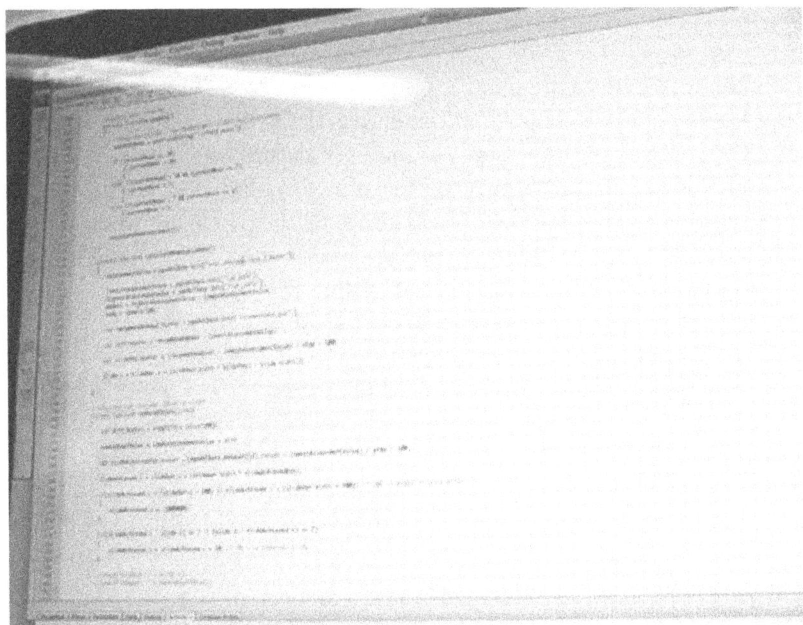

Figure 7.7 Software codes of the DirectLife goal adjustment interface. *Source*: Philips.

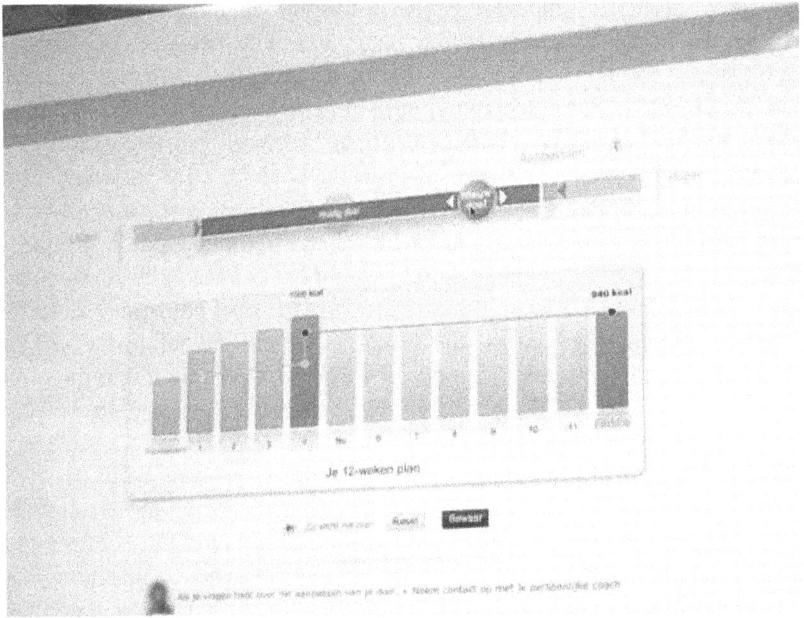

Figure 7.8 Demo server simulation of the DirectLife goal adjustment interface. *Source*: Philips.

anonymity. The demo server also ran a copy of the software that was currently used in the DirectLife website, to prevent messing up the online version with a still untested feature.

Despite the constraints pointed out above, demo server images were, in a sense, the "closest" designers got to the user experience of the goal adjustment interface. This is because of the almost complete overlap between what designers experienced on-screen and what they envisioned users would experience. But, from another perspective, software codes could present to designers an equally truthful rendition of the new user interface. This was because each demo server simulation was limited to what a single user would experience at one time. On the other hand, by inspecting software codes, web developers could know how the new interface would appear for all users, in every possible circumstance, without needing to build unique simulations for each case. Either way, the digital images involved in writing software codes and simulating the website interface expressed for the design team a high degree of "closure" regarding the final form of the goal adjustment interface.

Fifth Case of Variants: Trac Tickets

Before the improved DirectLife website went "live" for users, the goal adjustment interface had to undergo careful testing by members of the software development team. This was done to guarantee that software codes did not exhibit significant flaws, or "bugs," that could negatively affect user experience. Testing involved much iteration, from early-on manual exploration of Flash demos to later-stage automated scripts for comprehensive examination of programming codes. The general procedure adopted by software testers was to mimic expected (and less expected) behaviors for different types of users, in order to spot incongruences between what they saw happening on the screen and what they expected users would experience upon encountering that. Even if automated testing procedures for the goal adjustment interface were still incomplete at the time this research was carried out, testers did spot significant bugs in software codes before they were integrated into the online version of the website. These bugs were reported as "tickets" in Trac, the digital platform used for software development at NWS.

Trac tickets provide an outlook of the various types of bugs that were discussed by members of the software development team, some relating to the user experience of the DirectLife website: a broken background image, missing footer elements, and so forth. In the case of the goal adjustment interface, several bugs pointed to the algorithms that were used to calculate users' activity targets in the DirectLife program.

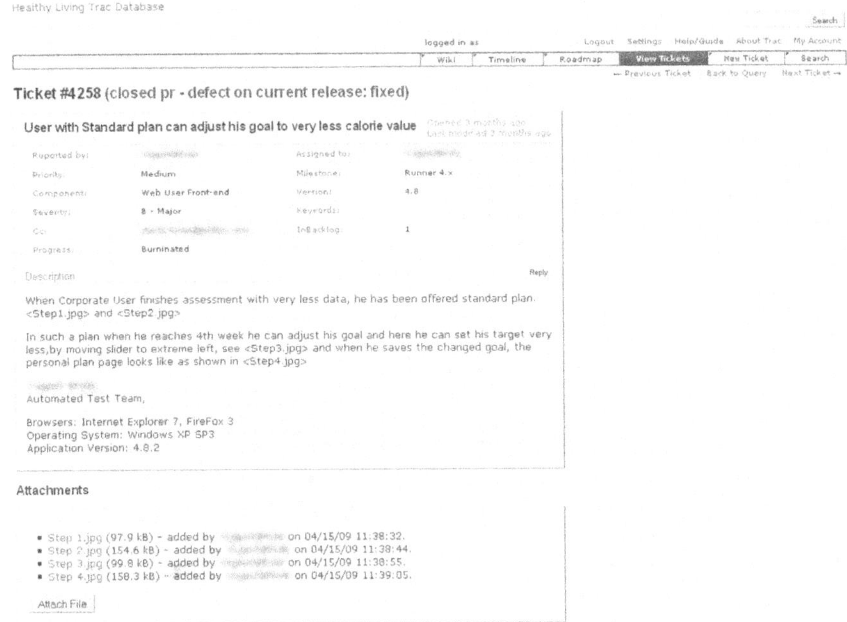

Figure 7.9 Ticket of a bug of the DirectLife goal adjustment interface. *Source*: Philips.

Ticket number 4258, illustrated in Figure 7.9, describes one of these bugs. In it, the software tester tried to convey the situation of a potential user as concretely as possible, by specifying the browser application, operating system, and website version that he was using. To further clarify the user experience of the bug, the ticket included references to files containing screenshots from the tester's own computer. Looking at file "Step 3.jpg" (Figure 7.10), it is possible to understand what concerned this tester. Here we had a user who might have forgotten to carry the activity monitor during the assessment week, when base levels of physical activity are estimated before starting the DirectLife program. This user therefore had very low measured levels of physical activity compared to his weekly targets (the grayed-out line that is partly overlapped by the pop-up to contact the coach). In week four, as the user was given the opportunity to adjust end targets for the activity improvement program, the interface locked him into setting them at absurdly low levels. For this user, the experience of a target line sloping down to 20 Cal would be highly counter-intuitive, considering DirectLife's promise to help bring his calorie expenditure up to a minimal level of healthy activity.

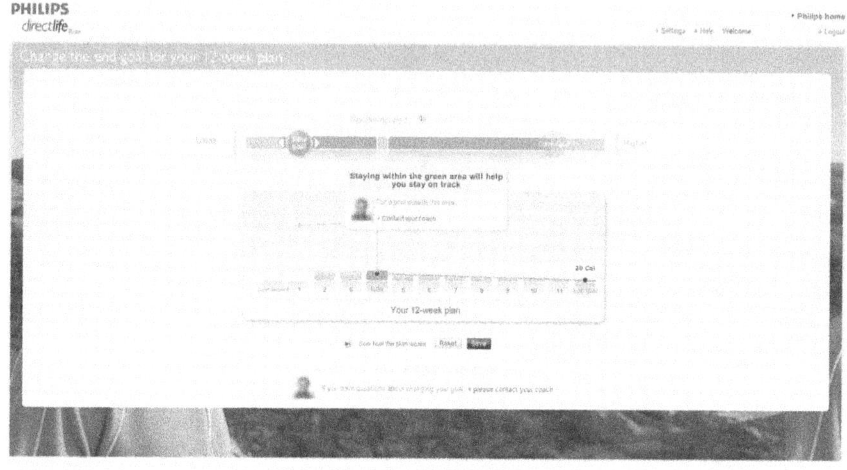

Figure 7.10 Screenshot of a bug of the DirectLife goal adjustment interface. *Source*: Philips.

The bug was solved within a day's time and the solution was included in a subsequent revision of the DirectLife website. However, as bugs like this started to pile up during the test procedure, software developers were forced to reconsider the underlying algorithms that were used to calculate targets. As the project manager of the software development team explains:

> We had to simplify the algorithms to avoid a lot of corner cases. Because of the clipping of goals, the setting of minimum and maximum [goals] on certain conditions, in combination with goal adjustment within certain bounds, that created a lot of non-linearities in the algorithms and a lot of situations where things would be strange. Like, people only being able to set the goal at a lower value than what they have currently, for instance. So, we were expecting a lot of issues from that. What we've seen in the past, if algorithms get too complicated, every time an issue comes up people need to analyze and to dive into them again, and to try to figure out what on earth is going on. So, we simplified that a bit, which made the system a bit more predictable. (Software Team Leader)

The simplification of target-setting algorithms did not happen immediately, but was the result of intense discussions within NWS. What is important to highlight is that the poor fit of the new goal adjustment interface with existing algorithms could not be predicted by designers just by examining the logical consistency of software codes. Instead, it was mainly discovered through digital images, following a test procedure that relied on the visual identification of what users might experience as undesirable manifestations of the goal adjustment interface.

DISCUSSION

I now return to the technological texture of digital media alluded to at the start of this chapter. Irwin (2016, 19) significantly elaborates Ihde's metaphor by relating it to the idea of a weave:

> In the craft of weaving, the warp is the tightly stretched lengthwise threaded core of a fabric and the weft is woven between the warp threads to create varied patterns [...] Each part contributes to the design, but the complete pattern is all that an observer sees on first glance. It takes further study, even possibly turning the textile over to see the underside, to reveal the whole of the weave.

If the goal adjustment interface can be seen as a completed pattern, then the present study revealed its "underside" by getting inside the setting where DirectLife was designed. The result from this immersion is an exploratory, richly descriptive account of the technological texture of digital images in design practice. Like the description of weaving above, each newly created image became a multistable variant that contributed to the whole of the goal adjustment interface by helping to imagine user-interface relations, serving as resource for bricolage, supporting social interaction within the design team, inscribing final solutions into software codes, or revealing unexpected behaviors of the designed object.

All of this to some extent matches Ihde's concept of technoconstruction mentioned earlier in the chapter. Similarly to how new scientific objects are co-constituted by the imaging technologies that scientists interact with, the form of the new DirectLife interface was determined by designers in instrumental phenomenological variations that involved various digitally created images. Staying close to Ihde's (1998) perspective on multistability in relation to technoscientific imaging practices, the present study shows how digital images, in addition to harboring divergent interpretations on the part of designers, can ultimately converge on the final designed object. In addition, while the extant studies following Ihde tend to presume the *finished* nature of such images (Hasse 2008; Rosenberger 2008), what is highlighted here is their progressive construction. In other words, digital images can be *intermediary* artifacts of design activity, more than just mediating artifacts.

Yet, the technoconstruction that takes place in design studios might be something "more" than what is witnessed in scientific laboratories. Ihde (2002, pxvii) once remarked that, differently from other professionals, scientists tend to hold on to the belief that their manufactured images portray reality as it exists "out there." This was not the case for DirectLife designers, for whom images were produced with clear intent of materializing for users an object that did not yet exist (at least, not in any experientially concrete form that was separate from those images themselves). At the core of these different approaches is the notion of *intersubjectivity*. The "reality" of the goal adjustment interface was perceived in each digital image in terms of fit between that which designers intended for users and what they imagined users would experience. If correct, that is a long way from the naïve view that truth in image interpretation rests on the presumed possibility of comparing technologically mediated and unmediated perception of what these images refer to.

NOTES

1. Interviews were conducted in English, which was fluently spoken by the researcher and all participants. The quotes included in this text contain light editing of verbatim transcriptions of the original interview data.

REFERENCES

Friis, J., L. A. Hickman, R. Rosenberger, R. C. Scharff, and D. Ihde. (2012). "Book Symposium on Don Ihde's Expanding Hermeneutics: Visualism in Science: Northwestern University Press, 1998." *Philosophy & Technology* 25 (2): 249–70.

Hasse, C. (2008). "Postphenomenology: Learning Cultural Perception in Science." *Human Studies* 31 (1): 43–61.

Ihde, D. (1986). *Experimental Phenomenology: An Introduction*. Albany: State University of New York Press.

———. (1990). *Technology and the Lifeworld: From Garden to Earth*. Bloomington: Indiana University Press.

———. (1998). *Expanding Hermeneutics: Visualism in Science*. Evanston, IL: Northwestern University Press.

———. (2002). *Bodies in Technology*. Minneapolis: University of Minnesota Press.

———. (2009a). "From da Vinci to CAD and Beyond." *Synthese* 168 (3): 453–67.

———. (2009b). *Postphenomenology and Technoscience: The Peking University Lectures*. Albany: State University of New York Press.

———. (2010). *Embodied Technics*. Copenhagen: Automatic Press/VIP.

———. (2012). *Experimental Phenomenology: Multistabilities*. Second Edition. Albany: State University of New York Press.

———. (2016). *Husserl's Missing Technologies*. New York: Fordham University Press.

Irwin, S. (2016). *Digital Media: Human–Technology Connection*. Lanham: Lexington Books.

Rosenberger, R. (2008). "Perceiving Other Planets: Bodily Experience, Interpretation, and the Mars Orbiter Camera." *Human Studies* 31 (1): 63–75.

———. (2011). "A Case Study in the Applied Philosophy of Imaging: The Synaptic Vesicle Debate." *Science, Technology & Human Values* 36 (1): 6–32.

———. (2013). "Mediating Mars: Perceptual Experience and Scientific Imaging Technologies." *Foundations of Science* 18 (1): 75–91.

———. (2015). "Postphenomenology: What's New? What's Next?" In J. K. B. O. Friis and R. P. Crease (eds.), *Technoscience and Postphenomenology: The Manhattan Papers*. Lanham: Lexington Books, 129–48.

Rosenberger, R. and P.-P. Verbeek. (2015). "A Field Guide to Postphenomenology." In R. Rosenberger and P.-P. Verbeek (eds.), *Postphenomenological Investigations: Essays on Human-Technology Relations*. Lanham: Lexington Books, 9–41.

Secomandi, F. (2013). "Thinking through the Service Interface: A Study of Philips DirectLife." *Design Philosophy Papers* 11 (1): 65–88.

———. (2015). "Bodies as Technology: How Can Postphenomenologists Deal with the Matter of Human Technique." In R. Rosenberger and P.-P. Verbeek (eds.), *Postphenomenological Investigations: Essays on Human-Technology Relations*. Lanham: Lexington Books, 105–121.

———. (2017). "Service Interfaces in Human-Technology Relations: A Case Study of Self-Tracking Technologies." In C. Hasse, J. Friis, J. Aagaard, and O. Tafdrup (eds.), *Postphenomenological Methodologies: New Ways in Studying Mediating Techno-Human Relationships*. Lanham: Lexington Books.

Secomandi, F. and D. Snelders. (2013). "Interface Design in Services: A Postphenomenological Approach." *Design Issues* 29 (1): 3–13.

Van Den Eede, Y. (2015). "Tracing the Tracker: A Postphenomenological Inquiry into Self-Tracking Technologies." In R. Rosenberger and P.-P. Verbeek (eds.), *Postphenomenological Investigations: Essays on Human-Technology Relations*. Lanham: Lexington Books, 143–58.

Whyte, K. P. (2015). "What Is Multistability: A Theory of the Keystone Concept of Postphenomenological Research." In J. K. B. O. Friis and R. P. Crease (eds.), *Technoscience and Postphenomenology: The Manhattan Papers*. Lanham: Lexington Books, 69–81.

Chapter 8

On the Immersion of E-Reading (Or Lack Thereof)

Robert Rosenberger

Like Twain, reports on the death of books have been greatly exaggerated. That is, although we have seen a dramatic increase in reading on-screen over the last decades with the rise of the Internet, email, social media, texting, and ebooks, people continue to also read from printed books.

Failed predictions abound. Against those who saw the skyrocketing sales of ebooks and assumed that printed books would soon be entirely crowded out of the market, we see evidence that the rate of increase in ebook sales has now plateaued and that sales overall may even be seeing a modest decline (Rosenberger 2013; Alter 2015; Tinvan 2016). Against those who have assumed that younger readers will prefer digital alternatives to traditional printed books, new data show otherwise (Rosenwald, 2015). And against those who have assumed that the digital revolution would lead the young to read fewer books overall, new findings reveal younger readers to be keeping up with and often exceeding the yearly reading of their elders (Pew Research Center 2016).

What to make of all this? We now find ourselves in a world in which different reading options are widely available. There has been a major shift to on-screen reading in our lives, including ebooks, online publications, and blogs, and of course digital communications such as email, social media, and text messaging. And yet even as printed magazines and newspapers struggle, printed books continue to thrive. In the philosophy of technology, one way to conceive of texts—both printed and digital—is as a mediating technology. Books, articles, and messages mediate our world and shape how we experience reading content. So it is important to step back and consider the different ways that these different reading platforms may shape reading experience differently.

My suggestion is that postphenomenology is an ideal philosophical perspective for approaching this topic (Ihde 1990; Verbeek 2011; Rosenberger and Verbeek 2015; Wellner 2016; Irwin 2016). With its adaptations of ideas from the history of phenomenological thought for use in describing user experience, and its adoption of commitments from the American pragmatist perspective, postphenomenology offers a framework of concepts that are helpful for conceiving of the ways that technologies mediate our lives. In particular, I will review Don Ihde's useful categorization of the different forms of human-technology relations (1990). And I will apply my own conception of how technology usage can reorganize a user's field of awareness, the overall totality of things that are under perception at a given moment (Rosenberger 2012; Rosenberger forthcoming). In this way, I begin a field theory of e-reading.

In what follows, I engage in a first foray into a postphenomenology of e-reading by taking a deep dive into an influential critique of e-reading with connections to this framework of thought, Anne Mangen's 2008 piece "Hypertext Fiction Reading: Haptics and Immersion." Through a review and analysis of Mangen's account, I consider the phenomenology of reading text in printed books and on-screen, and develop a description of the field of awareness associated with different reading platforms. This enables a critical engagement of Mangen's claims in particular, and an identification of some of the ways that bodily perceptual habits can come to shape our reading styles.

DO HYPERLINKS DISRUPT IMMERSIVE READING?

A cottage industry of lamentations over the ways that digital reading is changing humanity has developed in the popular press. For example, linguist Naomi Baron summarizes a main concern this way: "What are the three most critical drawbacks to reading onscreen? Distraction first, distraction second, distraction third" (2015, 210). On the topic of reading online, technology writer Nicholas Carr concludes, "Even as the internet grants us easy access to vast amounts of information, it is turning us into shallower thinkers, literally changing the structure of our brain" (2010). For a technical and phenomenologically informed version of this kind of critique, and one we can use as a jumping off point, let's turn to the work of reading specialist Anne Mangen.

In her seminal article, "Hypertext Fiction Reading: Haptics and Immersion," Mangen registers reservations about the emerging hype around "hypertext fiction," stories written in a digital medium that allow readers to click through for more information (2008). Many proponents have emerged, for example with N. Katherine Hayles writing that "learning to speak digital, it calls forth from us new modes of attending—listening, seeing, moving, navigating—that transform what it means to experience literature ('read' is no longer an adequate term)" (Hayles 2005). Against Hayles and others, Mangen identifies what may be sacrificed by these new modes of reading. To do so, she follows out an under-acknowledged dimension of the differences between digital and printed text: their concrete material affordances.

There is a multitude of effusive essays out there defending the printed word against a shift to screen reading by appealing to things like the crisp feel of pages, the smell, and the aesthetics of printed book design (fetishizations with which I'll admit I sympathize). But Mangen goes further to explore exactly what kind of reading is encouraged or discouraged, enabled or stymied, and made possible or made impossible by different reading platforms.

Mangen helpfully distinguishes between two types of immersion. One kind of immersion involves entering a "technologically enhanced environment," the kind of experience enabled by video games and virtual reality technology (2008, 406). The second kind, which she calls "phenomenological immersion," is when you are carried by text and by your imagination to a fictional world, the kind of experience enabled by books. She writes, "In this kind of immersion, the physical and technical features of the material support—the book—are ideally transparent in order to facilitate, and not disturb, phenomenological immersion" (ibid.). Her claim is that physical printed books enable this kind of immersion, and that digital technologies in general, and hypertext fiction in particular, instead are not well-suited for it.

Mangen reviews the psychological research findings that confirm what common sense has also already revealed: "we tend to *scan* text on screen" (2008, 409; original emphasis). Where printed text appears to lend itself to deeper, more sustained, and more reflective reading, screen reading instead appears to lend itself to quicker searches for information, jumping from article to article, and from website to website, and hastily glancing through the text. Mangen writes,

> Such a reading mode is highly vulnerable to distractions, particularly when these distractions are as easily available as a click with the mouse. Psychologists argue that we are psychobiologically inclined to resort to such means of rekindling our attention when our attention is, so to speak, exhausted—that is, when there is nothing left in view to maintain our interest. (ibid.)

She compares such distracted and disjointed reading to channel surfing, flipping through television channels with a remote control, looking over many viewing options at once, but only briefly for most.

How should we account for this difference in reading styles that tend to be associated with printed and on-screen text? Mangen notes that with regard to hypertext fiction, others have tended to offer explanations in terms of the disruptions to plot that come from jumping around the story. But she disagrees, suggesting that disruption to the phenomenological immersion that accompanies on-screen reading generally and hypertext fiction in particular, "has at least as much, if not more, to do with the sensory-motor affordances of distinctly different materialities than with plot" (2008, 407). The physical interface of book reading is of a compellingly different sort than using a computer or other screen-based reading device, like a dedicated e-reader. She observes that, "The tactility of a mouse click, of touch screen page turning or of a click with the e-book page turner bar is very different from that of flicking through the print pages of a book" (ibid.). In Mangen's account it is the different affordances made possible by those different platforms that are key. Where the static physical book inclines sustained engagement with its textual content, an Internet-connected screen allows a reader to easily disengage and jump to other content. And this affordance specific to screen reading becomes built into the phenomenological experience of the haptic affordance of the interface. This all comes together in the guiding example of the experience of hyperlinks.

Mangen writes, "our urge to click and the consequent impatient mode of reading can be at least partly explained by reference to psychobiologically hardwired dispositions of ours" (2008, 410). We tend to be unable to resist the temptation to respond to outside stimuli (such as, in the case of online reading, the temptation to jump to another website). That is, when the option is available to search for something more gripping, we take it, a tendency which Mangen refers to as a "psychobiological rule" (ibid.). Under this account, hyperlinks appear to us within the text in terms of their haptic affordance to open alternative content. As she puts it, "The links in hypertext fiction present themselves as an experiential potential, a latently accessible actualization of something currently unavailable, which becomes available with the click of a mouse" (ibid.). Thus, under this reasoning, hyperlinks must incite a disruption to immersive reading, disturbing the flow by offering a door to a different experience. Mangen writes, "We experience these as links to be clicked on, and such affordance is necessarily incompatible with phenomenological immersion" (ibid.).[1]

In what follows, I use the postphenomenological perspective to analyze Mangen's claims about the haptics of reading generally, and her points about the affordances of hyperlinks in particular. For the purposes of our concerns here, I do intend to engage a strawman version of Mangen's argument, at least somewhat. She has developed her argument specifically as a critique of the hype around hypertext fiction. But I am not specifically concerned with hypertext fiction. And I am not attempting to refute or even in any way deflate Mangen's particular contribution to that discussion. Instead, I want to engage her points here as if they are a critique of hyperlink-laden and Internet-connected text in general. In fact, it is not immediately clear why Mangen's claims shouldn't apply to other potentially immersive forms of text, such as non-fiction or written personal communications. So as a first attempt to develop a postphenomenological account of e-reading, we can assess Mangen's claims as they might apply to all reading, screens and print, hypertext-laden and hypertext-free.

THE FORMS OF E-READING EXPERIENCE

A key commitment of the postphenomenological perspective is that technology always can meaningfully transform the world in a multitude of ways. One way that Don Ihde has attempted to describe the variability possible for human relations to technology has been to outline the kinds of relationships that can occur. In part to distinguish Ihde's outline from my own attempt to develop a field theory in the next section, I have come to refer to this as Ihde's account of the different "forms" that human-technology relations may take. Mangen uses Ihde's description of these different forms in her own account of reading immersion, so it will be useful to review three of Ihde's main concepts here. Let's consider Ihde's notions of "embodiment relations," "hermeneutic relations," and "alterity relations."

Embodiment Relations

Building on moments in the history of the classical phenomenological canon in which figures like Martin Heidegger and Maurice Merleau-Ponty have described the experience of technology usage, Ihde uses the term "embodiment relations" to refer to cases in which a user's bodily perceptual capacities are transformed and extended through the device. Within an embodiment relation to technology, the device is at least to some extent incorporated into the user's bodily awareness (Ihde 1990, 73). The user and the technology together encounter the world with transformed capacities to perceive and/or act.

Standard examples include wearing eyeglasses and driving a car. In the case of the eyeglasses, a user looks out at the world through the device to attain a transformed visual experience. Of all the things of the world that this person sees before them, we would not say that the glasses themselves are simply another item that is seen; the glasses enable a transformed visual perception of those things. Driving a car is an example of a complex human-technology relation that greatly transforms a user's ability to travel. There is a way in which, as the driver becomes accustomed to the steering wheel and pedals, and comes to feel the tires on the street when the car is braking, and comes to have some sense of the space the car takes up on the roadway, she or he can be understood to embody the car.

Hermeneutic Relations

A second major way that humans experience transformed relations to the world via the use of technology is by perceiving the device itself and interpreting its readout. Rather than incorporating the device into our bodily perceptual awareness as in an embodiment relation, here instead we look directly at it, or listen to it, or otherwise perceive it directly. Ihde calls this a "hermeneutic relation." He writes, "Perceptually, the user's visual (or other) terminus is *upon* the instrumentation itself. To read an instrument is an analog to reading text" (Ihde 1990, 87; original emphasis).

The guiding example is human written language itself. If one knows how to interpret a form of writing, that is, if one can "read" it, then one experiences a transformed relationship with the world in the form of access to the writing's content. And in the case of Mangen's application of Ihde's ideas, this will be exactly what is at issue.

Of course it is not only the technology of written language with which we can share hermeneutic relations, but many other devices that bear readouts that we similarly (or perhaps analogously) must learn to read, from simple physical objects like a weathervane, to complex ones like scientific laboratory instrumentation. For example, if one knows how to read an analog clock, that is, if one can "tell time," then one understands the meaning of the numbers and hands on the clockface. And by engaging in a hermeneutic relation with the clock, by looking directly at it and interpreting its composition, one receives a transformed relationship to the world in the form of access to the precise time of day.

Alterity Relations

In a third form of human-technology relation, which Ihde calls "alterity relations," the device itself takes on a somewhat significant presence. It is like the way another human being is experienced as having a special and almost unignorable place within one's perceptual space, a kind of "Otherness." Some technological relations involve encountering the device as a significant object of awareness, though of course not on the level of the experience of encountering another human being, but in that direction, taking on, as Ihde puts it, a kind of "quasi-Otherness" (1990, 98).

A leading example that Ihde provides is videogames. Characters, and shapes, and avatars on-screen appear freighted with a special significance, as a meaningful endpoint of experience. Other instructive examples are those technologies fit with an interface scheme that is somewhat similar to interacting with another person. Examples include on-screen question-and-answer format exchanges like an ATM machine or a computer's "dialog box," and voice-interactive machines such as automated customer service representatives on the phone or smartphone personal assistant applications like Siri.[2]

Mangen uses these ideas to describe the act of reading generally, and reading hyperlink-laden text in particular. I will describe these relations in more detail below, but it seems correct to understand reading simultaneously both in terms of embodiment relations and hermeneutic relations. As the physical book is held and pages are turned, this can be conceived in terms of embodiment. A similar story of embodiment can be told about the haptics of mouse clicking, keyboard usage, and touchscreen interface in the case of on-screen reading. And in both cases the user develops a hermeneutic relation to the technology of the text itself, reading the content of the written language. In my view, this is what a standard account of the embodiment and hermeneutics of the technology of reading should look like.

Mangen agrees, but also goes further and stakes an intriguing claim about hyperlinks in tune with her analysis above. She writes,

> When reading hypertext fiction, however, the combination of the intangibility of the text and the prevalent haptic affordances of the computer make our hermeneutic relation—and hence phenomenological immersion—highly vulnerable to being captured by the haptic affordances of the computer, and, hence, making us relate to the computer in a primarily alterity rather than hermeneutic relation. (Mangen 2008, 415)

That is, according to Mangen, while the reading platform is approached as an embodiment relation and the text itself is read off through a hermeneutic relation, the hyperlinks within that text are encountered as an alterity relation. Rather than only encounter the hyperlinks as a word to be read (and symbol to be interpreted indicating the word's clickability), Mangen claims the hyperlinks should be understood as an unignorable significance; they maintain an alterity status.

I provide an alternative account to this experience below.

A FIELD THEORY OF E-READING

To expand the postphenomenological account of human-technology relations, I have attempted to develop what could be called a postphenomenological "field theory." That is, I have attempted to develop an account of what could be called a user's "field of awareness" as they use technology, that is, a description of the totality of what a user is aware of in a given moment (Rosenberger 2012; Rosenberger forthcoming).[3] The idea is to attempt to describe what stands forward within one's overall awareness, what stands back, how these things are arranged among one another, how deeply set these things may be within our habits of perception, and then also how all these things can change, or become "reorganized," as one's technology usage changes. I have identified four characteristics of a person's field of awareness subject to variation, although this need not be considered an exhaustive account: Ihde's notion of "transparency," as well as what I call "forefrontedness," "field composition," and "sedimentation."

Here I apply this framework to the experience of reading in both the printed book and on-screen contexts. If we share both embodiment and hermeneutic relations to our reading technologies, then we can also consider how those relations shape our fields of awareness.

Transparency

The notion of transparency is a key aspect of what is at issue in the question of ebook immersion. In Ihde's terminology, "transparency" refers to the degree to which a device itself (or parts of the device) grow less and less noticed as it is used. For example, if a person has grown accustomed to wearing a pair of eyeglasses, then what is present to the wearer is the world through the glasses, and not the glasses themselves. As Ihde puts it, the glasses "'withdraw' and are barely noticed, if at all." (1990, 73).[4] Driving a car is another everyday example of an act which typically involves a deeply transparent embodiment relation. For a novice driver still unaccustomed to the car's interface, its basic aspects will stand out as obtrusive features of the experience. The new driver may think actively about the steering wheel, pedals, et cetera. In contrast, the accustomed driver is more explicitly aware of the roadway ahead than the interface of the car. A central element of driving proficiency (that is, a central part of what it means to "know how to drive") is the ability to focus more on the road than on the steering wheel and pedals. Safe driving involves attaining a deeply transparent relation to the car's interface at most times (cf. Ihde 2014).

Crucially, Ihde distinguishes between the transparency involved in language interpretation and that of technological embodiment. Ihde describes the embodiment and hermeneutics of reading this way:

> Once attained, like any other acquisition in the lifeworld, writing could be read and understood in terms of its unique linguistic transparency. Writing becomes an embodied hermeneutic technics. [...] What is referred to is referred by the text and referred *through* the text. What now presents itself is the 'world' of the text. (1990, 84; original emphasis)

When one's hermeneutic relation to written language is deeply transparent, then the written text itself and the work of translating that text is less present to the reader than the text's content.

We can see this distinction at work again in the example of the interface of driving. If one can be said to embody the car as one drives, then one is focused more on the road than on the vehicle's bodily interface. This goes as well for those dashboard readouts with which we share hermeneutic relations: the speedometer, the gas gauge, et cetera. A driver becomes perceptually trained to direct her or his perception seamlessly back and forth between these dashboard displays and the road ahead and other information sources (such as mirrors). All of this can occur with more or less transparency. But this is true as well for the relation to the readouts themselves. Like reading alphabetic text and like "reading" the time displayed on a clock, a driver must learn to interpret the dashboard displays. These hermeneutic relationships can be more or less transparent. For the novice driver, the task of interpreting what the dashboard is saying may require some active and conscious work. In contrast, for the accustomed driver this work of interpretation occurs with a degree of transparency, and the meaning of the dashboard readout jumps forward to the driver all at once in the form of a perceptual gestalt. A similar account could be given for the driver's hermeneutic relations to many sources of information outside the car, from the brake and signal lights of other cars, to the icons displayed on roadside signage, to the stoplights overhead.

These distinctions should also hold for reading technologies, no matter the platform, "offline" printed books, ebooks, email, texting, online Internet articles, et cetera. We could first consider the varying levels of transparency that could accompany the embodiment of different reading technologies. For example, if one deeply embodies a printed book, then one's experience of the book's content might be uninterrupted by the action of physically turning the pages, and it may be easy to focus one's perception on the pages themselves and not on the other things outside the parameters of the book alone. That is, if one embodies the printed book with a high degree of transparency, then the facilitating material and haptic aspects of reading such as the page turning recede into the background. Mangen makes a similar point when she writes, "When reading a print book, the technological artifact—the book, the pages—partly withdraws, so that our intentionality is primarily directed towards the narrative fiction itself, and not to the technological objects as such" (2008, 415).

We can contrast this with the transparency involved in reading online. If one has a deeply embodied relation with, say, a desktop computer and is reading an article on a website, then many aspects of this experience may take on considerable transparency. The mouse under one's hand or the keyboard under one's fingers recede back as barely noticed elements of interface even as they are actively used to scroll through the article on-screen. For the user accustomed to this computer, the device itself may be experienced with a considerable degree of transparency during many moments of normal usage, including screen reading.[5]

We can also consider both of these examples in terms of their potential for hermeneutic transparency. If a reader shares a deeply transparent hermeneutic relation to the text in a printed book, then the act of reading the printed words themselves withdraws from awareness as the reader experiences the content of the writing. That is, although the reader's perceptual terminus, as Ihde put it above, is the words printed on the page, he claims that the hermeneutic relation will be one in which these printed words themselves will grow experientially transparent. A similar story could of course also be told about the potential transparency of the digital text of the article on the desktop computer screen. In either case the reader looks at the printed or digital words and through them experiences their content.

Now let's return to the particular issue of hyperlinks. Here's my suggestion: rather than conceive of the experience of hyperlinks in terms of alterity relations, we should instead conceive of them in terms of their place in a reader's field of awareness generally, and in terms of their level of transparency specifically. That is, perhaps we should not conceive of hyperlinks as an example of an alterity relation at all. Perhaps we should think of them in terms of embodied and hermeneutic relations to text that are encountered with varying levels of transparency. Recall that Mangen claims that hyperlinks appear in our experience in their potential to connect us to something else. They stand out in terms of this affordance, and Mangen suggests that by the concrete haptic nature of this potential, and also due to reasons of psychobiological inclination, such hyperlinks necessarily constitute an interruption, a disturbance of immersive reading. She claims that hyperlinks thus are encountered as a kind of alterity relation, taking up an obtrusive and significant presence. But perhaps another way to interpret this phenomenon—the purported immersion-shattering obtrusion of hyperlinks—is as the experience of an aspect of e-reading interface that, unlike the other words on the screen, refuses to take on a degree of hermeneutic transparency.

My suggestion is that shifting this account of the obtrusiveness of hyperlinks from a language of alterity to one of transparency is important because it introduces at least the possibility of hyperlinks taking on a less disruptive place within the experience of e-reading. And it implies the mechanism by which this would occur, were it to be possible: a reader could *learn* to experience hyperlinks with a degree of transparency, and this transparency could become set within the habits of our bodily perception. It may be possible that like the way the steering wheel and pedals are obtrusive aspects of experience for the novice driver and transparent aspects of experience for the accustomed driver, a feature of screen-based reading interface such as hyperlinks may stand out and be interruptive to immersion for someone newer to this form of reading and may take on at least some degree of transparency for someone accustomed to hyperlink-laden text. We could thus expect this experience to vary between individuals depending on the ways they've individually become accustomed to reading hyperlink-laden text.

There are buttons on many of the technologies that populate our everyday worlds. And there are a multitude of clickable items on the various screens we use, including those on which we read. And at least some of these buttons and other clickable on-screen items are aspects of interface that take on at least some degree of transparency at least some of the time. We can thus at least attempt to conceive of what it would mean for one to learn to also experience hyperlinks within reading materials with a degree of embodied and hermeneutic transparency.

Forefrontedness

While the transparency of the various aspects of a reader's relation to a reading platform seems important to an immersive reading experience, there is another important factor: what stands forward within that awareness, what resonates with significance, what jumps forth with meaning. Let's refer to these as "forefronted" aspects of experience. For example, there are many aspects of the roadway ahead that a driver is trained to experience with considerable forefrontedness. Among the many lights that pepper the landscape visible through the windshield, windows, and mirrors, certain ones such as the hanging traffic light or the brake lights of the car ahead stand forward as meaningful and as imparting specific urgently relevant information. Among the many noises of the soundscape present to the driver, the honking horns of other cars and the screeching sirens of emergency vehicles leap with significance to the foreground of awareness.

I suggest that we consider the experience of hyperlinks in terms of their forefronted status within digital text. Rather than think of hyperlinks in terms of alterity relations, we can think of them as standing forward as forefronted aspects of experience within the reader's overall field of awareness. Where the book itself and the text on its pages take on a degree of embodied and hermeneutic transparency, the hyperlinks may at times instead take on a degree of forefrontedness. And as a kind of variable, we can talk about how this experience may occur in different degrees for different people, and may be subject to change.

Field Composition

I have suggested that the description of human-technology relations at times requires more than only an account of those aspects of a device that withdraw. (Indeed, I suspect that the almost exclusive focus on this aspect of experience in many phenomenological accounts of technology owes itself to the fact that Heidegger so centrally thematized this issue, elevating it to foundational metaphysical importance.) There are many relationships to technology that can be better described in terms of a reorganization of our experience in greater ways than only the recession of some aspects into an experiential background and perhaps others highlighted in an experiential foreground. Some relationships with technology involve a more radical change to a person's overall field of awareness, a change which we can refer to here as "field composition" (Rosenberger 2012; Rosenberger forthcoming).

Consider the experience of watching a movie in the movie theater. There are many aspects of the experience that Mangen might consider an example of entering a "technologically enhanced environment." As the lights dim, the screen lights up. Our seats are directed toward that screen and are bolted to the ground. The screen itself is enormous, taking up much of our visual field if our eyeballs are pointed to the center. Many theaters include surround sound speakers, putting viewers in the middle of the movie's audio space. These enhanced environmental elements can incline a form of phenomenological immersion, one that can be helpfully described with an appeal to the notion of field composition. It could be said that as the movie becomes engrossing, many aspects of the theater begin to take on a degree of transparency. The experience of sitting in those forward-facing seats withdraws into the background. But more, the content of the movie stands forward, and in moments in which the viewer is largely enthralled, the movie content comes to be the majority—if not in some moments the near totality—of what the viewer is aware of. In those moments in the unlit theater, with its transparently embodied seating, and with its booming sound, the viewer is not much aware of the fact that the movie itself appears on a large rectangular screen enframed by darkness. In those moments in which she or he is absorbed in the viewing experience, "immersed" in the movie's content we might say, this viewer's field of awareness is largely composed of the relation to the movie's audio and visual content. At least part of what it means to be immersed in movie viewership is to have one's field of awareness largely composed by a relation to the content of the movie.

Another example of a technology whose normal usage often involves a considerable reorganization of a user's field of awareness is the cellphone. For a user accustomed to talking on a particular cellphone, the phone itself in hand may take on a considerable degree of transparency. But in those moments in which a user is deeply engaged in phone conversation and captivated by it, "immersed" we might again say, something more radical occurs than only the transparency of the phone itself. For those moments when one is engrossed in phone conversation, we could say that conversation comes to positively occupy the whole of the user's field of awareness. When absorbed in conversation, in that moment the content of that conversation and the presence of the interlocutor overtake much of what the user is aware, coming to constitute the practical entirety of that person's field of awareness. This point is driven home by the fact that it is possible for a person to be so engrossed in conversation that she or he does not even see the things in front of them, even if this person's eyes remain open.[6]

This notion of the occupation of one's overall field of awareness may be helpful for conceiving of some aspects of what it means to be fully immersed in reading. If one is immersed in reading, then one's attention is captured by the content, and/or one is lost within the book, and/or one's mind is "on" that content. One part of the phenomenology of this experience seems to be that much of a reader's field of awareness is composed by the reading content. That is, at least part of what we mean when we say that someone is immersed in reading is that the reader's entire field of awareness has been significantly reorganized. Immersive reading can be then in part defined as an experience in which much of the reader's overall field of awareness is taken up by the reading material's content. Reading immersion includes significant field composition. (But I doubt that immersion requires total composition by the reading content at all times, at least in principle.)

This potential for reading immersion seems generally the same for printed paper and screen reading. The remaining questions going forward are whether any particular platforms incline or disincline reading immersion, and if any platforms (or distinct aspects of particular platforms) incline distraction and disruption to this kind of immersive reading. And if so, then why?

Sedimentation

The term "sedimentation" is used throughout the history of phenomenological thought to refer to how our past experiences remain in our minds in such a way that our present experiences can occur already imbued with meaning. That is, the continued presence of our past experiences in our minds enable the thing we are currently experiencing to appear as immediately significant, as instantly meaningful, as already in context. The metaphor is of course to sedimentary rock, a kind of rock that is formed as many deposits of sediment collect and harden together over time. Our past experience accumulates in our minds and forms into our immediate perceptual context. But as Merleau-Ponty is careful to note, we should not let this metaphor extend too far and imply that the contextualizing effects of our sedimented past experiences are somehow static or inert; sedimentation is a continually active process of setting experience within an immediate context of meaning (1945, 131).

I have been pushing for greater appreciation of this aspect of experience within postphenomenological accounts of human-technology relations (Rosenberger 2012; Rosenberger forthcoming). I advocate using the term sedimentation to refer to the particular level of strength of the bodily perceptual habits associated with the organization of a particular human-technology relationship. So, for example, for one with a deeply sedimented relationship to one's eyeglasses, one may be able to casually maintain a transparent relation with one's glasses despite a smudge on the lens. The strength of the bodily perceptual habits, developed over time, enable this wearer to easily look past the smudge.

I suggest that sedimentation should be a factor in the story we tell about the differences in reading styles that are associated with different reading platforms. As an individual uses, say, a desktop computer, or a tablet, or a dedicated e-reader, or a smartphone to engage in reading, she or he may develop a habitual inclination toward reading in a particular way on that device. If this person spends most of the time scanning articles on this device, then they may develop the habitual inclination to approach the device in the same way in the future. Something similar can be postulated about the experience of hyperlinks. Insofar as they are forefronted within a reader's experience, that relation may become sedimented in habit, and hyperlinks encountered in the future will similarly be immediately experienced as forefronted, all out of a force of habit. Again, an advantage of this language is that it introduces a degree of individual variability, and it allows for the possibility for changes; habits can be broken.

For example, contrast the experience of someone reading something on an Internet-connected device on the one hand, with the experience of that same person reading on a platform not connected to the Internet (such as a printed book, or dedicated e-reader). Let's make the example more specific: contrast on the one hand the experience of this person reading an article as a pdf opened within a desktop computer's web browser, with the experience of this same person reading this same article printed out on paper. Let's also say that the pdf article read on-screen does not have any hyperlinks. To assess this case, we would need to know about this individual's personal history with these devices. What habits of reading has this person developed in terms of each of these reading platforms? If like most people this person tends to use the computer to skim through blogs and news articles and social media posts on the Internet, jumping from one webpage to another, then this tendency may become set in habit. When this person now encounters the on-screen pdf, this experience may occur in terms of a habitual inclination to skim, and to move on to other options, and to jump over to another webpage. This same person may have a different habitual relationship to reading offline. Without the built-in capacity to offer easy alternatives that is presented by Internet-connected devices, this person may have developed a different relationship to offline reading platforms like this printed out article, one that might include a habitual inclination toward more sustained reading.

CONCLUSION

It is surely true that technologies of reading can give shape to reading content. They can incline certain styles of reading. And certain reading technologies lend themselves to particular forms of communication over others. But it is also possible that one of the main reasons that we experience the content of writing in a particular way when reading from a particular device is because we have *learned* to do so. This may be the result of perceptual training. That is, our reading technologies shape reading content not only because of the contingencies of those devices, or the contingencies of our psychobiology, but because of the relationships we as readers develop with our reading technologies.

These relationships are in part volitional; we read certain ways on purpose, as part of conscious choice. (For example, we may intentionally scan through a bunch of articles on the Internet, skimming for main points, and then choosing a particular piece for closer reading.) And these relationships are in part automatic, sedimented within the long-developed habits erected through each reader's individual history of experience with a particular reading device. The ways we have purposefully engaged a particular reading device (or kind of reading device) in the past become sedimented in perceptual habit and experienced as contemporary reading-style inclination when we approach that device again in the present.

This final point has practical consequence. That is, the question of why reading technologies shape reading content has implications for normative issues regarding how we should evaluate reading devices, and how we should approach the practice of reading with various technologies. Here's the rub: if—as Mangen seems to suggest—the material designs of reading devices entirely *determine* our relationship to reading content, or if—as she additionally appears to suggest—that relationship is *determined* by psychobiological factors, then the choices a reader can make about this relationship reduce only to those over which reading platform to prefer. For example, if screens place inherent restrictions on the kind of immersion possible for e-reading through haptic affordance and psychobiology as Mangen suggests, then we are left with only the choice between accepting the limitations of e-reading, or abandoning it for the printed word. But if instead the contingencies of reading devices themselves and the inherent structures of human psychobiology only *incline*—and do not entirely determine—our relationship to reading content, then there is elbow room for the reader her- or himself to decide to approach reading content in a chosen manner.

Enter the additional factor of bodily perceptual habituation. Insofar as our approach to e-reading is open to elements of individual choice, the effects of those choices can calcify into established habit over time. Thus, it is at least possible that a large part of the reason why certain aspects of reading technologies appear to demand to be experienced a certain way—for example, that hyperlinks appear to necessarily shatter immersion, or that reading on an Internet-connected device appears disposed toward skimming—is not because this is compelled by the device design or by psychobiology, but because it is inclined by individual learned habits.

This has implications for the question of just how much choice we as readers have over the reading style associated with our experience of different reading technologies. If habit were to turn out to be a major reason why readers automatically approach a particular platform in terms of a particular style (e.g., Internet articles in terms of an inclination to skim, hyperlinks in terms of an interruption to immersion, printed books in terms of the possibility for sustained immersion, et cetera), then this approach remains open to change, at least in principle. A reader could attempt to break the habits associated with the approach to a particular reading platform in terms of this automatic style inclination. Though in principle possible, the actual accomplishment of such habit breaking may turn out to be exceedingly difficult. It would depend on the individual case. It could involve extensive retraining. It could involve not only developing the alternative approach to the reading device, but also unlearning the habits that incline this particular reader to automatically approach this device in a particular way.[7]

Mangen's work insightfully and persuasively shows the indelible importance of the bodily haptics of reading, especially as screen-based forms of reading continue to evolve, and continue to become more and more integrated into our daily lives. But her account may understate readers' potential to approach these haptics in different ways.

This is all to say that even if we are inclined to agree with critics like Mangen who claim that e-reading compels certain styles of reading in general, and that hyperlinks interrupt immersion in particular, there is still room to disagree about the strength of this inclination, and about why this happens in the first place. I believe there to be open questions about exactly why we are inclined to experience reading content differently when read through different media, screen vs. print, hyperlinked vs. not, Internet-connected screens vs. unconnected e-readers. And our answers to these questions have implications for just how compelled we are to experience reading content on particular devices in particular ways.

NOTES

1. Another argument Mangen appears to make regards the printed book's abject materiality itself. I either don't entirely understand this point or am deeply unconvinced by her line of reasoning on this. She provides a quotation from Merleau-Ponty in which he writes that "objects are really there for me, and *their invisible aspects have reality* precisely because I can move around so as to bring them into view and touch them" (her quote comes from Moran and Mooney 2002, 425) (Mangen 2008, 408; original emphasis). I take this to mean something like: if we are looking at an apple and we only see one side of it from where we are standing, the entire apple has a fuller reality than only the part we happen to see because we could in principle walk around and see the rest of it. Mangen uses this observation to draw a distinction between the reality of printed text and on-screen text. She writes that for a printed book,

> Such phenomenological depth, thickness and dimension are—factually, and by definition—absent in whatever we read on screen, due to its intangibility. The digital text has no material substance; hence it has no invisible dimensions. By definition, the digital erases all traces of tangibility, and, hence, invisibility. (2008, 408)

Since the printed book is itself a physical enduring substance and the digital text is not, Mangen appears to claim that the vanishing digital text does not support the invisible aspects of experience that make something real. The digital text's lack of material reality then somehow disables immersive reading.

Again, it is possible that I am misunderstanding the point here, but it seems as if Mangen is committing a category mistake. When reading a story in a book, printed or otherwise, the content of that book can be real to us—in whatever way the things we read are real to us—because we can imagine them to be real. This is based on our experience in the real world, a real world with parts that we retain memories of experiencing, including invisible aspects that we do not perceive, but could perceive. That is, the reality of what we read is *not* based on the invisible aspects of the materiality of the printed book itself. The content of the printed book is not experienced as real—in whatever way the things we read have some reality—because the book itself is a physical object with a front and back. The reality of the text content, that is, the way we experience text content as plausibly related to the real world in such a way that we can imagine that content as if it were real, comes from the way that we apply our own individual experiences in the actual world to the text. And that text could be printed or digital.

2. There are other forms of human-technology relations possible to articulate, although I do not go into them in detail here. For example, Ihde has also identified "background relations" to describe technologies that actively make up our environmental context, such a home's central heating system or a kitchen refrigerator (1990, 108). Peter-Paul Verbeek has attempted to expand Ihde's categorization of the forms

of human-technology relations to also include devices which are implanted into the human body, and also actively responsive background devices (2011).

3. There is a broad kinship here with the classical phenomenological work of Aron Gurwitsch who wrote about the "organization" or experience within the "field of consciousness" (1964).

4. For a helpful comparative analysis of the different ways that the idea of transparency occurs in different theoretical frameworks, including postphenomenology, see Van Den Eede 2011.

5. I have discussed the transparency of desktop computing elsewhere (Rosenberger 2009) and its potential to drop suddenly in particular unexpected situations.

6. This account of phone usage, in which a phone user's overall field of awareness can become largely occupied by the conversation, and at times compelled involuntarily and unknowingly into this experiential organization through the force of long-developed bodily habits, is a central feature of my account of cell phone-induced driving impairment (Rosenberger 2012).

7. I take one crux of the debate between Galit Wellner and myself over the issue of cellphones and driver distraction to regard similar dynamics. She remains unconvinced by the decades-long accumulation of empirical evidence showing people to be bad at driving safely while using the phone, and claims that drivers are able to split their attention in an effective way. As a postphenomenological philosopher, I am committed to the idea that a variety of coherent human-technology relationships are always possible. So I agree that such a split attention version of cellphones and driving could be possible, at least in principle. But I argue that the distracted version of cellphone use and driving is set in habit, habits established over an individual's lifetime of phone usage, habits that may be prohibitively difficult to break. And I argue that it would be dangerous to try, especially considering the sly way that habits can unconsciously influence our behaviors. See the 2014 special issue 18(1–2) of the journal *Techné* for more on this debate.

REFERENCES

Alter, A. (2015). "The Plot Twist: E-Book Sales Slip, and Print is Far From Dead." *New York Times*. 9.22.2015. http://www.nytimes.com/2015/09/23/business/media/the-plot-twist-e-book-sales-slip-and-print-is-far-from-dead.html?_r=1

Baron, N. (2015). *Words Onscreen: The Fate of Reading in a Digital World*. Oxford: Oxford University Press.

Carr, N. (2010). "Author Nicholas Carr: The Web Shatters Focus, Rewires Brains." Wired.com. 5.24.2010. https://www.wired.com/2010/05/ff_nicholas_carr/

Gurwitsch, A. (1964). *The Field of Consciousness*. Pittsburgh: Duquesne University Press.

Hayles, N. K. (2003). "Deeper Intro the Machine: The Future of Electronic Literature." *Culture Machine* 5. http://www.culturemachine.net/index.php/cm/article/view/245/241

Ihde, D. (1990). *Technology and the Lifeworld*. Bloomington: Indiana University Press.

———. (2014). "Embodiment and Multi- Versus Mono-Tasking in Driving-Celling." *Techné: Research in Philosophy and Technology* 18 (1–2): 147–153.

Irwin, S. (2016). *Digital Media: Human–Technology Connection*. Lanham: Lexington Books.

Mangen, A. (2008). "Hypertext Fiction Reading: Haptics and Immersion." *Journal of Research in Reading* 31 (4): 404–419.

Moran, D. and T. Mooney. (2003). *The Phenomenology Reader*. London: Routledge.

Merleau-Ponty, M. (1945). *The Phenomenology of Perception*. Trans. D. Landes. London: Routledge.

Pew Research Center. (2016). "Book Reading 2016." September, 2016.

Rosenberger, R. (2009). "The Sudden Experience of the Computer." *AI & Society* 24: 173–180.

———. (2012). "Embodied Technology and the Problem of Using the Phone While Driving." *Phenomenology and the Cognitive Sciences* 11 (1): 79–94.

———. (2013). "Why Don't People Want to Read Ebooks on Tablets?" *Slate*. 8.15.2013. http://www.slate.com/blogs/future_tense/2013/08/15/ebook_sales_decline_do_people_not_want_to_read_books_on_tablets.html

———. (forthcoming). "The Organization of User Experience." In A. Shew and J. Pitt (eds.), *Spaces for the Future: A Companion to Philosophy of Technology*. Routledge.

Rosenberger, R. and P.-P. Verbeek (eds.). (2015). *Postphenomenological Investigations: Essays in Human–Technology Relations*. Lanham: Lexington Books.

Rosenwald, M. S. (2015). "Why Digital Natives Prefer Reading in Print. Yes, You Read That Right." *The Washington Post*. 2.22.2015. https://www.washingtonpost.com/local/why-digital-natives-prefer-reading-in-print-yes-you-read-that-right/2015/02/22/8596ca86-b871-11e4-9423-f3d0a1ec335c_story.html

Tivnan, T. (2016). "E-book Sales Abate for Big Five." *The Bookseller*. 1.29.2016. http://www.thebookseller.com/blogs/e-book-sales-abate-big-five-321245

Van Den Eede, Y. (2011). "In Between Us: On the Transparency and Opacity of Technological Mediation." *Foundations of Science* 16 (2–3): 139–159.

Verbeek, P.-P. (2011). *Moralizing Technology*. Chicago: Chicago University Press.

Wellner, G. (2016). *A Postphenomenological Inquiry of Cell Phones: Genealogies, Meanings, and Becoming*. Lanham: Lexington Books.

Part III

Shaping Postphenomenological Media Theory

Chapter 9

Sublime Embodiment of the Media

Lars Botin

Our bodies are slow and media is fast. According to Paul Virilio's theory on dromology (1977), our bodies will succumb in the whirl of speed, where time and space collapse in a constant state of simultaneity that externalizes and alienates the body forever. The critical theorist Hartmut Rosa echoes the dystopian vision of Virilio in a more recent publication (2010) on the dangers of acceleration, which has perverted our modern capitalist society. Contemporary society, he claims, constantly focuses on growth, efficiency, and competition, especially in the case of emergent information technologies and social media. In this chapter I will argue for a sublimation—as from *sublime*—of the body through information technologies and social media. The notion of sublimation allows us to identify meaningful embodiment of technologies that we now mainly conceive as detached and distanced from our bodies, that is, as producing inert and inactive bodies.

Virilio's critique of technological development and the role of media is on a phenomenological and existential level. It is hard to see how we as humans can maintain our authenticity and autonomy. It is the final dissolution of humanity as we know it. Rosa, on the other hand, is concerned with our social beings, where we disappear into the machine of growth and efficiency and become numb components of an evermore-accelerating technological progress that actually leads us nowhere and has totalitarian outlines. In order not to end up in this state of totalitarian utopia (no-place) we have to slow down and hold back the evolution of technology, according to Rosa.

The question is whether there is an alternative path to that presented by Virilio and Rosa, a path in which human-technology relations and evolutions lead toward a "eutopia" (eutopia = good-place) where our bodies reside and operate with technology on a meaningful and beneficial level. In this eutopia we are embraced by and embrace technology, in this case media, and we evolve new identities and bodies that might be cyborgs, goddesses, and/or monsters (Haraway 1985; Barad 1999; Smits 2006). If we are able to track and lay out the path for eutopia, then it is possible to see salvation, and not condemnation, in our being together with technology. This can be an alternative to the vision of Rosa and Virilio who encourage us to stop technology and get out of the determinist race toward extinction and annihilation.

This chapter will discuss the "saving part" in our being together with technology, and how we should direct our attention toward eutopia. We can become monsters, cyborgs, or goddesses in this travel, but if there is directedness in our moves and decisions then these hybrid beings will transcend the possible dangers of speed and acceleration. If successful, we will be able to embody speed and acceleration in a way that makes sense to our co-constructed and co-constituted bodies. Speed and acceleration will be positive determinants for our new bodily being. We will leave the "slow body" behind in our strive toward eutopia, where we are not enslaved (Rosa) by technology, but on the contrary have a possibility to be emancipated through and with technology (Feenberg 2002). This emancipation is not liberation from the physical constraints and limitations of the body and the senses, but rather a sublimation of them.

In order to develop this argument, we need to elaborate a concept of the sublime where technology plays an integrated part of the body, without being determining in a classic way. On the contrary, it is—in line with postphenomenological ontology—co-constituent for body-making and for the construction of the good-place, or in other words, of reality.

This chapter is composed of three sections. First I will address what I have coined as sublime human-technological ecstasy. This section will mainly deal with the body's translational and transformational being and becoming in relation to media. Secondly I will discuss more specifically the possible co-constitutions of body and media. How do our bodies handle these transformations in our search for a new reality? I end the investigation looking at how we, through that embodiment, create new sublime realities that supplement current definitions and conceptualizations of reality.

SUBLIME HUMAN-TECHNOLOGICAL ECSTASY

Marshall McLuhan wrote *Understanding Media* in 1964, the same year as when Herbert Marcuse published *One-Dimensional Man* and Jacques Ellul's book *The Technological Society* was translated into English. Marcuse's and Ellul's perspective on human-technology relations are rooted in the technological development in a post-war period and hence are rather gloomy. By contrast, McLuhan acknowledges the Janus face of technology: where there is danger there is also salvation.

"The medium is the message" is not a nihilistic statement in the sense of "there is nothing outside of the medium," but rather it suggests that we are constantly in touch with the medium/media (cf. Van Den Eede 2012). This is in line with what Peter-Paul Verbeek has coined mediation (2011), in the context of which we have practices and interpretations that we make on an everyday basis. Medium is, in the particular reading offered here, the phenomenon of the sublime toward which we are attuned with all our bodily senses, and which we incessantly try to grasp as well as hold back. Accordingly, we perceive reality through the media, be that social media or any sort of media that we co-construct ourselves with and through. According to McLuhan, speed "always operates to separate, to extend, and amplify functions of the body" (McLuhan 1964/2001, 110). McLuhan is in this specific quote aiming his attention at "lower reaches of mechanical order" that were dominant centuries ago, but Ellul's ideas on technological extension and amplification and the impact on humans (1964) show that this is also the case for higher and more complex mechanical orders like the media, that transcend by far the speed of horse wagons, cars, trains et cetera. *Extension* and *amplification* are crucial concepts when it comes to how the body can be together with media-technology and I shall extensively address this in this section on the concept of the sublime.

The spider constructs the web that becomes a fulfillment of the bodily being of the spider: extension and amplification. The web mediates the world to the spider. The web is the mouth, the ears, and the eyes, yes the whole bodily and sensorial system of the spider, what Don Ihde would call a fully embodied technology relation. It is also a hermeneutic relation because the spider "reads" the environmental and social context and condition of the world through the web. The relation between spider and web is truly multistable (Ihde 1990), because the affordances of the web are multiple in relation to the spider's practices and interpretations.

The metaphor of the web is usually associated with electronic and digital networks, which is why the spider-web relation can be used in order to show how human-media relations can be addressed in order to find appropriate solutions that constitute new paths and realities. This is the reason why the sublime being of the spider is relevant in this case; the spider-web relation constitutes the foundation for possible ecstatic embodiment of media. In the following I shall address the historical and philosophical interpretations of the concept of the sublime in order to explain why the being of the spider-web relation is of such character, and why embodiment of the media is ecstatic.

Throughout centuries the origin of the concept of the sublime has been ascribed to the Greek rhetoric teacher Longinus or Pseudo-Longinus (1st or 3rd century AD). In a treatise titled *Peri Hypsous*—written in letter form, in Greek, and dedicated to the learned *Postumius* Terentianus—Longinus attempts to account for the content and form of the sublime (Rhys Jones 1899). The Latin translation of Longinus' Greek document was done by the Venetian professor of rhetoric Francesco *Robortello* in 1554, and the problems related to the process of translation were analyzed by Martin Heidegger in "The Origin of the Work of Art," where he states that the translation of Greek words into the Latin language is not without consequences as it is still to this day considered to be. Quite the contrary, because behind the apparent word-for-word and thus credible translation hides a translation of the Greek experience to a different sort of thinking. "*Roman thought takes over the Greek words without a corresponding, equally authentic experience of what they say, without the Greek word.* The rootlessness of Western thought begins with this translation" (Heidegger 1935–36/2001, 23; original emphasis).

"Peri hypsous" is usually translated into English as "on the sublime," but the primary meaning of "hypsous" is a sort of vertical height or rise both in a literal and a figurative sense (Rhys Jones 1899, XI). At the same time Longinus also speaks of a form of horizontal expansion. It follows from this that an axiomatic construction can be identified, where the vertical ascent dominates the horizontal expansion. It will become clear throughout the following what this means.

As implied, with Longinus we see a dominant vertical force in the interpretation of the concept, which is rediscovered in the German translation of "hypsous," where in addition a sort of human intervention is emphasized since something is raised/elevated in relation to/above something else: "erhaben" from the verb "erheben." As already mentioned, the concept—the sublime—gains a different meaning in the English translation which comes from the Anglo-Saxon adoption of the Latin concept of interpretation/reading. The concept is here given the topographic meaning "sub limine," which can mean under the border, at the border, on the border, and/or crossing. Not all meanings are word-for-word or literal translations of the Latin concept, but focus on the prefix "sub-," which often takes on the meaning of transition from one stage to another. Thereby, the concept takes on metamorphic characteristics in focusing on transition and transformation, whereas Longinus, to a much larger extent, saw qualities of metaphysical nature in the appearance of the sublime. The metamorphic quality of the concept makes way for the body to enter and be active, because metamorphosis is corporeal and physical in its essence.

The Latin identification of the sublime can therefore be ascribed to the dynamic relationship between matter and form, while the original Greek term, to a much larger degree, emphasized the intervention of the spiritual and thus the potential presence of a religious manifestation.

Longinus' definitions of "hypsous" as a metaphysical-religious ascent—ascendance—were dominant up until the break of Enlightenment, when the

English parliamentarian and philosopher Edmund Burke made the concept central to his investigation of the sublime and beautiful. Meanwhile, the German philosopher Immanuel Kant searched for the core of the sublime, yet taking other epistemological roads. Kant claimed that the sublime, in contrast to the lovely/beautiful, is characterized by the absence of an actual object and in sum can be identified as a representation of reason as an unrestricted concept (Guyer 1979, 265). Kant maintains his focus on the sublime's independence from the senses and argues that only reason is capable of "capturing" the boundless and shapeless existence of the sublime. To Kant, we are dealing with the setting of a mood where the imagination and reason come into play in a relationship of hierarchical nature.

The imagination registers the presence of the sublime, while reason enables us to express and acknowledge its being. At the same time, the sublime exposes the relationship between imagination, mind, and reason, where man in intense moments realizes—through reason—a possible connection to higher powers. Kant seeks to document a basic mathematical substance in the sublime, from which abstract and less than substantial reflections are generated.

Edmund Burke gives another, and in this connection more fruitful, definition of the sublime, because even though it is our soul that is moved and touched by the presence of the sublime, we are heavily influenced on a bodily level. In Burke's *A Philosophical Enquiry into the Sublime and Beautiful* (2008), the presence of the sublime is described as primordial in nature—and not as an abstract mathematical principle. The sublime can be seen as related to space and time and thus it requires presence. Burke attacks the metaphysical and superficial, which Longinus and to a certain degree Kant identified in "hypsous"—remember that the German translation is an extension of the original Greek concept, while for Kant it was the power of imagination that could recognize the sublime.

For Burke, the acknowledgement of the sublime is not dependent on intellect or reason, but manifests itself openly and unmasked in the sense-dependent life of emotion:

> The passion caused by the great and the sublime in *nature*, when those causes operate most powerfully, is Astonishment; and astonishment is that state of a soul, in which all its motions are suspended, with some degree of horror. (Burke 2008, 57; original emphasis)

As if struck by lightning (astonish: most likely from the early *astonen*, from Middle English *astonen*, *astonien*, from old French: *estoner*, from Vulgar Latin: *extonare*, from Latin: *ex* + *tonare*—to lighten) the subject is paralyzed when meeting the sublime nature, the sublime object, and/or the sublime action.

Burke looks at the concept from a phenomenological perspective, where bodily/physical presence is needed in order for the phenomena to occur. One of the 20th century's most significant thinkers, Martin Heidegger, who has dealt with concepts which in many respects compare with the sublime, recalls the imperative in Burke's interpretation of the concept. In the essay "The Origin of the Work of Art" (1935–36/2001), Heidegger pleads for the "raison d'être" of art and science, as man's chance to create something, which makes us stand apart from the ordinary, which thrills, which again moves us to move ourselves.

The sublime in technology is meant to metaphorically transport us in space and time, it is meant to move us and change us through excitement. We are, thus, talking about a transformation and transportation in time and space which contrasts with Burke's perception of the concept, where we can still catch a glimpse of a metaphysical existence through the intervention of the soul. Whereas Kant identifies God-given reason as a means for acknowledging the abstract essence of the sublime, Burke gives a quasi-sacral description of the existence of the sublime in nature, while Heidegger talks of things as the carriers of a sublime potential. Longinus, Burke, and Heidegger respectively have literature, nature, and art as the subject areas of their studies, where mental metamorphosis and metaphysics are present in varying degrees. In this perspective media seems to always be able to cover both aspects and, thus, seems to have no problem dealing with the sublime in both the Greek and the later Latin production of meaning.

In order to patchwork from the hitherto analyzed definitions and interpretations of the sublime in relation to embodiment of media, these meanings stand out and become emergent:

- The vertical on behalf of the horizontal (Longinus), because the active body is vertical/perpendicular in grasping reality;
- Imagination, horror and reaching the inexplicable (Kant and Burke) in an attempt to foresee possible realities, consequences, and situations;
- Mental movement and change (metamorphoses) in order to bodily perceive and connect to the reality of media (Heidegger).

The latter conceptualization will be the starting point for the section on "Embodying the media." In the final part of this discussion on the sublime I shall introduce some modern/postmodern conceptualizations, which relate to and complement the list above.

Metaphysics in relation to technology, following the breakthrough of the modern and, hence, the explosion in technological development, has become marginalized together with astrology and alchemy. The American technology historian David Nye (1994) emphasizes that technology has no trouble realizing the sublime as a physical expansion in the search for a transgression of boundaries. This is how the sublime as a physical expansion manifests itself in an artifact, that is, media. Nye also points out that the sublime is not a constant and definite entity, but that it changes constantly over time and space, which is why the metamorphic is a basic component in the modern technological sublime (Nye 1994, xvii). Thus, Nye implies that the American perception of the concept is different in nature from the European, which is still to this day tied up to the original version of "hypsous," which contains a high degree of transcendental metaphysics.

Nye identifies different modes of the sublime in more recent American history, where a chronological, sequential progression can be observed. The most essential modes are, according to Nye, definitely what he refers to as the dynamic, technological sublime and the geometrical sublime. The dynamic, technological sublime is tied up to the large horizontal expansion, which characterized the 19th century with the arrival of the railroad and the electrification of the American continent. Nye writes: "the dynamic form of the technological sublime had emphasized the movement of information over wires and railroads across the natural landscape, transforming it into a mere backdrop" (Nye 1994, 77). The static geometrical sublime, on the other hand, is characterized by the vertical rise of the skyscraper at the beginning of the 20th century and represents domination over nature: "All these structures expressed the triumph of reason in concrete form, proving that the world was becoming in Emerson's words, 'a realized will'—'the double of man'" (Nye 1994, 77). The dynamic technological sublime *transforms* the world into backdrop, whereas the geometrical sublime, through reason, *conquers* and *dominates* the world. In both cases technology mediates new realities and new worlds, and radical change is at stake.

Longinus', Burke's, and Kant's definitions of the sublime appeal only to an elite through their focus on literature, fine art (i.e., *Kultur*) and reason, where the American sublime is at its outset democratic and follows very closely the tendencies and developments in society as a whole. The American version of the sublime can be identified in cities budding on the prairie and their twinkle in the night. It is the skyscrapers' flight to the sky and the longing of bridges for distant shores. However, Nye stresses that the democratic, shallow structure corresponds to an Olympic, vertical perspective on reality, which can be translated directly into a sense of total power over nature. This is diametrically opposed to both Burke's and Kant's perceptions of the relationship between nature and culture in the domain of the sublime. Nye explains:

> Kant's sublime humbled the individual to nature, whereas the technical sublime emphasized and fortified the feeling of having conquered nature. The electrical sublime [...] dissolved topographically the boundary between nature and culture. (Nye 1994, 152)

A third aspect in Nye's analysis of the sublime reinforces the perception of the American technological, geometrical, and electronic sublime. This third aspect differs from the Kantian interpretation of the concept, and concerns the fact that the sublime materializes itself, and that it paradoxically is able to represent the infinite and the formless (Nye 1994, 294). This way, there is, after all, a sense that the sublime is not strictly a rational construction, but that it also contains a transcendental purpose, which Nye, in fact, admits when he is confronted with the reality of Las Vegas where everything is senseless simulacra and escapism from the world.

The ascendental, transcendental, and metaphysical principle, which Longinus, Kant and to a certain degree Burke and Heidegger find in the sublime is, however, not completely forgotten in contemporary philosophy. Transcendence is a concept which is central in Jean-François Lyotard's postmodern approach to the sublime. In the essay "The Sublime and the Avant-Garde" (1993), Lyotard describes how the sublime is tied up to the question: "does it happen?" The sublime is vague, fragile, and uncertain. The sublime is a time-related sense of an obscure and inexplicable and unexplainable nature, where "hidden meaning, talking silence (and) feelings transcending all reason" (Lyotard 1993, 54; my translation) are present.

In his interpretation, Lyotard uses a translation of the French poet and literary critic, Nicolas Boileau-Despréaux, who in 1701 published an annotated edition of Longinus' text. Boileau believes that he is able to identify a definite indefinable character in the formation of the concept—a feeling of "je ne sais quoi," which manifests itself in the meeting with the original work and makes it possible for the connoisseur to make qualified distinctions. Adopting Boileau's "je ne sais quoi" logic, Lyotard defines much late modern and postmodern art as sublime, and he rarely responds to the axiomatic features which his predecessors have tried to identify in the concept; that is the dominant, vertical ascent, and the expansive, horizontal "sounding board." Lyotard's "indefinable" definition of the sublime seems to be more consistent with terms such as: peculiar, strange, and odd. Nye points out that Lyotard does not acknowledge the technological sublime nor does he understand the (American) historic roots of the concept, when he compares the postmodern avant-garde with the alleged rationale of technology: "he is writing [Lyotard] not about the sublime but another form of the unspeakable [H]e sets his form of the sublime in opposition to what he (mis)conceives to be the rationality of the technicians" (Nye 1994, xx). The rationality of American engineers of modernity is inflated with various types of the sublime (technological, geometrical, electrical), which had the purpose of transforming, conquering, and dominating nature and the world in order to make way for the good place and the good life.

In sum, the sublime was originally a phenomenon of nature that instantly and radically moved and shook us in unpredictable directions or, perhaps even more frightening, left us in a position where all motions were suspended. In Nye's definition of the modern sublime it is mankind, through technological innovation and development, that controls and dominates nature, which is a position that this chapter challenges, because humans are constantly moved and shaped by technology and cannot maintain a static controlling poise. I have called this constant motion and shaping for ecstatic embodiment, according to the definitions that I address in embodying the media, and in what follows I shall dwell on this concept in relation to how we embody the media and how the media becomes flesh in this meeting.

EMBODYING THE MEDIA—AND VICE VERSA

Let me introduce another concept that is able to bridge the different axiomatic qualities of the sublime: ecstasy. Ecstasy is according to the Greek philosopher Plotinus the *culmination of possibility*, and conjoined with Levinas' definition of the notion as the moral demand of exteriority toward the Other (1981), it can tie together the different strands that have been developed—through Plotinus' "culmination" and the qualities of the real, through "possibilities" and "exteriority toward the Other." This topic I shall address in the final part of this chapter.

In my attempt to bridge the body and media I also turn my attention toward Gilles Deleuze and Félix Guattari. Specifically I focus on their elucidations on the rhizome in *A Thousand Plateaus* (2007), because the rhizome is both media and body at one and the same time.

The rhizome is a structure that is striated and smooth. It sits in the world as a membrane through which things pass without frictions and/or difficulties. Deleuze and Guattari describe this process as similar to the vital osmotic process of plants. At the same time the rhizome is a sort of organ that allows for transformation, translation, transmission, transition, and transport where the body is crucial as mediator for these constant flows of becoming. Deleuze and Guattari write:

> A rhizome has no beginning or end; it is always in the middle, between things, interbeing, *intermezzo*. [...] The middle is by no means an average; on the contrary, it is where things pick up speed. *Between* things does not designate a localizable relation going from one thing to the other and back again, but a perpendicular direction, a transversal movement that sweeps one and the other way, a stream without beginning or end that undermines its banks and picks up speed in the middle. (Deleuze and Guattari 2007, 27–28; original emphasis)

What is mediated in the rhizome is speed, where the body is an integrated part in the perpendicular direction and transversal movement, where *desire* is what directs the movement. We move on *desire lines* or *lines of flight* in the rhizome, and these lines or paths are made by and for the body. The body is speed. Not in the measurable meaning of the concept, but exactly as sublime transformational and metamorphic understanding of how we constantly become in the rhizome. How we constantly regenerate in the media and how these regenerations are micro-manifestations of the macro-rhizome.

Peter-Paul Verbeek would call these micro-manifestations manifestations of *mediation* toward which we relate physically and mentally, through practices and interpretations (2011, 99). In this particular perspective the main mover is our body, which has the capacity to both interpret and practice the reality of the media. We may not be reflectively conscious of this bodily being and becoming on the desire lines in the rhizome, but our bodies pass here and there in this "stream without beginning or end" (Deleuze and Guattari 2007, 28) and they evolve and revolve as we move.

Deleuze and Guattari define the body in the following terms:

> On the plane of consistency, *a body is defined only by a longitude and a latitude*: in other words the sum total of the material elements belonging to it under given relations of movement and rest, speed and slowness (longitude); the sum total of the intensive affects it is capable of at a given power or degree of potential (latitude). (Deleuze and Guattari 2007, 287; original emphasis)

This definition of the body is inspired by Spinoza and echoes the spatial and temporal qualities of the sublime. It is what opens the paths for the apparent slow, weak, and fragile masses of bone, organs, flesh, and skin in the rhizome of the web—because we—like the spider—are the web and at the same we are what passes through and moves in the web on longitudinal and latitudinal desire lines. This is sublimation of being/becoming in a reality, where we as humans constitute context and text at one and the same time, just like the spider-web relation. It also means that we are in a position to co-create, co-constitute, co-construct, co-design, and co-shape the way we are in co-relations with media, because we *are* through and with the media.

According to Maurice Merleau-Ponty we are always positioned in relation to world and our body determines this position. This body has been characterized as schematic and prenoetic, which means that it operates beyond our consciousness and intentionality. This does not mean that the body schema is but a conglomeration of neurophysiological capacities of an "ignorant" body, but rather that the body is ready to connect to any sort of temporal and spatial reality. In the preface to Merleau-Ponty's *The Visible and the Invisible* (1968) the editor John Wild writes: "But the postural schema is not a particular image; it rather gives the body to itself as an 'I can,' as a *system of powers organized as according to transposable schemes for movement*" (Merleau-Ponty 1968, liv; my emphasis).

This, then, mirrors the definition of ecstasy by Plotinus—the culmination of possibilities, and here is also where the rhizomatic quality of in-between speed and the body schema's directedness toward the world, through "I can," co-constitute each other. This co-constitution is based on an *attitude* (postural schema) of the body, which is not just spatial and temporal, but extends into aesthetics and ethics. We can summarize movement of the body in rhizomes and schemes that are inseparable from the body itself in the following list:

- General quality and capacity of the human body;
- Common attitude and perception of the body;
- Universal and cyclical perception of time and space, hence fusion of past, present, and future (Botin 2015).

In order to understand how the body is more than a conglomeration of bits and parts we must keep a focus on Merleau-Ponty's elucidations on the body and flesh, because in these we find how body/flesh and media are not antipodes or dichotomies. On the contrary, the body is always and already in the media as the media is always and already in the body.

In the chapter "The Intertwining—The Chiasm" in *The Visible and the Invisible* Merleau-Ponty stresses that there is no antinomy between the body, the things, and the world. They are intertwined and act together: "My body model of the things and the things model of my body" (Merleau-Ponty 1968, 131). This intimate relation of the body with the world and the things is co-constitutional and co-constructive, and the intimacy cannot be broken. We cannot separate ourselves from the things and the world. The things and the world are body/flesh and we are things in the world. Merleau-Ponty talks about the sublimation of the flesh in the sense and logics of Longinus, where the body transcends the ordinary physical limits of bones, organs, muscles, and skin and is raised vertically into the realm of ideals, without losing touch with world and reality. Conversely, world and reality are also made out of this bodily connection to ideals, which I tried to sketch in the attitude of the postural schema of the body (see above). Merleau-Ponty writes:

> There is a strict ideality in experiences that are experiences of the flesh: the moments of the sonata, the fragments of the luminous field, adhere to one another with a cohesion without concept, which is of the same type as the cohesion of the parts of my body, or the cohesion of my body with the world. Is my body a thing, is it an idea? It is neither, being the measurant of things. We will therefore have to recognize an ideality that is not alien to the flesh, that gives it its axes, its depth, its dimensions. (Merleau-Ponty 1968, 152)

These axes, dimensions, and depth that are ideally co-created in between body, things, and world are present in the definitions of the postural schema of the body, and as we have seen they are present in the things and in the world as well because they are flesh. In all of this I also see the seeds for Ihde's conceptualization of multistability, because this relation is characterized by multiplicity, differentiation and/or, to use a concept from Deleuze and Guattari, a constant flow of becoming.

The media is flesh because the body is in the media as the media is in the body. They cannot be separated. The body models the axes and the dimensions of the media and the sublime depth of the media touches and moves the body in constant "intra-action." Here I use the concept of the American feminist researcher Karen Barad, which I find illuminating in relation to how our bodies materialize, or how "matter comes to matter." Barad writes: "*materialization is an iterative intra-active process whereby material-discursive bodies are sedimented out of the intra-action of multiple material-discursive apparatuses through which these phenomena (bodies) become intelligible*" (Barad 1999, 108; original emphasis). Our bodies become matter, hence visible and intelligible, through our intra-action with material-discursive apparatuses. The reason why intra-action is possible is that both the body and the apparatuses are material-discursive (in multiple ways), which means that there is a common playground, hence no antinomy or dichotomy in between bodies, things, and world.

Deleuze and Guattari described and analyzed the nature of the rhizome and how bodies move on desire lines without difficulty and how bodies are part of an osmotic process of constant becoming. I have tried to combine this ontological understanding of the body/world relation with a similar understanding present in the work of Merleau-Ponty and in the concept of intra-action as defined by Barad.

In the following conclusive lines of this section on embodying the media I will turn my attention to how this patchwork of ideas elucidates the sublime co-existence of body and media, or as Merleau-Ponty writes: "The thickness of the body, far from rivaling that of the world, is on the contrary the sole means I have to go unto the heart of things, by making myself a world and by making them flesh" (Merleau-Ponty 1968, 135).

Multiplication and Amplification of Body in Media

New media technology is based on algorithms and structured architecture of logics and mathematics, referring to the Euclidean paradigm of geometrical space and chronological time. And yet, media is in almost every way phenomenological in its intensification, amplification, and expansion. It constantly opens up possibilities, where intimacy, distance, inclusion, exclusion, friendship, hostility et cetera exist independent of Euclidean space and time.

The postural body schema with its axiological and dimensional qualities of aesthetical and ethical character is met by similar qualities and properties in the media. Media is no longer just a message or an extension of the human body, to paraphrase McLuhan. Media is flesh/body, rhizome and material-discursive, which means that the speed and acceleration of media is flesh/body, which finally constitutes the sublimation of the body and media.

The "thickness of the body" (Merleau-Ponty 1968, 135) cannot be maintained in media, nevertheless it is how we get to "the heart of things." In meeting "the heart of things," sublime instant metamorphosis occurs and a new entity, or to use Merleau-Ponty's term, "element" is born: a monster, a cyborg, a goddess, or most certainly the materialization of a hybrid/composite agent is generated.

Now back to Virilio and Rosa: their reading of the consequences of media is paradoxically based on Euclidean rationality, ignoring the possibilities and potentials of the metamorphosis in, of, and by the media, where our bodily experiences get expanded and intensified simultaneously. This is why the concept of sublimity is crucial in order to understand the affordances of multiplication and amplification of body in media.

The simplistic drawing in Figure 9.1 is an attempt to show how extension, expansion, amplification, and multiplication take place in media. There are multiple possible bodies and embodiments as technology evolves and works. What you are and who you are is interdependent with the forces of the web/rhizome and as such multistable in its essence, which the vertical "bodies" try to represent. It might be fully embodied like the spider or how we are in the rhizome, and at the same time a way in which we try to understand and relate to an external technology/world relation (hermeneutic).

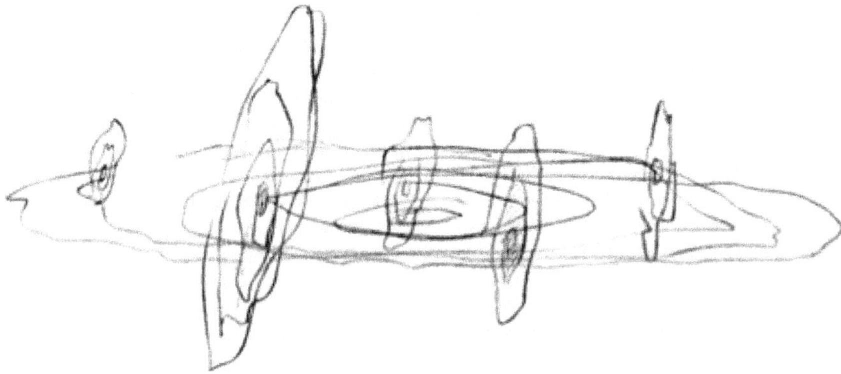

Figure 9.1 Latitudinal and longitudinal becomings of multistable beings in media.

In the following, concluding comments I'll try to expand, finally, on how reality can be re-conceptualized within this framework of embodiment of media and sublime power of human-technology interdependency.

EUTOPIA OR NEW REALITIES

Reality is multiple, or in postphenomenological terms, multistable. It changes according to the potentials, possibilities, and constraints that we meet as we move along the paths of our existence. Reality is in this particular reading tied to the grammatical realm of verbs, where relational practices and processes are performed. Reality is in this perspective not the conglomeration of nouns or things (*res*), because even though these are malleable and dynamic entities they do not point toward the stream or flow of becoming that constitutes the core essences of the real.

There is a difference between the world of things and the flow of the real. This difference stands out clearly the moment we look at the German term for reality: *Wirklichkeit,* which means space and time where things work, that is, practices, processes, actions et cetera. This is not the Anglo-Saxon definition of reality which points exactly to the things (nouns) and indicates a closer relationship between world (*Welt*) and reality (*Wirklichkeit*).

The constructionist view, which is embedded in the German interpretation of reality (*Wirklichkeit*), is in this perspective perceived as social practice, where possible typologies are continuously constituted. This points toward the concept of multistability, where possible stabilizations of media-reality are continuously constituted and hence *become*. The stabilities can be fast, slow, near, far, intimate, alienating, and interdependent with the way we embody the media. Is there something stable in reality, having acknowledged that it is multistable? First, we count on the fact that there is a world and there is a body in the world. This is the starting point, also in a reality of digits and numbers. Second, reality, in this perspective, points toward multiple possibilities. The Danish philosopher Lennart Nørklit states that without possibility we are dead (2004). Being alive is dependent on a world of facts and a reality of possibilities. These possibilities are multistable, yet common practices can materialize, which means that even though our situation is complex we are not in a state of anarchy or chaos. Nørklit argues that facts and possibilities are not enough for the constitution of reality (2004, 36–45). Choices are at stake, and choices are based on values. Some possibilities are better than others, and we make hierarchies in between different possibilities. What connects facts, possibilities, and choices/values are our bodies. In relation to possible choices/values in the reality of media we have to listen to the body and understand how the media is a multiplicity of ways our bodies are in the world. Listening to the body is also listening to the body's being and becoming with and through the web, to how mediation takes place and how this mediation cannot be separated from the body. The body is not caught in the mediation of the media, but *is* the media, as Merleau-Ponty pointed out through the concept of schema. Another way of listening more closely to the body is to specify what is meant by choices/values in relation to the hybrid composite body-media. This should be done in order to create possibility of choice for the body as a worldly fact and at the same time mold the media in order to extend, amplify, and sublimate the physical body. The relation is as such dialectical and co-constitutional and there is no conflict or confrontation in between the body and the media, because they are, like the spider and the web, together in the world.

In order for all of this to make sense, and for us to cling to our bodily being, we have to address sense-making. We make sense of mediation through practices and interpretations (Verbeek 2011, 99), where our bodies are both in the mediation and "outside" trying to get in, that is, ecstatic. There is a here-body and a there-body (Ihde 2002) in a simultaneous performance, which is precisely how embodiment takes place. The technological extension, amplification, and sublimation of the body that happens in the media are performative as it (the body) bastes the patchwork, threads the web and, in doing this, produces sense.

This new body is a co-construction of media and flesh, where the directedness (intentionality) of the monster, cyborg, or goddess is characterized by an exteriority toward the Other (ecstasy). We do not lose the "thickness" of our bodies as we are radically and rapidly transformed and transported in the media. We gain and cumulate possibilities that culminate in meetings and encounters with the Other, which make our bodies visible and intelligible in radically new ways. Alphonso Lingis addressed this in *Foreign Bodies*, where he writes:

> Existential philosophy defined the new concepts of ecstasy or of transcendence to fix a distinct kind of being that is by casting itself out of its own given place and time, without dissipating, because at each moment it projects itself—or, more exactly, a variant of itself—into another place and time. (Lingis 1994, 6)

We do not dissipate or disappear as we co-cast variants of ourselves in other places and times. Our new ecstatic bodies are variants of the "thick" body. They are technological mediations of our bodies that follow the lines and paths of media toward the Other.

Virilio, Rosa, and other pessimist technological determinists foresee how our bodies will succumb in the meeting with speed and acceleration of media. Their prediction is made from a Euclidean and dualistic perspective, where media is conceived as a systemic, mechanical, and in-human technical construct where the body gets devoured and annihilated. I have offered a "reality check" concerning media and body and in it a different and more positive image appears, because what is needed is what Verbeek (2011) has coined "moral imagination," where we, together with technology, try to design the possibilities for the body to be slow, near, intimate, and caring in the media, and at the same time allow for sublime extension, amplification, and acceleration of both the media and the body.

Bruno Latour, relying on the Heideggerian *Gestell*, encourages us to erect a scaffold in order to assure care and caution, and suggests that technology is the extension with which we co-compose in engaged ways, "in the task of maintaining and nurturing those fragile habitations" (Latour 2004, 43). These fragile habitations, in which we dwell, are intra-active, sublime, and multistable in their essences.

In this way media becomes eutopia, because it provides a constant opening toward possibilities and potentials for our body to perform in multiple, meaningful, and responsible ways.

REFERENCES

Barad, K. (1998). "Getting Real: Technoscientific Practices and the Materialization of Reality." *Differences: A Journal of Feminist Cultural Studies* 10 (2): 87–129.

Botin, L. (2005). "Om det sublime i kunst og teknologi" (On the Sublime in Art and Technology). *Nord Nytt. Kultur og teknologi* Nr. 90, August 2004: 91–116.

———. (2013). "Techno-Anthropology: In-betweeness and Hybridization." In T. Børsen and L. Botin (eds.), *What is Techno-Anthropology?* Aalborg: Aalborg University Press.

———. (2015). "Hospital Architecture and Design in Postphenomenological Perspective." In J. K. B. O. Friis and R. P. Crease (eds.), *Technoscience and Postphenomenology: The Manhattan Papers*. Lanham: Lexington Books.

Burke, E. (2008). *A Philosophical Enquiry into the Sublime and Beautiful*. New York/London: Routledge.

Deleuze, G. and F. Guattari. (2007). *Thousand Plateaus: Capitalism and Schizophrenia*. London/New York: Continuum.

Ellul, J. (1964). *The Technological Society*. New York: Vintage Books.

Feenberg, A. (2002). *Transforming Technology: A Critical Theory Revisited*. Oxford: Oxford University Press.

Guyer, P. (1979). *Kant and the Claims of Taste*. Cambridge, MA: Harvard University Press.

Haraway, D. J. (1985/1991). "A Cyborg Manifesto: Science, Technology and Socialist Feminism in the Late 20th Century." In D. J. Haraway, *Simians, Cyborgs and Women: The Re-Invention of Nature*. New York: Routledge.

Heidegger, M. (1935–36/2001). "The Origin of the Work of Art." In M. Heidegger, *Poetry, Language, Thought*. New York: HarperCollins Publishers.

———. (1977). "The Question Concerning Technology." In M. Heidegger, *The Question Concerning Technology and Other Essays*. New York: Harper Perennial.

Ihde, D. (1990). *Technology and the Lifeworld: From Garden to Earth*. Bloomington: Indiana University Press.

———. (2002). *Bodies in Technology*. Minneapolis/London: University of Minnesota Press.

Latour, B. (2003). "The Promises of Constructivism." In D. Ihde and E. Selinger (eds.), *Chasing Technoscience*. Bloomington: Indiana University Press.

Levinas, E. (1981). *Otherwise than Being or Beyond Essence*. New York: Springer.

Lingis, A. (1994). *Foreign Bodies*. New York/London: Routledge.

Lyotard, J.-F. (1993). *On the Sublime (Om det sublime)*. Viborg (DK).

Marcuse, H. (1964). *One-Dimensional Man*. London/New York: Routledge.

McLuhan, M. (1964/2001). *Understanding Media: The Extensions of Man*. London/New York: Routledge.

Merleau-Ponty, M. (1945/2005). *Phenomenology of Perception*. London/New York: Routledge Classics.

———. (1968). *The Visible and the Invisible*. Evanston: Northwestern University Press.

Nye, D. (1994). *American Technological Sublime*. Cambridge, MA: MIT Press.

Nørklit, L. (2004). "Hvad er virkelighed?" (What is Reality?). In J. Christensen (ed.), *Vidensgrundlag for handlen*. Aalborg: Aalborg University Press.

Rhys Jones, W. (1899). *Longinus on the Sublime*. Cambridge: Cambridge University Press.

Rosa, H. (2010). *Alienation and Acceleration: Towards a Critical Theory of Late-Modern Temporality*. Aarhus: Aarhus University Press.

Smits, M. (2006). "Taming Monsters: The Cultural Domestication of New Technology." *Technology in Society* 28: 489–504.

Van Den Eede, Y. (2012). *Amor Technologiae: Marshall McLuhan as Philosopher of Technology—Toward a Philosophy of Human-Media Relationships*. Brussels: VUBPRESS.

Verbeek, P.-P. (2011). *Moralizing Technology: Understanding and Designing the Morality of Things*. Chicago: Chicago University Press.

Virilio, P. (1977). *Speed and Politics: An Essay on Dromology* New York: Semiotext(e).

Chapter 10

Thinking Through Media

Stieglerian Remarks on a Possible Postphenomenology of Media

Pieter Lemmens

> The essence of technology pervades our existence in a way we still barely surmise.
>
> —Martin Heidegger, *Was heisst Denken?*[1]

This chapter will stage a brief encounter between postphenomenology (mostly Ihde and Verbeek) and Stieglerian technophenomenology, with a view to one of the key questions of this volume, that is, whether postphenomenology or "mediation theory" could be extended into a true philosophy of media. My contribution to this question is, rather modestly, that for this purpose it could greatly profit from a dialogue with the philosophy of Bernard Stiegler and most specifically from considering the latter's views on the status of media—or in his terminology: mnemo- or memory technologies—as not just instruments or channels of human communication and information exchange but as retentional devices that shape human thought and rationality *in a most fundamental way*, that is to say as *empirical yet transcendentally operative* conditions of possibility of *any* "life of the mind" (Arendt 1971).[2] As Marshall McLuhan might have suggested: thinking through media first of all means realizing that we think through media.

Postphenomenology has shown in great detail how all kinds of technologies co-shape human experience in myriad ways, focusing mostly on bodily experience. However, it has been less concerned with, and also less capable of analyzing the impact of *media* technologies on the human mind. In my view this is the case not only because its conceptual toolbox, in contrast to that of Stiegler, seems less suited for dealing with media. It also, and most importantly, appears to me that it lacks sufficient insight into the fundamental role of media, at the most original level, in the transcendental constitution of human subjectivity or consciousness *as such*, that is to say in its *essential technicity*, not in the least as its very methodological foundation. Therefore Stiegler's work could be considered as a possible complement to the postphenomenological framework.

In order to show this, I will first discuss postphenomenology's and Stiegler's respective re-interpretations of "classic" phenomenology. Then I will demonstrate that although the former stresses the central role played by technologies in subject and world constitution, it seems less capable of grasping the extent to which *media* technologies specifically are constitutive of the very domain of constitution of phenomenology itself, that is to say of the immediately intuited essential elements of consciousness ("the things themselves"). Hence, it manifests insufficient awareness of the fundamental importance of media for a truly postmetaphysical, that is, technical-material understanding of the proper philosophical dimension in which it situates itself. Next, I will compare its phenomenology of human-technology relations with Stiegler's organology of media. Then I will discuss its central concept of multistability vis-à-vis Stiegler's notion of metastability and compare its related idea of technical ambiguity with the latter's pharmacology of technology from the perspective of media.

In addition, I will criticize postphenomenology's dismissal of what it disapprovingly calls "*technology uberhaupt* [sic]" (Ihde 2009, 22; original emphasis), thereby questioning its rather dogmatic adherence to the "empirical turn." Finally, I will advance some critical remarks regarding its apparent refusal to seriously consider the phenomenon of technical "alienation" and failure to recognize what Stiegler theorizes as the inherently "proletarianizing" nature of all technologies, especially *media* technologies, that is to say: in a transcendentalist sense.

TECHNOLOGIZING PHENOMENOLOGY

Both Ihde and Stiegler present themselves explicitly as heirs to the philosophical tradition of phenomenology as it originated from Edmund Husserl and was further developed and expanded into an existential hermeneutics by Martin Heidegger. Both have, each in their own original way, fundamentally contributed to this tradition by renewing it critically yet positively, principally through the implication of the technical artifact into phenomenological thought, that is, by giving technologies in the broadest sense, and for Stiegler most specifically media, the place they deserve in the center of the phenomenological analysis. They show how human perception, cognition, and action are all fundamentally shaped, and in a very intimate sense—although the degree to which this "intimacy" is recognized and theorized differs quite substantially as I will try to point out—by the technical artifacts that furnish the human lifeworld and via which human beings continuously interact with their environments and themselves. In so doing, both have in their own manner "technologized" phenomenology.

There are important differences, though, in the specific ways both authors engage in the dialogue with Husserl and Heidegger and in how they reconceive phenomenology accordingly. Both propose, and demonstrate the necessity of, a "technological turn" of phenomenology (and for Stiegler more generally of philosophy *as such*), but their conception and execution of it diverges significantly. To put it provisionally and in a somewhat simplified way here: whereas Ihde primarily urges phenomenologists to become *more empirical* and investigate the various roles that *concrete* technologies play in human life (Ihde 2009, 23), Stiegler primarily wants phenomenologists and philosophers generally to recognize the structurally forgotten or neglected transcendental role concrete technologies, especially media technologies, play in human thought and being-in-the-world more generally. He urges philosophers to not just empirically analyze particular roles played by particular technologies in particular lifeworlds or cultural situations but to show phenomenologically that media technology *as such* must be understood as fundamentally shaping or constituting the domain of the transcendental, or in Heideggerian terms the ontological difference, which has traditionally always been conceived in an idealist-transcendentalist fashion. I will further elaborate on this important difference in the next section. Suffice it to say for the moment that this transcendental status of technology in the sense of media is certainly somehow acknowledged by Ihde,[3] but it is not explicitly theorized *phenomeno-logically*, only partially demonstrated and elaborated empirically.

Another manifest difference between Ihde's and Stiegler's approaches concerns their references to other philosophical and/or scientific disciplines and traditions in their correction or refinement of the "classic" phenomenological perspective they criticize and the construction of their respective conceptualizations of the human-technology relation. As for Ihde, his critical re-interpretation of classic phenomenology rests predominantly on adopting a pragmatist perspective on experience, substituting Dewey's organism-environment interaction framework for Husserl's perceptive consciousness model and embracing Richard Rorty's anti-representationalism, anti-essentialism (Ihde 2009, 10), and anti-foundationalism (Ihde 2012, xvi). This incorporation of the pragmatist framework is so crucial for Ihde that he characterized his position once with the formula: "pragmatism + phenomenology = postphenomenology" (Ihde 2012, 117). Although "retaining the rigorous techniques of phenomenological variations" (Ihde 2012, xv), he favors "a pragmatic American approach to things" (ibid., 98), also implying an adherence to the so-called "empirical turn" and a focus on case studies from STS (ibid.).

As for Stiegler, he incorporates a variety of theoretical perspectives in his overall approach. His re-interpretation of Husserl's and Heidegger's phenomenologies basically extends the deconstructivist reading offered of these perspectives by his principal mentor Jacques Derrida. In Stiegler's early, most purely theoretical analyses conducted in the first three volumes of *Technics and Time* (TT) this deconstructivist perspective is always leading. Another crucial and consistent backdrop in these analyses is formed by the views on human-technology co-evolution of the French paleoanthropologist André Leroi-Gourhan, whose ideas of hominization as technical exteriorization and the shared external artificial memory unique to the human species are crucial to understanding Stiegler's general philosophical enterprise.

ORIGINAL TECHNICITY AND TECHNOLOGY AS THE EMPIRICAL TRANSCENDENTAL

As for the "intimacy" of the human-technology relation alluded to above, that is, *the extent* or "depth" to which technology is shaping human existence, it is true that Ihde as well as Peter-Paul Verbeek show how technical artifacts fundamentally shape human being-in-the-world by constituting *both* the poles of the traditional subject-object dichotomy such that not only the object but also the subject gets "shaped" through the mediating technologies that relate them. However, they've never really focused on media technologies and most importantly their account of the reciprocal subject-object constitution remains essentially empirical, principally consisting of analyses of concrete examples and focused on empirical characterizations of typical human-technology relations, notwithstanding the early Ihde's elaborate and instructive exercises in "doing phenomenology" from *Experimental Phenomenology* (EP), which are not concerned with human-technology relations, though, but with the perception and variational analysis of visual images and simple optical illusions. Media *do* receive explicit attention in the recent work of the editors of this volume: Wellner (2016) on cellphones and Irwin (2016) on digital media as well as Van Den Eede (2012) on human-media relationships in general, although the latter is more indebted to McLuhan. These authors no doubt enrich the scope of postphenomenology into (new) media territory yet they remain in my view firmly within its predominantly empirical orientation, notwithstanding the breadth and profundity of the analyses offered.

Postphenomenology certainly stresses that subject and object are technologically co-shaped or co-constituted and have no pre-given "identity," as it were, prior to their technological interrelation. The arguably central conceptual notion of postphenomenology, *mediation*, must therefore be regarded as a little inaccurate (see also Van Den Eede 2012). Verbeek is most clear about this in fact when he elaborates, quite helpfully, that *mediation* must not be understood in the usual sense as a relation between poles that are themselves already what they are prior to the relation, but inversely as a relation which precedes these poles and first of all shapes or constitutes them mutually, that is, in the sense of a co-shaping or co-constitution. Correcting earlier formulations of Ihde in which the latter seems to remain within the subject-object dualism that postphenomenology is actually designed to overcome, Verbeek states: "By saying that mediation is located 'between' humans and world (as in the schema I-technology-world), Ihde seems to put subject and object over against one another, instead of starting from the idea that they mutually constitute each other" (Verbeek 2005, 129). It is this mutual constitution however that is the proper postphenomenological viewpoint: "When analyzing the mediating role of artifacts, therefore, this mediation cannot be regarded as a medium 'between' subject and object. Mediation consists in a mutual constitution of subject and object" (ibid., 130).

Stiegler could certainly agree with this way of putting it, but then Verbeek goes on, employing Ihde's terminology, to concretely explain what this mediation involves. Verbeek writes that technologies *transform* human perception, either by *amplifying* it or by *reducing* it in some sense, that is to say either by strengthening or weakening specific aspects of the reality that is perceived, in contrast with the way it shows itself to "naked perception" (ibid., 131). The ways in which the microscope and the telescope simultaneously amplify and reduce (certain aspects of) our visual perception of reality provide obvious examples. Technologies can further also open up new ways for reality to manifest itself, as in infrared photography and electron microscopy (ibid., 134). Yet these are not exactly examples of co-constitution in the phenomeno-*logical* sense, I would argue, but more of mediation in the empirical sense. Moreover, what needs to be demonstrated—from a Stieglerian view on such co-constitution, which proceeds through *media*—is that the very phenomenon of perception *as such*, and that is to say of human perception—even in its "naked form" (whatever that may be)—as a *noetic* (and not just aesthetic) phenomenon, is always already, to use the Heideggerian expression, constituted technologically, yes *originates* from the coupling between human biological sense organs and technical media. And it is exactly what Stiegler aims to show when he claims that *all noesis* is *technesis* (Stiegler 2015a, 31), which means in more Heideggerian terminology that the very movement of transcendence of being-there as the "performance" of the ontological difference is enabled and conditioned by technological media.

Postphenomenologists do frequently claim that the human is a technological creature right from the start and that humanity and technology are thus to be understood as co-extensive. But what is lacking in their work is not only a genuinely phenomenological account of the deeply constitutive nature of technology for human existence *as such*, that is, for its *very way of being* and not only its perception, action, cognition, and various experiences of itself and the world. Postphenomenology also misses an anthropological account of the human's "original technicity," as Stiegler calls it, as well as an understanding of the very genesis of the human life form as a fundamentally technical life form, that is, an account of anthropogenesis as a process of technogenesis. The latter may not necessarily belong to a technologized phenomenology, but the former certainly forms one of its principal tasks I presume. And in that regard, Stiegler has gone much farther in rethinking phenomenology, investigating the phenomenological implications of humanity's original technicity—or original constitution through media in the sense of *milieu*—at the most fundamental level.

Surely, Ihde starts off *Technology and the Lifeworld* (TL) by showing, via his heuristic Rousseauesque phantasy of a non-technological Garden, that a humanity without technology can exist only in the imagination and that empirically and historically humans have always possessed technologies, if only very minimally (1990, 11). As cultured creatures humans are inevitably technologized creatures and, as Ihde writes, "*human activity from immemorial time and across the diversity of cultures has always been technologically embedded*" (ibid., 20; original emphasis). Yet, despite the many interesting excursions into cultural and historical anthropology TL features, and notwithstanding its elaborate phenomenology of human-technology relations and the two flanking programs of "cultural hermeneutics" and "lifeworld shapes," what is missing is a truly techno-phenomenological account of the very phenomenological "things themselves"—those which the so-called "classic" or transcendentalist phenomenologists used to think independently of any technology or media artifact—in the sense of demonstrating the artificial, and therefore thoroughly accidental (instead of essential and eternal) nature of these elementary phenomena. This original prostheticity and accidentality of the phenomenological "things themselves" remains unthought in the analyses of the still traditional metaphysical thinkers. And with the "things themselves" I mean here not technologies, as postphenomenologists do. I take these in a very classic sense as denoting the most basic phenomena of classic phenomenology, like intentionality, noesis, being-in-the-world, existence, temporality, historicity, et cetera.

Such an account, though, forms the very core, and admittedly also the most difficult part of Stiegler's technophenomenological enterprise as laid out foremost in his grand magnum opus TT, an as yet unfinished multivolume work most explicitly dedicated to thinking time, in the Heideggerian sense, as the horizon of the understanding of being and the ontological structure of being-there, from the perspective of technics. Since it is impossible to cover Stiegler's rethinking of all these phenomena here, let alone in any detail,

I have chosen to focus on just two key aspects of his "techno-logical" reinterpretation of (1) the phenomenon of intentionality or attention (a term Stiegler more frequently uses) and (2) the phenomenon of being-there or being-in-the-world as a dynamic of ekstatico-horizontal temporality and historicity. My aim is to show that intentionality and existence as the human mode of being in which it is always embedded (i.e., being-there or being-in-the-world) is *originally*, that is to say *always already* constituted by technology, even in its allegedly naked form and way before the appearance of today's technological culture (Ihde 1990, 9; Verbeek 2011, 1). Hence, these elementary phenomena are not historical constants but historically (and initially evolutionary) evolving variabilities.

It is my impression, from my reading of the work of Ihde and Verbeek, that despite their emphasis on what they call "technological intentionality" or "instrumental intentionality" (Ihde 1990, 48, 102, 32; Verbeek 2005, 114), both still seem to assume some human intentionality "baseline," if only implicitly since its intrinsic, original technicity is never theorized. That intentionality, according to them, can either be technologically mediated or not, humans in our modern "maxi-technological culture" of course being much more technologically mediated than in "technologically minimalist cultures" (Ihde 1990, 15). However, what I would like to show with Stiegler is that *all* and *every* human intentionality is technically constituted, through what Stiegler has theorized as "tertiary retentions." By this he means all technical memory prostheses that underpin and condition both the primary and secondary retentions as well as protentions (anticipations) which Husserl distinguished in his analysis of the temporality of transcendental consciousness (and I will return to this below). Therefore, it is not only "in our technological culture" that "humans and technologies do not have separate existences anymore" (Verbeek 2011, 16). Instead, humans as existent beings and technology have been unseparated from the outset.

Human *ex*-istence, in the Heideggerian sense as standing-out-into the clearing of being, *presupposes* technical *ex*-teriorization since both projection (*Ent-wurf*) and re-petition (*Wieder-holung*) in the Heideggerian sense *originally* rely on technologies as *pros*-theses. It is thanks to its intimate relation with the technical supplement that the human life form is not merely a sub-sistent mode of being (like that of animals) tied to a closed environment (*Umwelt*) but an ek-sistent and con-sistent being open to a meaningful world (*Welt*), consistence meaning being-there's orientation toward ideas and ideals (Stiegler 2010, 9). Stiegler illustrates the original technicity of the human and in particular of human thought or *noesis* in many ways throughout his work through techno-logical re-interpretations of a host of Western thinkers, from Plato and Aristotle via Kant and Hegel to Husserl and Heidegger. But since we're dealing with phenomenology here I'll try to explain this now only through a brief exposition of his re-interpretation of Husserl's analysis of internal time consciousness as well as his reconsideration of the role of so-called world-historical entities—things bequeathed from the past—in the very constitution of being-there's original temporality (a role hinted upon but nevertheless thoroughly rejected by Heidegger in *Being and Time*'s analytic of historicity).

The internal flow of consciousness Husserl called intention and Stiegler mostly refers to as attention, consists of a fabric of protentions (anticipations) and retentions (recollections). Now in Husserl's famous analysis of inner time consciousness from 1928 (Husserl 2008), executed on the basis of repeatedly listening to a melody via a gramophone, there is a distinction between primary and secondary retentions or memories. Primary retention refers to the retention of a perception (e.g., a just heard sequence of sounds); secondary retention refers to a memory and accordingly a product of the imagination (e.g., when the same sequence of sounds is called up from one's memory during a second listening). Stiegler adds to these a third form of retention: the *tertiary* retention, which is technical and artificial, like a piece of writing, a book, a record, or a CD, indeed what we nowadays call media. Stiegler shows that only these kinds of external retentions allowed Husserl to distinguish between primary and secondary retentions in the first place (Stiegler 2014, 52). What he claims more generally, however, most elaborately in an extensive analysis of Husserlian intentionality (Stiegler 2009, 188–243), is that tertiary retentions are fundamental to *any* intentionality or attention in the sense that they are originally constitutive and conditional for the production of the primary and secondary retentions (and protentions). Moreover, tertiary retentions underpin all forms of intentionality and make up the flow of intentional consciousness. All technical milieus are in fact assemblages of retentional devices, either implicitly or explicitly, consisting of tertiary retentions. Such milieus are a condition of possibility for human intentionality *as such*, and for the human mind more generally, since without such a milieu of external technical retentions, the mind would be no more than an ephemeral "vapor" (Stiegler 2011, 80).

As for being-there's original temporality, Stiegler shows that technical artifacts are also constitutive of the human's relation to time, in the sense of the ecstatic-horizontal structure of temporality of being-there as described in *Being and Time*. In the first volume of TT, Stiegler shows that what Heidegger called "facticity" or the "already there" of being-there, its historial (*geschichtlich*) "having-been-ness" or the ecstasis of the past, is only accessible thanks to the technical artifacts originating from that past. These function as artificial memories which give being-there a *media-specific* access to a past that it has never been and that it has never experienced itself, but that nevertheless fundamentally determines its being. It does so by appropriating this past in its future, which is typical of being-there's historical mode of being: repetition (*Wiederholung*). Although Heidegger in his analytic of historicity explicitly mentions technical artifacts when he speaks of "antiquities" which can be found for example in museums as relics of the past and which he describes with the term "world historial," he does in no way attribute to them any role in the constitution of the ecstatic-horizontal structure of being-there's being. They are for him just innerworldly beings that are only historial because they belong to the world of being-there, entirely constituted by that world and thus in no way constitutive of it (Stiegler 1998, 204).

Stiegler, however, shows that technical media are not only empirically given in the sense of intra-temporal but are constitutive of the *original*—read: transcendental—temporality of being-there (ibid., 27). Also, the ecstasis of the future as the projecting of being-there on its own possibilities is itself only possible, Stiegler shows, because of being-there's fundamental prostheticity. This means that also being-there's understanding, which is nothing else than its projection on its own possibilities and which is founded primarily in the *ecstasis* of the future, is fundamentally constituted and conditioned technologically through tertiary retentions. Since the emergence of mnemotechnologies this means: through media. Thus, technologies have not only "always been part of our lifeworld" (Ihde 2009, 38), they constitute that lifeworld *as such*, and from the very start. Paraphrasing an expression of Ihde regarding the inherently technical nature of all science—"No instruments, no science" (ibid., 35)—we could say "No technologies, no lifeworld." Technology is not just "part of the human condition" (Verbeek 2011, 155), it *is* the human condition. As Stiegler puts it most succinctly: "Man *is* technology" (Stiegler 2016, 360). The human exactly *ek-sists*—and con-sists—through what Ihde, following Latour, calls the "nonhumans" (Ihde 2002, 98), although their relation is anything but symmetrical.

IHDE'S PHENOMENOLOGY OF TECHNICS VERSUS STIEGLER'S ORGANOLOGY OF TECHNICS

Arguably the two most important and influential strands of Ihde's overall view on technology are his phenomenology of technics, analyzing the structural features of human-technology relations, and his cultural hermeneutics, analyzing the various ways in which technologies are culturally embedded (Ihde 1990, 124). In this chapter I will only focus on the first strand, his most widely known phenomenology of human-technology relations. I will compare this strand with Stiegler's *organological* view of the human condition as a technical condition. Organology analyzes the *transductive*[4] relations between the three organ systems that together constitute the human life form as a fundamentally technical life form. These are: the biological or physiological organs, the artificial or technical organs, and the social organs or organizations. The latter result from but also negotiate and regulate the articulation of the other two and are understood by Stiegler most basically as *systems of care* (Stiegler 2014, 5).

An important initial difference between these two conceptualizations is that Ihde's focus is primarily (yet not exclusively) on the relation between the *body* and technology, whereas Stiegler is mainly interested in the relation between technology and the *mind*, the *psyche* or *spirit,* and more precisely the *noetic*, what Husserl called *noesis*. Stiegler's prime interest is in what he calls "mnemotechnologies" or in other words *media* like writing, printing, radio, cinema, television, computers, and iPhones. These technologies support (or undermine) the human psyche and mind as either "psychotechnologies," which operate on or at the cost of the human psyche in order to steer or control it, or "nootechnologies," which serve the elevation and emancipation of the spirit as the collective mind. Nootechnologies further the development of the intellect or *nous*, as the ancient Greeks called it. This is not an individual phenomenon for Stiegler but a *trans*individual one, that is, transcending individual psyches as both the result and the condition of their continuous collective interaction *as* articulated through a mnemotechnical milieu (Stiegler 2013, 427–8).

I will not elaborate Ihde's famous quadruple of human-technology relations here, since I consider them well-known: embodiment, hermeneutic, alterity, and background relations (Ihde 1990, 72–123). Verbeek adds two allegedly "posthuman" relations to this arsenal, namely composite and cyborg relations (Verbeek 2008, 140). Remarkably, and for our purposes highly interesting, is the fact that in *Postphenomenology and Technoscience* Ihde mentions a fifth element as addition to the original quadruple, one that is not so much another distinct new human-technology relation but more of a general characteristic of all four relations, and that is the fact that all these relations do instantiate a relational ontology. It means that they all show that humans and technologies are co-constituted as the entities that they are *in* and *through* the relation. Because technologies, via their mediating operations, transform both perception and action and therefore the experience of the world, humans themselves become transformed in the process as well. Technologies are thus not neutral instruments utilized by a pre-given and stable subject. Instead, the subjectivity of the subject changes as a result of technological mediation, as does the world and the objects therein as encountered through this mediation. In this regard, Ihde writes: "And it is here that histories and any empirical turn may become *ontologically* important, which will lead us to the pragmatist insight that histories also are important in any philosophical analysis" (Ihde 2009, 44; original emphasis).

Although it's not clear to me exactly why the philosophical importance of histories is a specifically pragmatist insight, I read the first part of this assertion as suggesting that technical artifacts must be granted an ontological status *in their very facticity* or *onticity*, to use the terms of Heidegger. This is to say: they co-shape what the latter called our *understanding of being*, that is, of the being of beings, what Stiegler refers to as the dimension of the *noetic*, which therefore cannot be conceived as an ontologically pure origin as the thinker of being nevertheless insisted upon, but must instead be understood as itself ontically or empirically constituted. And this is exactly the crux of Stiegler's techno-logical critique of Heidegger and by extension of the whole philosophical—*as* metaphysical—tradition as such, which has consistently neglected technical artifacts or denied them any role in its attempts to understand the mind, thinking, *logos*, the subject, et cetera, but also *critique*, due to its persistence in "a transcendental discourse" (Stiegler 2009, 5).

Another difference between Ihde's phenomenology of human-technology relations and Stiegler's general organology of transductivity is that the former approaches the relationality and relativity involved in the human-technology nexus as a *bipartite* relationship between two poles (humans and technical artifacts), whereas the latter stresses the fact that the human condition as a technical condition involves a *tripartite* relationality. Stiegler's three poles, again, are psyches or psychosomatic beings (the psychic organs), collectives or social organizations (the social organs), and technical artifacts or technical systems (the technical organs). For both Ihde and Stiegler, humans and technology co-determine each other in these relations, yet Stiegler insists, following Simondon, that the individual cannot be thought except to the extent that it belongs to a collective and a collective history, the adoption of which is necessary for the individual to constitute itself in the first place (Stiegler 2014, 50). This is crucial for Stiegler since what defines humanity for him is exactly the possession of a *collectively shared* external technical memory or inheritance system, the so-called "epiphylogenetic," which allows for the transmission of individual (*epi-*) experience to the species (*phylo-*), that is, for culture, and is just as vital and determinative for the individual *as* individual as its genetic memory (Stiegler 1998, 140ff.).

As Ihde writes in *Bodies in Technology*: "all human-technology relations are two-way relations. Insofar as I use or employ a technology, I am used by and employed by that technology as well" (Ihde 2002, 137). He then goes on to say that "our bodies adapt to different kinds of technologies and technological contexts," but that it is equally true that "technologies must also adapt to us" (ibid., 138). This seems to yield a kind of "co-adaptation" of humans and technology. We change as a result of our changing technologies and vice versa, and this entails that "our bodies have an amazing plasticity and polymorphism that is often brought out precisely in our relations with technologies. We are bodies in technologies" (ibid.). Stiegler would agree, although his focus lies more on "minds in technologies." He would add that (1) the body is always a social/socialized body; (2) humans do not (and certainly *should* not) *adapt* to their technologies but *adopt* them on the basis of social and political criteria. And in that regard I am not sure what to think of the suggested symmetry between "we using technologies" and "technologies using us," notwithstanding the fact that technologies can evidently be employed to control and manipulate humans.

Whereas Ihde describes the "plasticity and polymorphism" principally in terms of the transformation of experience (of self and world), Stiegler's organology attempts to understand the changing transductive relations between the three organ systems in terms of a continuous *reciprocal de- and re-functionalization* of the psychosomatic organs and social organizations as a response to mutations in technical artifacts or at the level of technical systems, and vice versa of course. Yet for Stiegler technical exteriorization comes first as it were since "techno-genesis is structurally prior to socio-genesis" (Stiegler 2009, 2). The co-evolution of the human and technology can be understood as a continuous "cycle of functionalizations and refunctionalizations" (Stiegler 2015a, 118), probably commencing in pre-hominid times with the defunctionalization of the paw becoming a hand or a foot (ibid., 120).

Lastly, Stiegler's general organology conceives of human-technology relations as inherently dynamic, or what is more: as temporal and historical *processes*. Instead of using the classic pair of subject and object as co-constituting *entities* still extant in postphenomenology, he follows the poststructuralist trend of thinking in terms of processes of subjectivation (and objectivation) or, in his preferred Simondonian terminology: of *individuation*. That is to say, he speaks in terms of structurally open-ended processes continuously tending toward but never achieving individuality and where the principle of individuality is the process of individuation itself and not some pre-existing ground or *ousia*. The three organ systems that constitute organological configurations are in fact three processes of *co*-individuation. What Heidegger termed "being-there" as "being-with" is understood by Stiegler as a process of psycho-social co-individuation always conditioned, pace Heidegger, upon a process of technical individuation. The latter means that psycho-social co-individuation unfolds *as* a process of *adoption* of technical artifacts (Stiegler 2014, 50–51). In my view, this conceptualization of the human-technology nexus is more powerful and does more justice, for instance, to the deeply temporal and historical nature, emphasized by Heidegger, of the ek-static human life form as one that is ultimately moved or animated by technics.

MULTISTABILITY VERSUS METASTABILITY AND "TECHNOLOGY WITH A CAPITAL T"

Another important postphenomenological concept originating from Ihde yet widely employed among his disciples as well is that of *multistability*. This concept was first developed, or in his own words "discovered" (as against Husserl's invariant essences) in the context of his then still experimentally (not yet post-)phenomenological variations of visual images and illusions in EP. Only later, in TL, it was applied to the analysis of human-technology relations. Ihde employs this concept to express the fact that the same technology (same as in being identical in a purely material sense) can assume different functionalities or give rise to different uses depending on the particular use context or cultural context in which it finds itself employed or embedded. An Acheulean stone tool officially categorized as a "hand axe" for instance can act just as well as a projectile or something else altogether (a ceremonial scepter for example), depending on the context in which it is used (Ihde 1990, 68–69). A technology can have a multiplicity of uses in different use contexts and this means that there exists no such thing as a "thing itself" in the domain of technology. Instead: "There are only things in contexts, and contexts are multiple" (ibid., 69). Multistability holds "even more strongly in the complexities of technology-culture gestalts" (ibid., 146). Different cultures can and do interpret the same technologies in different ways and so embed them differently, a phenomenon termed "variant cultural embeddings" (Ihde 1990, 144). Both use-context and culture-related multistability entail for Ihde that the human-technology *relation* is decidedly a "human-technology *relativity*" (Ihde 1990, 70; my emphasis) and postphenomenology could very well be called the relativity theory of human-technology interaction.

Stiegler would acknowledge the importance of multistability in the sense of Ihde but only to a certain extent. In fact, he himself often uses the term "metastability," adopted from Simondon, who derived it from thermodynamics. According to Simondon, it is a state transcending the classical opposition between stability and instability in the sense of being charged with potentials for becoming. It is used to characterize the indissociable, transductive relation between humans and their technologies and between humanity and technics *as such*. This means: the relations between the psychosomatic, technical, and social organ systems always have the form of a *tension*, an irreducible tension that drives the process of psychic, social, and technical co-individuation. This process can be understood in terms of a dynamic "metastable equilibrium" that is nothing other than the temporality of human existence tracking the advance of technics as the process of technical exteriorization (Stiegler 2009, 2). All organological configurations are metastable and all three organological levels have their own logics and tendencies but they cannot be considered in isolation from one another (Stiegler 2010, 104–5). Human societies for Stiegler are in fact therapeutic *systems of care* functioning through the continuous adoption of new technologies. As systems, societies undergo constant arrangement, combination, and economization, through socio-political norms and prescriptions, of the various tendencies and counter-tendencies that weave and metastabilize the dynamic systems shaping the three organological levels that constantly co-individuate (ibid., 121).

The principal driving factor however, and here Stiegler's view differs substantially from Ihde's apparent "anything goes" conception of multistability, is what Stiegler refers to as the "technical tendency," which has certain similarities with the Heideggerian notion of technical destining (*Geschick*) but is derived from Leroi-Gourhan. The latter's paleoanthropological studies in human-technology co-evolution have demonstrated the existence of quasi-universal, transcultural *technical tendencies* that differentially sediment as *technical facts* in different ethnic groups and later in societies. These technical tendencies exhibit a certain "teleologism" (Stiegler 1998, 54) and can therefore definitely be counted upon to anticipate the process of technical becoming. However, one should not confuse them with the technical facts, which can always temporarily contradict the tendency. One of the principal problems today for Stiegler is how to liberate the processes of technological innovation in the contemporary *hypermediated* societies from their adaptive subjection to the market by a short-term capitalism that intensely exploits the media landscape and thereby frustrates the possibility of anticipating the future of human societies and blocks opportunities for long-term investment based on predictions of long-term technical tendencies that definitely do exist (Stiegler 2010, 124–5).

Stiegler readily acknowledges that there is ample space for negotiation within the metastable equilibria formed constantly through the organological configurations resulting from the interaction between the bio-anthropological dynamic of the *who* (i.e., being-there) and the techno-logical dynamic of the *what* (i.e., technical artifacts). It is the latter as technical tendency that catalyzes this interaction, "insofar as it is already there, and insofar as it tends spontaneously to differentiate itself in advance from the differentiation of the *who*, since the *who* is always inscribed in a system of *whats* overdetermined by technical tendencies" (Stiegler 2009, 7; original emphasis).

Thus, for Stiegler, it is not only concrete technical media that "form intentionalities and inclinations" (Ihde 1990, 141): there's a more general tendency operating at the (systemic) level of the much despised—that is to say: in postphenomenological quarters—"'Technology' with a capital T" (Verbeek 2005, 4; cf. Ihde 1990, 6, 144) or "*technology uberhaupt* [sic]" (Ihde 2009, 22; original emphasis) as well. This does not mean that Stiegler subscribes to a rigidly determined, autonomously operating "single or unified trajectory" (ibid.) of Technology, often associated with the work of Ellul and Heidegger. Yet he fully admits with the latter that the trajectory of Western technics, as a process of epiphylogenesis, can be understood in terms of a metaphysical destiny, though not one rooted in a forgetfulness of *being* but of *technology* as the *thoroughly accidental condition* of possibility (and impossibility) of *all* understanding of being and *all* relating to beings.

It often seems as if postphenomenology considers technologies in complete abstraction of the politico-economic context in which they occur—a "use context" decisive like no other I would argue—thereby lacking not so much a normative stance (see for instance the work of Verbeek), but more objectionably in my opinion, a *truly critical* ambition or engagement. It also appears to have no interest in what could most simply be called the "negative" and, dare I say, "de-humanizing" aspects of everything that is involved in human-technology relations, not in the least those related to new media. There seems to be an almost methodical aversion among postphenomenologists for everything that even resembles an alienation critique of technology. After having once and for all disqualified Heidegger's supposedly "monolithic, abstract, and nostalgic" philosophy of technology deemed "inadequate" (Verbeek 2005, 60)—a criticism also leveled against Ellul, Jaspers, and Marcuse—and after having rejected wholesale the "excessively gloomy picture" (ibid., 4) of technology supposedly maintained by those authors, postphenomenology has lost sight of the *systemic* and *systemically conditioning* nature of technology, in particular of contemporary media. And it has also discarded the thinking of technological change more generally in its insistence to focus on describing concrete technologies. This to the point almost of receding into an empirical discipline hardly distinguishable anymore from, say, science and technology studies (Zwier et al. 2015). And sometimes it appears a little too satisfied with a priori dismissing more critical analyses of technology that it deems "pessimistic" (Ihde 2009, 27).

TECHNICAL AMBIGUITY AND PHARMACOLOGY OF TECHNOLOGY: THE ISSUE OF PROLETARIANIZATION

Postphenomenologists, despite their talk of the co-constitution of the human and technology and perceptive awareness of the inclining effects of technologies (Ihde 1990, 183) tend to underestimate the *conditioning* nature of technology, that is, of particular technologies and even more so of larger (socio) technical systems (which are hardly taken into account anyway), both at the individual and societal level. Moreover, postphenomenologists fail to see—or at the very least gravely underestimate—what Stiegler calls the inherently *proletarianizing* character of technology, a crucial notion within Stiegler's general conception of technology that I will explain in a moment.

In my view, both these shortcomings can be imputed to postphenomenology's lack of appreciation of what Stiegler theorizes as the "original default of origin" (*défaut d'origine*). This means humanity's *original lack* of intrinsic qualities, which compels it to constantly (re)invent itself through technical *accidents* that it vitally needs but that always remain ambiguous—to use the term that Ihde employs almost synonymously with multistability. As *artificial* organs they do not belong to the human organism organically as traits but only organo-*logically* as adoptions and therefore demand the learning and constant maintenance of skills, of a practice, of technical *intelligence* if you like, a techno-*logos*. These artificial organs can be ap*propri*ated for better or worse but they will never truly become its "*proper*ties." They are artificial, accidental compensations for the original and therefore insurmountable lack at the heart of human existence as "being-there" and *as such* they can *both* support or elevate *and* undermine or degrade that existence.

This is technical ambiguity in the sense of Stiegler. For him, ambiguity is thus not understood as the mere possibility of technical objects to function differently in different use contexts or vary according to the culture in which they are embedded, which is what Ihde means when he writes that "technologies are non-neutral and essentially, but structurally, ambiguous" (Ihde 1990, 144). The notion of ambiguity constitutes the core of Stiegler's understanding of technology just as the notion of multistability arguably does for postphenomenology. When Stiegler uses the notion of ambiguity, he refers to the fact that *all* technologies, in their relation to the human, or more precisely its way of being, have the character of what he calls, after Derrida and Plato, a *pharmakon*, a Greek word meaning both poison and medicine. Applied to the human condition as a technical condition it means for Stiegler that technologies, as compensations for the original default, can both support and undermine human existence in all its dimensions. They remedy or cure as it were the human default in all kinds of ways but *simultaneously* deepen it and can as such also frustrate human existence. Herein lies the essential ambiguity of technology for Stiegler: it is *at once* and *irreducibly* poisonous *and* beneficial to humans.[5] This "at once" is the core meaning of the *pharmaco*-logical nature of technologies: they are curative or healing *precisely insofar* as they are toxic or destructive (Stiegler 2013a, 4) and it is precisely because of their empowering effects that they can be disempowering. And that is why technologies are always in need of a *therapy*, that is, of practices and not just uses prescribed by marketing campaigns for constantly adapting consumers to the newest media gadgets.

This distinction between simple use and practice is very important for Stiegler since the former, dominant in today's media-saturated consumerist and service societies, deprives users of their knowledge and know-how, frustrates genuine *adoption* of technical media. In fact, "use" represents sheer *adaptation* to the marketized media commodities of a capitalist media industry exclusively interested in amassing surplus value through maximizing the sale of such media (and their content). This *loss of knowledge and know-how*—that is, of *noetic* capacity—is the core meaning of what Stiegler calls "proletarianization," a notion adapted from the Marxist tradition but understood more in a Simondonian fashion as a process of *disindividuation*—noetic but of course also somatic—due to the *short-circuiting* of psychic and collective individuation processes. The short-circuiting is performed through technical organs or organ systems like machines, assembly lines, automated factories, service centers, and today most decisively indeed through so-called *social media* (that actually destroy the social fabric). All these exclude the producer/worker and/or consumer from participating in the evolution and transformation of the conditions of the media environment in which he or she operates and exists (or rather: simply subsists). These important functions are now delegated to engineers and marketeers primarily serving the needs of capital (Stiegler 2010, 37).

The 19th-century proletarianized *producers* and passed their know-how into machines, thereby reducing them to units of labor power. The 20th century proletarianized *consumers* and eroded their *savoir-vivre* to substitute it with the lifestyle prescriptions and pre-fab user-guided experiences of an omnipresent marketing industry, thereby reducing themselves to units of buying power. The nascent 21st century is in the process of also proletarianizing the *engineers*, the intellectuals and generally the "conceivers." This happens not only by forcing them to adapt their noetic capacities to the media networks of cognitive capitalism but also by resolutely subordinating academic and scientific research to the dictates of the market, thereby reducing researchers to units of "invention-power" or "innovation-power." Even trading and financial speculations are today fully automated, turning even political and economic leaders such as Alan Greenspan into proletarians, "*deprived of knowledge* of *their own logic* and *by their own logic*—a logic reduced to calculation without remainder and leading as well to a market of fools" (Stiegler 2010, 47; original emphasis).

Most important for our purposes is that for Stiegler all technologies, as *pharmaka*, are essentially proletarianizing, that is, inherently toxic (Stiegler 2013, 42). Yet, for the same reason, they also have an inherently *deproletarianizing* potential. Taking the large-scale, systemic, sweeping view of "Technology with a capital T," downplayed by postphenomenology, Stiegler's account of anthropogenesis as technogenesis basically distinguishes two phases or *epochès* in "the process of technological becoming" that constantly pervades the human and needs to be integrated in its mode of being. The first *epochè* is the emergence of a new *pharmakon* as it suspends or interrupts the institutions and programs based on the existing system of *pharmaka*, thereby realizing what Stiegler calls "the first redoubling" (since a new technical reality "doubles upon" the existing one and thereby relegates it to the past, which then indeed becomes the *Gewesenheit* in the Heideggerian sense of *Geschichtlichkeit*). This opens up a new *epochè* in more or less the sense Heidegger gave to this term, and which is principally toxic since it short-circuits the existing programs that co-regulate the three organological levels, thus pathologizing them. Think here of the disruptive effects of the Internet today. The second phase consists of the *therapeutic adoption* of the new *pharmakon*—through politics and the invention of new practices of self and freedom, new sciences, new modes of thought, and generally new ways of living enabled by it—thus turning it into a curative. This then establishes the new *epochè* in the proper sense, as a new process of psycho-social individuation based on a new process of technical individuation (Stiegler 2013, 35). Think of the many new possibilities for socializing, producing, researching, experimenting, artistically expressing, et cetera opened up by the Internet. This is called the second redoubling—which today mostly fails (Stiegler 2011, 7)—transforming the process of technical becoming (*de-venir*) into a genuine future (*a-venir*) (ibid.), that is to say a new socio-cultural "project" in the Heideggerian sense, or *Daseinsprogramm* (with a term from Hans Blumenberg).

TECHNOGENESIS AS PATHOGENESIS AND THE INHERENT *HYBRIS* OF *TECHNE*

With Georges Canguilhem, Stiegler considers the human being to be "a sick animal" (to use Nietzsche's famous expression) in that he understands the technogenesis of the *anthropos* as a *patho*genesis. As fundamentally pharmaco-organological—the *pharmakon* being at the very heart of being-there's organologically constituted existence (Stiegler 2016, 139)—the human being is periodically, and today chronically, confronted with destabilizations or disruptions caused by the upheavals of its technological, today most prominently digital *media* milieu, which are experienced as "pathologies" of its technical organ systems. This requires the invention of new *sociotherapies*: new ways of living and existing, new desires and "new beliefs" (Nietzsche), that is, a new state of mental health enabled through the new *pharmaka*. Becoming sick can also be related to the heteronomizing or alienating tendency inherent in all *pharmaka*, but as always these carry within themselves the potential and promise of offering the supports for a new, yet inevitably always relative autonomy, that is, relative to technical heteronomy (ibid., 41; Lemmens 2015). With, though also against Heidegger, Stiegler describes this pathogenesis of the human also as an interminable being-put-into-question of being-there by the *pharmakon*—more original, and in fact the very condition of possibility (but also impossibility) of being-there's ability to question being.

Postphenomenologists write that they "analyze technology as a constitutive part of the lifeworld rather than as a threat to it" (Verbeek 2011, 14) and are no doubt right in claiming that technologies "provide many varied and enriched ways in which that world can be encountered" (Verbeek 2005, 143–5). They state that "[r]ather than thinking in terms of alienation [postphenomenology] thinks in terms of mediation" (Rosenberger and Verbeek 2015, 11) and that "against the idea that technology alienates human beings from the world and from themselves it places the idea that technologies help to shape human subjectivity and the objectivity of the world" (ibid., 12). In doing so they may surely provide a corrective to the possibly all-too pessimistic view of their forefathers. Yet, what I would like to point out in closing is that they tend to underestimate the fact that technology can *very well* pose a threat to the lifeworld, "to human authenticity and to the meaningfulness of reality" (Verbeek 2011, 3), and indeed *does* have alienating or dehumanizing effects. However problematic these terms might be, this only means they have to be *rethought* from an understanding of the human condition as an *originally* technical—and thus irreducibly heteronomous—condition instead of prematurely dismissed. Technology frequently *does* engender desubjectivation, desocialization, stupidity, immiseration, a loss or impoverishment of world-openness, and an occlusion of what Heidegger called the "clearing" (which should also be rethought as technologically constituted). Who can deny, to provide a media-related example, the distractive and often even destructive effects on attention and rationality of today's cognitive capitalism's media landscape, not to mention the ruinous effects on the economy and the social fabric through the ever growing implementation of technical automatisms of all kinds in our still so-called lifeworlds.

What this is meant to convey is that technology is not only *constitutive* of human subjectivity and the world, it is also at the same time—and necessarily so from an organo-pharmacological perspective—a *destitutive* and heteronomizing force. Hence, it is a constant factor of alienation, disruption, and most fundamentally of what the ancient Greeks knew as *hybris*, which was their *first and foremost* association with what they named *techne*. This word has been interpreted by Heidegger once as "a mode of proceeding *against physis*" (Heidegger 1994, 155; original emphasis) or as a "violence doing" (Heidegger 2000, 170) against the "overwhelming" (*dike*) of the *physis*. This qualifies the *anthropos* (the technical life form) as "the uncanniest of the uncanny" (*to deinotaton*) (ibid., 159), as that "monstrous" "event of appropriation" (*Ereignis*) that changes the face of the Earth in its attempt to "enframe" it and that has ultimately unleashed a global crisis threatening its very planetary life support system. This is in truth the "return" of *hybris* on a scale unimaginable to the ancient Greeks. It is this fundamentally "hybristic" nature of technology that seems almost if not totally absent in postphenomenology.

BY WAY OF CONCLUSION

Postphenomenology is without doubt an important and extremely useful way of thinking about technology, having developed some powerful tools to explore the human-technology nexus in the past, as it is doing in the present, and will surely keep doing in the future. It certainly has a lot of merits and great practical utility and can without doubt be further elaborated to think about concrete human-technology interactions in our increasingly mediatized life-worlds. Yet, especially when it comes to thinking in and of the realm of media, I claim that it could profit from re-considering its emphasis on the empirical turn and recognize the thoroughly transcendental—albeit of course empirically transcendental or aposteriorically conditioning—operativity of media in the sense of retentional devices that originally constitute and condition the protential-retentional flux of so-called transcendental subjectivity. Emerging from the interiorization of a process of technical exteriorization, this subjectivity is always constituted in turn by that which it constitutes, which means in Stiegler's words "that it is constructed only as an after-effect and that it is always caught in the problematic of its own re-constitution; it is originarily a re-constituted subject and in that sense synthetic" (Stiegler 2011, 80). And this syn-thesis is always a pros-thesis or an originary prostheticity (ibid., 1). Needless to say that from such a perspective the massive industrialization, digitization, and automation of the entirety of retentional devices currently underway globally—and nothing else is going on, one might say, with the intense and ubiquitous "mediatization" of our lifewords—has huge consequences for the future of subjectivity. One does not have to share Stiegler's own rather bleak diagnosis that the current digital "prosthetization of consciousness" (ibid., 4) has been so far largely destructive in its effects on consciousness, to understand that the stakes of this event are enormous if not outright uncanny and deserve the utmost concern by any post- or techno-phenomenologist.

To conclude: apart from lacking a critical politico-economic as well as a truly ontological (cf. Zwier et al. 2016) perspective on technology, what I feel is most palpably (and in my view problematically) absent in postphenomenology is an awareness, a recognition, and yes an appreciation of the "uncanny" or what Stiegler calls the *heimlich-unheimlich* character of Technology (Stiegler 2013, 111) as that which constitutes not only the "grounding" of the human but also its "ungrounding," its fundamentally hybristic, "titanic" yet fragile and precarious ontological openness. This is something not to be trivialized now that we're in the midst globally of a "total technological make-over" as it were in which all three organological systems are disruptively metamorphosing simultaneously and we are entering what geologists call the Anthropocene, which summons humanity to completely rethink and reconstruct its technological modus vivendi on a highly damaged planet in a fragile biosphere, indeed in what Heidegger called the *Gestell*—only much more urgent now. And the question of "new media," which constitute the digitized global *noosphere* that is without doubt indispensable for dealing with our planetary crisis, is of the utmost importance here. Some "upscaling" of the postphenomenological toolbox toward this urgent planetary predicament could possibly be one of its most promising future agendas, but this is a topic for another occasion.

NOTES

1. Heidegger, Martin, *Was heisst Denken?* Tübingen: Max Niemeyer Verlag, 1984, p. 53. Translated by the author.
2. Obviously, this suggestion resonates to some extent with Dominic Smith's plea for a more "transcendental empiricist" approach in postphenomenology—which is inspired more by Deleuze, though (Smith 2015).
3. Cf. "Technologies can be the means by which 'consciousness itself' is mediated. Technologies may occupy the 'of' [in the sense of "consciousness *of*," i.e., intentionality] and not just be some object domain" (Ihde 2009, 23).
4. Transduction is a term derived from Simondon and denotes a relation in which the relata acquire their identity only from within the relation or in other words are co-constituted relationally.
5. Of course, Stiegler's pharmacology has a superficial similarity with Ihde's scheme of amplification and reduction, that is, the fact that technologies always weaken and strengthen certain human capacities or aspects of perception or interpretation of the world (or of the engagement with it), yet the organological toxic-curative duplicity of the *pharmakon* is more complicated, if only because it involves the very organogenesis of human existence.

REFERENCES

Arendt, H. (1971). *The Life of the Mind.* San Diego: Harcourt Inc.

Heidegger, M. (1994). *Basic Questions of Philosophy: Selected "Problems" of "Logic."* Indianapolis: Indiana University Press.

———. (2000). *Introduction to Metaphysics.* New Haven: Yale University Press.

———. (2004). *What is Called Thinking?* New York: Harper Perennial.

Husserl, E. (2008). *On the Phenomenology of the Consciousness of Internal Time (1893–1917).* Dordrecht: Kluwer.

Ihde, D. (1990). *Technology and the Lifeworld: From Garden to Earth.* Bloomington: Indiana University Press.

———. (2002). *Bodies in Technology.* Minneapolis: University of Minnesota Press.

———. (2009). *Postphenomenology and Technoscience: The Peking University Lectures*. Albany: SUNY Press.

———. (2012). *Experimental Phenomenology: Multistabilities*. Second Edition. Albany: SUNY Press.

Irwin, S. (2016). *Digital Media: Human–Technology Connection*. Lanham: Lexington Books.

Lemmens, P. (2015). "Social Autonomy and Heteronomy in the Age of ICT: The Digital *Pharmakon* and the (Dis)Empowerment of the General Intellect." *Foundations of Science*, October 17.

Rosenberger, R. and P.-P. Verbeek. (2015). *Postphenomenological Investigations. Essays on Human–Technology Relations*. Lanham: Lexington Books.

Smith, D. (2014). "Rewriting the Constitution: A Critique of 'Postphenomenology.'" *Philosophy of Technology*, August 26.

Stiegler, B. (1998). *Technics and Time 1: The Fault of Epimetheus*. Stanford: Stanford University Press.

———. (2009). *Technics and Time 2: Disorientation*. Stanford: Stanford University Press.

———. (2010). *For a New Critique of Political Economy*. Cambridge-Malden: Polity.

———. (2011). *Technics and Time 3: Cinematic Time and the Question of Malaise*. Stanford: Stanford University Press.

———. (2013). *What Makes Life Worth Living: On Pharmacology*. Cambridge-Malden: Polity.

———. (2014). *Symbolic Misery 1: The Hyperindustrial Epoch*. Cambridge-Malden: Polity.

———. (2015a). *Symbolic Misery 2: The* Katastrophe *of the Sensible*. Cambridge-Malden: Polity.

———. (2015b). *States of Shock: Stupidity and Knowledge in the 21st Century*. Cambridge-Malden: Polity.

———. (2015c). *La société automatique 1. L'Avenir du travail*. Paris: Fayard.

———. (2016). *Dans la disruption. Comment ne pas devenir fou?* Paris: Les liens qui libèrent.

Van Den Eede, Y. (2012). *Amor Technologiae: Marshall McLuhan as Philosopher of Technology—Toward a Philosophy of Human-Media Relations*. Brussels: VUBPress.

Verbeek, P.-P. (2005). *What Things Do*. University Park, PA: Penn State University Press.

———. (2011). *Moralizing Technology*. Chicago: University of Chicago Press.

Wellner, G. P. (2016). *A Postphenomenological Inquiry of Cell Phones: Genealogies, Meanings, and Becoming*. Lanham: Lexington Books.

Zwier, J., V. Blok, and P. Lemmens. (2016). "Phenomenology and the Empirical Turn: A Phenomenological Analysis of Postphenomenology." *Philosophy of Technology*, May 25.

Chapter 11

I-Media-World

The Algorithmic Shift from Hermeneutic Relations to Writing Relations

Galit Wellner

INTRODUCTION, OR WHY WE NEED A NEW TYPE OF POSTPHENOMENOLOGICAL RELATIONS

Digital technologies manage to do things we thought only humans can do. Unlike industrial machines that exceed the human body's capabilities—move faster, function more accurately, exercise more physical force—digital technologies seem to target another horizon. Instead of attempting to surpass humans' physical limits, they aim to outperform the mind. This trend is accelerated by smart algorithms, also known as Artificial Intelligence (AI). Some of the algorithms imagine, like Deep Dream Generator, that produces dreamy variations of a given picture (see Figures 11.1a–1b).[1] Others improvise, like Shimon the robot who plays jazz with four hands.[2] And some others function as robo-journalists writing dozens of news articles per minute, albeit mostly reporting on sports and financials.[3]

These digital technologies display their output (pictures, music, text), and they thereby produce media. Media, like technologies, mediate the world for us, hence the name media.[4] But sometimes media also means technology; the words "media" and "technology" are used interchangeably when referring to television or to the Internet, for instance; and when Marshall McLuhan states "the medium is the message,"[5] the word medium is usually interpreted to denote technology or the coupling of technological device and displayed content. Frequently the artifact and the content are coupled so tightly that the distinction is not easy or simple (Van Den Eede 2012, 27–29, 168). The media-technology mix reflects the dominant role of technology in content production and display; yet it cannot blur the distinction between displaying content for reading *versus* writing that content. In the case of AI this distinction is important, as different software engines perform each action. When

Figures 11.1a–b Deep Dream Generator, 1a is the source, 1b is the 6th iteration.

combined in a single product, the combination raises concerns, because the calculation-writing processes remain opaque. We can see, listen, or read the media-output and examine it, but cannot assess the writing phase in which these technologies produce media.

Likewise, in postphenomenology the focus is on reading, while writing tends to remain in the fringe. Most of the references to media are grouped under the notion of hermeneutic relations that describes how the world is experienced through the act of reading a "text." And "text" is understood in the widest sense: "text" can be a written text, as well as a graph, a dashboard, or an image taken during a medical test. The analyses describing hermeneutic relations frequently overlook the act of writing, and when they do refer to writing, it is in order to explain the reading phase, or as an introduction to embodiment relations. For example, when Ihde analyzes the invention of writing as part of the explanation of hermeneutic relations, he depicts the evolution of the alphabet as the development of "*embodied* hermeneutic technic" (Ihde 1990, 84; my emphasis). Writing in this context means the "*embodied* form of language" (ibid., 82; my emphasis). The analytic focus shifts from hermeneutics to embodiment.

In this chapter, I would like to distinguish between reading and writing and suggest a new type of postphenomenological relations that take into account the fact that writing is an act of leaving a trace in the world. While embodiment relations stress the impact of technology on the user's body, the relations I envision seek to complementarily accentuate the impact on the world. Take for example a video recording of a child's fifth birthday party. Postphenomenologists would suggest it is important which point of view is selected, which lighting is used (e.g., turning off the lights in the room when the cake with the candles is rolled in), at which height the camera is placed et cetera. All these parameters are related to the body of the photographer and hence usually studied with embodiment relations. However, the centrality of the recording body comes with a price. Such an analysis overlooks the results of the recording act. When video recording a birthday party, it is no less important that a movie came to the world, functioning as a trace that will be available for years after the event has faded away. An object is added to the world, thereby changing the world.

If we look at writing, it extensively involves technology; a text is always produced by a technology, from a simple pencil to a radio telescope, a space camera, or an electronic microscope (Ihde 1990; Rosenberger 2008; Forss 2012). Reading may also require technology but to a lesser extent and with greater flexibility. Think of the way a piece of paper is held when writing—usually on a hard surface and approached from above with a writing tool like a pen. Now compare this situation to reading in which the piece of paper can be held in any direction, even above the head when we read on the beach!

In AI, the separation between reading and writing is clearer and sharper. Unlike people—at least literate people—that can read *and* write, AI technologies can perform either reading or writing. The acts of reading and writing are done by different algorithms: a robo-journalist may write a review on a football game, but cannot read articles; Shimon the robot can play jazz but cannot hear others playing. Therefore, even if hermeneutic relations attempt to cover human reading and writing, the need for an analytic separation between reading and writing becomes apparent. Reading can still be analyzed with hermeneutic relations while writing urges us to seek a new type of relations. I name this new type "writing relations."

Here is the chapter's outline: if "writing relations" are a new type of postphenomenological relations, then the first step should be a detailed overview of the "parent" relation, that is—hermeneutic relations. Then I will briefly draw the border between reading and writing while pointing at their intersections, overlaps, and affinities. Next comes a sketch of the new type of writing relations, including the necessary alterations in the postphenomenological scheme of "I—technology—world." As the digital age has dramatically transformed reading and writing, I will discuss these changes. One major difference is that the entity that reads/writes is not necessarily human, and both actions can be delegated to algorithms. I will discuss the possible roles of human beings and AI in the digital variations of reading and writing.

FROM INTERPRETIVE TO PRODUCTIVE HERMENEUTIC RELATIONS

Generally speaking, hermeneutic relations engage the user's linguistic and interpretive capacities. The postphenomenological scheme for hermeneutic relations is:

$$I \rightarrow (\text{ technology—world })$$

The world is seldom directly accessible. In hermeneutic relations, it is mediated by a technology-text. Don Ihde explains: "the world is first transformed into a text, which in turn is read" (Ihde 1990, 92). Andrew Feenberg stretches Ihde's transformation ingredient and regards hermeneutic relations like a screenplay in which "the interpreted message stands in for the world, is in effect a world" (Feenberg 2006, 194). According to Ihde and Feenberg, "technology" and "world" are not just two parts of one logical unit but rather "technology" replaces "world" by a message-text. The role of the "I" is to impute meaning to that message-text. This way the postphenomenological scheme can be logically divided into two parts—"I" and text; they are separated by an arrow indicating human intentionality that is directed toward the combo technology-world.

As an interpretation-oriented relation, hermeneutic relations are centered on text. It is assumed that somebody wrote a text; that the text exists; and that now the "I" reads it. These are three stages stretching along a timeline—writing, displaying, and reading. It should be noted that before the emergence of digital technologies, only writing and reading were relevant; digital technologies introduced a middle stage of display. Most of the postphenomenological analyses of hermeneutic relations focus on the latter stage of reading, and pay less attention to the earlier writing phase. One of the few references to writing can be found in Ihde's early study on the evolution of signs as part of his explanation of hermeneutic relations (Ihde 1990, 82–83). He describes how specific visual cues were selected to represent the corresponding words or sounds. Yet the act of writing is analyzed via its embodied aspects. There is hardly a reference to the traces in the world created in the act of writing.

The case study of the evolution of signs reminds us that hermeneutic relations are not the only way a media technology mediates the world. Sometimes media also function as part of the experiencer's body, thereby maintaining embodiment relations in parallel to hermeneutic relations (see also Rosenberger 2008; Forss 2012). Embodiment relations highlight the technological element and disregard the content element(s). Another type of postphenomenological relation is alterity, in which media is referred to as a quasi-other. Here the "I" approaches the technological artifact or the displayed content in and of itself, thereby maintaining a form of a dialog with it (see Wellner 2014). Nevertheless, hermeneutic relations are the main postphenomenological vehicle to understand our special association to media technologies, those that produce and present "text." Take for example Ihde's study of writing tools (Ihde 2010, 128–39) where he expounds their evolution: from "hard" tools for inscribing cuneiform tablets (this is the original sense of a tablet!), through "soft" tools like a brush serving to write on parchment and paper, to the "virtual" phase of a keyboard, in which both hands are in use. In his analysis he explores the ways in which a writing tool is held on the bodily level, but he does not mention the intellectual effort that is required at the writing phase, an effort that runs in parallel to the embodied effort. More importantly, there is no discussion on the change in the world.

Some postphenomenological analyses attempt to model how a technology that "writes" influences the ways in which content is read and understood. For example, Robert Rosenberger studies pictures taken by the Mars Orbiter Camera modified to incorporate data from other instruments such as thermal emission detector and laser altimeter (2008). He details a technology-intensive multi-phased translation process that runs from an analog real-world picture to a digital image, through its transmission in space, integration of information from various instruments into a single coherent image, and finally to a reverse translation back to a picture that can be seen by humans on a computer screen (rather than a long series of numbers).[6] He shows how the combining algorithms shape the content and allow multiple interpretations. Rosenberger invests much effort in explaining the technical details of the production of these digital images in order to analyze the reading stage. He remains committed to the centrality of the interpretive aspects; the detailed analysis of the "writing" of the image-text serves as no more than an explanation of the multiple choices of its reading.

This focus on reading in hermeneutic relations follows the cultural inclination, with McLuhan, toward "a literate worldview" which centers on the figure/content and leaves the ground/form in the background (see Van Den Eede 2012, 167). The writing stage is left in the background partially modeled, with some elements covered by embodiment relations. In the next sections I will portray what writing relations may look like. Later I will show that the need for such new postphenomenological relations intensifies once digital technologies start reading and writing.

SEPARATING WRITING FROM READING

In *Of Grammatology* Jacques Derrida (1976) deconstructs the speech-writing dichotomy. Here I deal with the adjacent dichotomy of reading-writing. And while reading and writing are usually treated together due to their mutual interest in text, my aim is to separate them and reveal the distinctions. I map the dissimilarities between reading and writing according to the three constituents of the postphenomenological scheme—"I," "technology," and "world."

Starting with the "I" perspective, writing is done in a given period of time and by a few, whereas reading is recurring and can be *en masse*. A text can be written at once or rewritten over weeks (as I did for this chapter), months or even years. And it can be subject to additions that explain it and eventually become part of it. A good example is the Jewish *Talmud* that was written during several hundred years, probably from the 3rd to the 5th centuries. Each page of the Talmud is built of "boxes" (see Figure 11.2), where the central box is the original text of the *Talmud,* usually conveying a religious rule, and the surrounding boxes contain texts from various leading authors who interpret and contemplate on the central text. The *Talmud* was formed during approximately 300 years, but now it is stable and fixed. The number of authors, although exceeding one, is still low enough to be listed and counted. The readers, by contrast, are innumerable. Looking at the *Talmud* today, its reading phase lasts until now and the number of readers still cannot be quantified.

ב ברכות פרק ראשון מאימתי

מאימתי

Brahot T. 1 אלף (ברכות)

Figure 11.2 Babylonian *Talmud*, Vilnius edition, showing the first page of the first tractate. *Source:* https://commons.wikimedia.org/wiki/File:First_page_of_the_first_tractate_of_the_Talmud_(Daf_Beis_of_Maseches_Brachos).jpg.

After examining the dissimilarities between reading and writing from the "I" perspective, let us examine the gaps from the "technology" perspective. Basically, the technologies of writing are different from those of reading: pens, pencils, and keyboards vs. eyeglasses and other optical technologies.

Even when both reading and writing are delegated to technologies as evidenced today, the algorithms that read are distinct from those that write. Those that read use technics like word count and word proximity to analyze a written text (see Hayles 2012). Those that write are trained by humans (e.g., journalists) to turn data, preferably structured like financial reports or sports tables, into human-readable text (e.g., articles). The technologies are different: writing tends to involve tools such as hammers (for cuneiforms), pens, keyboards, and big data technics; reading may demand a surface on which the text can be displayed, as well as sight aids like eye-glasses. But those reading technologies are also needed for writing! Moreover, writing technologies seem to be more robust, so that they require more resources in terms of physical, thermodynamic, and economic aspects. Writing with a keyboard, a pen and certainly with a hammer entails physical labor, especially in comparison to reading actions like looking at a wall, looking at a shelf in the library or looking at Facebook's Wall. The thermodynamic elements are more significant in the creation of a text that consumes more energy than reading. This is true since the Stone Age when "text" (i.e., image) was inscribed on stones, all the way to writing a computer file that is electronically "inscribed" on magnetic or optical medium. The economic implications correlate with the energy consumption; the bigger the effort, the higher the price of the action.

The distinction between reading and writing resembles that between content and medium. Reading tends to foreground the content, writing tends to foreground the medium. Yet, in both reading and writing, it is difficult to separate the medium/technology on which and with which the text is written from the contents of the text, especially in light of McLuhan's well-known idiom: "the medium is the message." Yoni Van Den Eede explains this difficulty: "Content we consciously perceive; but form escapes our attention" (2012, 23). We need to analytically separate form from content, technology from media, and writing from reading.

Lastly, from a "world" perspective, the act of writing is a form of recording (see Stiegler 1998), whose target may be an event, a discussion, a mood, or a thought, to name a few. As recording, writing leaves a physical trace in the world, a trace which can be read and re-read by others. By contrast, reading leaves only faint traces: fingerprints, "ears" at the corners of book pages, or written underlines and notes. Digital reading is no exception and it leaves just a few bits designating who read, when and which pages or parts were displayed (still it cannot detect which parts were actually read). Moreover, reading's traces rarely have meaning without the text to which they refer; they are like parasites that need the "host" text.

Integrating into postphenomenology the notion of the trace may call for a new perspective on other postphenomenological relations. Take for example embodiment relations. If I abruptly stop my car, the car might leave a physical trace on the road marking the sudden deceleration of the vehicle. In the age of the Anthropocene we realize that even merely driving a car leaves gas emissions in the world. Only if my car is electric and the electricity is supplied from wind or sun am I more likely to avoid emission traces. These traces, neglected and even non-visible before we realized we live in the Anthropocene, add a hermeneutic dimension to embodiment relations. It is complementary to Ihde's emphasis on embodiment aspects in hermeneutic relations of the invention of early alphabet and in writing practices.

In this section I showed the differences between reading and writing "I's," between the technologies that enable these actions and between the types of traces left in the world. These differences may justify a change in the postphenomenological scheme to separate between reading, which is covered by the existing hermeneutic relation formula, and writing which is absent. The next section includes a few attempts to provide a postphenomenological scheme for writing relations.

WRITING RELATIONS

If a new type of relation should be added to represent writing, then what should the corresponding variation of the postphenomenological scheme look like? In this section I will playfully attempt to move in some directions, gathering variations from previous postphenomenological analyses, arranging them in a logical order, somewhat different from the order in which they were written or published.

The first attempt to represent writing relations is an extensive deployment of the arrow that indicates intentionality. It enables me to represent the technological intentionality of writing that places a trace in the world. This tactic is based on the work of Peter-Paul Verbeek (2008) expanding the four postphenomenological relations into a framework which he names "cyborg intentionality." Of relevance here might be his notion of "composite intentionality" that refers to situations in which intentionality is distributed between humans and technologies.[7] He suggests replacing the dash sign between "technology" and "world" in the postphenomenological scheme with an arrow, thereby creating a permutation on the classic hermeneutic relations:

I → (technology → world)

This variation can model writing relations because it represents how writing technologies create a trace in the world. It reflects the active role of a text as a trace. However, it does not solve the ambiguities of content-artifact and reading-writing.

The second attempt to model writing relations is based on the work of Nicola Liberati (2016) who uses curly brackets in order to denote where the user's attention is directed: that which is positioned within the curly brackets withdraws to the background. He also differentiates between the physical technological artifact and non-physical technological representations. This divide reflects the Janus face of media as form and content. The divide, as explained before, may be difficult in some situations, and is mostly for analytical purposes. In his terms, "technology" is the technological artifact and "object" or "label" is the technological representation, or the text. He presents a set of two variations:

Subject → ({Object}—Technology)
Subject → (Object—{Technology})

In the first instance the text withdraws to the background, and the user's attention is directed to the technological artifact—a paper, a screen, or a writing tool. This situation reflects a mode of writing that focuses on the format, like in Japanese calligraphy or the experience of those who begin to use a computer and look for the letters on the keyboard. In the second instance, the technological artifact that enables the reading/writing withdraws to the background. It is a variation of the postphenomenological hermeneutic relations in which the attention is focused on the text ("object" in Liberati's terminology) and represents the act of reading. It can also represent a mode of writing in which the assisting technologies withdraw to the background and the user-writer concentrates on the text itself. However, Liberati does not refer to the world component; his variations are partial.

The third attempt combines the previous two. It is based on the work of Heather Wiltse (2014) who splits the "technology" element into device and content, which she terms substrate and trace. Substrate denotes the enabling medium on which the text is written (or otherwise inscribed) and trace indicates a text (or anything that can be interpreted). This differentiation can also be found in Liberati's solution—see Table 11.1. Although Liberati develops a different argument, his observation is very similar to that of Wiltse.

Wiltse explains that in digital environments the trace and the substrate are separated so that contents are produced by a device different from that with which they are displayed. She demonstrates the trace-substrate dichotomy with the thermometer. In its traditional form the mercury measures and

Table 11.1

	Technological artifact	*Text*
Liberati	Technology	Object, label
Wiltse	Substrate	Trace

shows the temperature at the same time. It functions as both substrate and trace. From a simple classic mercury thermometer she proceeds to a digital thermometer in which the measurement and the display are done by two different components. Her final example in this "set" is a weather website that provides temperature information for remote locations, as if these locations are right outside the door. The technology that inscribes the information has no direct link to that which presents it. Wiltse concludes that the functional uncoupling of writing and display is paradigmatic to digital environments. This separation is represented by a vertical separator in her variation to the postphenomenological scheme. What Wiltse suggests can be regarded as a combination of Verbeek's double intentionality and Liberati's differentiation between artifact and text. In postphenomenological terms, the substrate is facing the "world" while the trace faces the "I":

I → ([trace | substrate] → world)

Her revised postphenomenological scheme includes both writing and displaying-reading. It is intended to replace hermeneutic relations in the context of digital environments. It is a solution specifically tailored to digital technologies. I prefer to focus on a solution that will capture the unique characteristics of writing as a general act, applicable for analog and digital environments alike. This strategy will allow me to leave the hermeneutic relations unchanged and apply them for acts of reading, remaining faithful to their interpretive mission (in the strict and narrow sense).

My last attempt combines all three previous variations: split "technology" into "tech" (for technological artifact) and "text," so that the new basic scheme will look like this:

I—tech—text—world

Hermeneutic relations representing reading will simply bracket together technology, text, and world, in a manner very similar to the existing "triptych" scheme. For writing relations, however, the arrow moves away from the "I" and separates between technology and text:

(I—tech) → (text → world)

This variation assumes that in the process of inscription the technology withdraws to the background, as in embodiment relations, and the focus of the writing entity is on the combined text-world. The arrow between "text" and "world" represents the creation of a trace in the world, as suggested by

Verbeek. Note that here "tech" is facing the "I," and not "text" as proposed by Wiltse and Liberati.

There is another possible variation of this quad-scheme: I self-reflexively write this chapter; I find myself thinking of the text, interacting with it, while the world withdraws to the background; I realize this situation resembles alterity relations. In this mode of writing, the scheme can be:

(I—tech) → text (→ world)

In this exercise, it becomes apparent that the brackets in the postphenomenological scheme have two functions. In the left combo, they denote that two entities function together in close symbiosis, as in embodiment relations. It is the "I" and the "technology" ensemble that writes. In the right combo the brackets signify that something withdraws to the background such that the world becomes temporarily irrelevant—a mute environs. Combining the two parts and meanings of the brackets, the result is a mix of embodiment, alterity, and hermeneutic relations. Indeed, all of them are relevant to the writing process! However, there is a price for this mega-convergence: the elegance and simplicity of the postphenomenological "triptych" scheme evaporates.

The four directions presented here use brackets and arrows to enrich the basic postphenomenological scheme. My attempt presented as the last direction is specifically designed to deal with the complexities of writing while being applicable to both analog and digital practices.

WHY DOES THE DIGITAL AGE REQUIRE US TO RETHINK MEDIA? OR, AGAINST SIMONDON'S CONCRETIZATION

Digital technologies change the rules of the game. Why? Here is one possible explanation: Take a piece of paper in your hand. You can turn it, fold it into an airplane-like flying thing or crease it into a ball. When treated this way, it basically behaves like a hammer. Both maintain (mostly) embodiment relations with you. And as paper was invented in China in the 2nd century BC as a wrapping material for delicate objects, both were originally intended for purposes other than media. But if something is written on that paper, it immediately changes and maintains with you (also) hermeneutic relations. The paper turns into media. Now, instead of a paper, let's take a screen. It is media from the start. Yes, it can serve as a weapon, like the hammer, but this stability is rare and not the common use. The multistability of a screen is mostly located on the level of content, and reflects its ability to display text, drawings, maps, photographs, movies et cetera. It is not an embodied multistability but one that works on the hermeneutic level. Put differently, digital technologies' multistability is more of the text-content and less of the technological artifact.

The digital is changing the rules of the game also due to the differences between digital and analog writing. Digital writing is composed of two stages: the first stage is writing the software code that runs the digital media, preparing the ground for the next stage—which is done by that software—of selecting content and displaying it, that is, "writing" the content (see Wiltse, 2014). A simple example is a LED in a car's dashboard functioning like a text: when it is off, we continue driving uninterruptedly; when it is on, we interpret it as an alert to stop and check the car. In analog systems, turning the led on is part of the flow and the operations. In digital technologies, there is a special software code—an IF-THEN loop—that decides if the LED is on or off. In the analog situation the LED is embedded into the technology, whereas in the digital realm a hermeneutic element is introduced. It is not a coincidence that in digital technologies the LED indication can be easily turned into a text (displayed on a screen or heard via a speaker) explaining the fault, and possibly directing to further instructions on how to proceed or even how to fix the problem.

This concept of a two-stage writing is elaborated by Wiltse (2014) as a gap between how things work and how they are experienced. She regards the first stage of writing the software code as setting the stage for "work." It is followed by a stage of writing the text to be displayed which prepares the "experience." She matches "work" with the substrate (i.e., technological device) and "experience" with trace (i.e., text). Next she contrasts between the two stages in terms of opacity and transparency. The digital work is opaque and the digital experience is transparent. We don't know how algorithms calculate the result they show us. We can just read their output.

In this context, Wiltse's example of the evolution of the thermometer is illuminating as she demonstrates how the temperature measurement components are broken down to measurement, writing, and display functions. It can be interesting to compare between the digital age's breakdown to work/experience and Gilbert Simondon's notion of concretization (Simondon 1958). Concretization is a key process in the evolution of a mechanical system in which some elements come closer over time, thereby acquiring functions from each other until they fully merge into one mechanism. Recently re-discovered, concretization is heralded as "one of [Simondon's] most important and lasting philosophical contributions" (Iliadis 2015, 86). Feenberg (2016) calls it "elegance." And Iliadis elaborates: "A technological object is charged with overabundant functions when it concretizes; each individual element fulfills additional functions that increase while the total amount of elements decrease, leading to a deceivingly complex yet 'simple' object" (Iliadis 2015, 88). As a result, "the technological object becomes (oddly) less complex, particularly in regard to its quantity of physical elements, as it develops" (ibid.). Simondon's famous example of concretization is the Guimbal turbine which is an engine that cools itself while working in the water.[8]

Whereas for Simondon the fulfillment of two functions at once by the same technological element is regarded as a higher order of mechanology, the logic of the digital age is inverse: each action should be performed by a distinct code/engine. In the digital non-concretize evolution, functions are broken to discrete elements or software engines. It is anti-concretization that characterizes digital technologies. These two models seem to follow the modernity vs. postmodernity discussions: modernity idealizes efficiency and coherence (as evidenced in the Guimbal turbine for example); postmodernity praises the multiplicity even at the price of disorganization and inconsistency (efficiency and speed are targets of critique and not necessarily ends to be pursued; see Paul Virilio and Zygmunt Bauman, to name a few). Hence, if concretization is modern by its nature, the suggested split of technology in the postphenomenological scheme into text and device can be classified as postmodern.

Moreover, attempts to reach concretization in the digital sphere invoke worries. For instance, when Facebook allows users to login to other web services with the user profile thereby bypassing the need to provide (again) personal information, it can be regarded as a concretization, but it also raises concerns for privacy. The same occurs when the smartphone integrates information across applications so that phonebook records are shared with the email address book and the navigation app. The automatic links the smartphone offers are convenient yet fuel anxieties. These concerns and anxieties can be imputed to the opacity-transparency dichotomy described by Wiltse (2014): unlike the Guimbal turbine whose work is visible (and so Simondon could detect its elegance), software engines are hidden and we cannot assess the efficiency and "elegance" of such shared records and cross-linking, nor can we determine who else has access to these data records behind the technological veil.

ALGORITHMIC READING AND WRITING

Digital technologies introduce a new paradigm into the logic of engineering a system, moving from concretization, which was typical to modern mechanics, to fragmentation and specialization. In an ecology governed by fragmentation and specialization, it is conceived natural and inevitable that reading and writing are performed by different software algorithms. AI introduces a deeper step into this paradigm by moving from linear argumentation and reasoning to a mesh-like rhizome reading, writing, and reasoning. While the shift from concretization to fragmentation occurs inside technologies, the move from linear to mesh-like argumentation has a more visible effect on humans, although most of the actions remain hidden. In this section I will review how reading and writing function differently when digital technologies—and especially AI—are involved.

N. Katherine Hayles (2012) explores the possibility of "machine reading" as part of a larger framework in which she examines new modes of reading. In machine reading the "machine" is a software algorithm which may work with some hardware devices (e.g., scanners for "reading"), but these are not a must. The software counts words, calculates proximities between phrases et cetera. Hayles positions machine reading in digital humanities as a major component that works side by side with human researchers. For Hayles, digital humanities cultivates the collaboration between "human cognition" and "machine cognition" to extend the former's "scope, power, and flexibility" (ibid., 41–42). Machine reading extends human cognition not by imitation. It does not resemble human reading, just as a rolling wheel of a bicycle or a car does not resemble running. The human and the technological complement each other, co-shape each other. The consequences can be dramatic, such as the replacement of traditional linear argumentation based on hermeneutic interpretation by what Hayles terms "digging potatoes," scattered here and there (ibid., 38). When the "potatoes" are piled, a rhizomatic argument is built, with more than a single starting point, developing into many directions.

An illuminating example of a hybrid reading can be found in Stacey Irwin's *Digital Media* (2016). In chapter 10 Irwin portrays digital journalism as a close collaboration between human journalists and data mining technologies. She highlights the affinity between journalism's telos to reveal information and bring it to the public on one hand, and big data's efforts to reveal a hidden pattern in masses of information and bring it to people in a digestible form on the other. Beyond affinity in telos, in practice data mining enables journalists to produce new stories leading to "data-driven or data-centric journalism" (Irwin 2016, 130). Data-driven journalism becomes a must to cover Wikileaks releases; it is impossible to read all the documents, as their numbers are in tens of thousands and sometimes even hundreds of thousands. Searching for interesting emails is like looking for a needle in the haystack. Computerized text analysis tools are needed to discover meaningful insights. This practice illustrates how machine reading assists humans and saves the effort to read huge amounts of text as well as time. They also have the potential to find surprising stories, beyond the keywords searched after. Another way of implementing data mining technologies in journalism is to produce a story based on the mere analysis of bits and bytes. Irwin explains: "Data journalism is about finding the story in the data. Embedded data is about finding more of the story or an additional story in data that is not specifically part of the shared facts" (ibid., 137). For instance, a user's location in coordinates is just a set of numbers automatically produced. As such, these numbers are meaningless. But when combined, they may indicate, for example, how many people attended a manifestation. This is how data mining technologies may "bring forward an entirely new story" (ibid.).

So far for reading by algorithms. What about writing? Ten years prior to her analysis of machine reading and digital humanities, Hayles experimented in writing a printed book in the digital age. Her book, *Writing Machines* (2002), has a unique visual design, frequently resembling computer screen layouts. This is one of the tactics which Hayles uses to explore the complex relations between media and materiality, especially in light of the (false) assumption that digital media has no materiality. But the text of *Writing Machines* was not written by a machine. Hayles meant to show how writing practices have changed. As I write this chapter I am inspired by her work and think how the text will be read through digital displays. I remind myself that when I read a paper book I have visual cues like the page layout that help me scan it quickly in a second reading and find the parts I liked or found relevant. I can remember if a sentence was on the right or left page, up or down the page. But when reading a text on an ebook reader or on a computer screen, the cues are different. It is likely to be subtitles, as well as an unusual structure of the paragraph (i.e., bullets, a very long paragraph or very short) or several words in italics in the middle of the paragraph. In *Writing Machines* Hayles imports some of these practices back into the printed version. The result is not always clear, but the effect is remarkable. Hayles' experimental *Writing Machines* can be regarded as an early phase of a paradigm shift. It raises writers' awareness to the unique characteristics of digital human reading, that is, reading through digital technologies.

The next phase of machine writing can be found in the writing of notifications, small pieces of text that can be displayed one-by-one or together as a tendency. Usually in the framework of mobile apps, notifications indicate an action, a location, or a state-of-mind. When the app notifies, the user as well as others can "read" the notification. What is interesting for the evolution of machine writing is the automated notification apps. Here it makes a difference who posted the "away" notice on an instant messaging app (see Wiltse 2014, 173)—was it written by an algorithm, and hence the person might still be at her desk? Or was it written by the person, by intentionally setting her status to "away"? The app CouchCachet (mentioned by Wiltse) provides a similar dilemma as it "checks-in" at a location of a party, even if the user did not attend it. The purpose is to build a certain reputation to the user. The target reader is not the user but his or her acquaintances and followers.

Down the road of digital writing's evolution, I am reminded of Lev Manovich's *Software Takes Command* (2013) where he shows how media architecture is shifting from document to performance. While a document is fixed and can be accessed in an identical way over and over again, performance is the unstable representation we see when we access online navigation maps, scenes in games, or real-time stock exchange data. Because algorithms "write" these texts (frequently based on notifications as explained before), they keep changing according to the time they are produced and frequently according to the person who operates the app. Unlike traditional documents which one (human) could read time and again, under the performance regime the displayed text cannot be re-read. It will always change the next time it is displayed. Hayles' *Writing Machines* was a baby step in this direction.

If we agree with Manovich on the shift in media architectures, we need to understand how machines write. Let's return to journalism. There we can find robo-journalism in which algorithms scan huge amounts of data and quickly build articles out of them. Today robo-journalism is done mostly in the areas of financial reporting and coverage of sports events. These areas were selected for the table-like data structures so that algorithms can easily read them. It is interesting to note, however, that today's automated article writing technics have human origins, as they use "machine learning" technologies. It means that human journalists "train" the system with sample writings and "teach" it how to write various articles. It is necessary as long as the articles are produced for human reading. While most human readers will not be able to notice if a financial news article was written by a human or by an algorithm, sometimes there is a difference. Ethical, moral, and intellectual property issues arise.

How should the postphenomenological scheme look like in this situation of machine writing? Here Verbeek's work on technological intentionality is of prime importance and the examples brought in this section can highlight the role of the arrow that is not directly linked to the "I." In this variation of the postphenomenological scheme the "I" is in brackets:

(I—) tech → text → world

Bracketing the "I" means the human withdraws to the background at the stage of writing. This variation is complemented by the classic formulation of hermeneutic relations in which the text is read and interpreted, no matter who or what wrote it.

SUMMARY AND SOME OPEN QUESTIONS

In this chapter I made three moves: In the first I reviewed the postphenomenological hermeneutic relations to show how they are limited to reading, and to explain why they cannot represent writing. My main thesis was that there is no reference to the trace left in the world resulting from the act of writing, and that writing in the postphenomenological research ends up in embodiment relations that stress the changes in the "I" and not those in the world. The focus on the reading phase overlooks the writing phase. It takes the writing as a given, and there are hardly any discussions on the writing as such. Future research can develop the postphenomenological scheme to answer questions like: who wrote? Was it a "who" or a "what"? Or is it a combination of them, like in the case of a dashboard that reflects not only the technical assemblage that "writes" a certain notification, but also the designer and the engineer who programmed the system to alert a specific condition in a specific form. Is it a LED that changes its light, so that the color functions as a "text"? How to model such a cue that urges the user to look elsewhere—in a brochure or on a website—for explanations and meaning?

My next move started with a mapping of the differences between reading and writing according to the constituents of the postphenomenological scheme—I, technology, and world. Reading and writing are different modes of mediation. They can take place in different times and places, and frequently by different people. This is true not only for digital media but also for traditional media like printing press, television, and radio. It was an opportunity for me to start exploring the situation in which embodiment relations may end up as hermeneutic relations, taking into account the rise of the Anthropocene. In this age, we identify traces that were not visible before, or were not noticeable, and "read" the consequences of embodiment relations, such as gas emissions.

The mapping served as a launching pad to the last move. Here I developed the main thesis of this chapter starting with an investigation of possible variations of the postphenomenological scheme to represent writing relations. Through these variations, I attempted to model the trace created in the world by the emergence of text in the act of writing, as well as the need to differentiate between the technological device and the content.

In light of recent developments in digital technologies, and mainly AI, the third step seemed to be a must. For this purpose I reviewed the paradigm shift from Simondon's concretization in which a certain element performs more than one function, thereby increasing the overall system's efficiency, to an opposite digital paradigm in which each function is performed by a discrete software code. AI deepens this paradigm shift by breaking the linear argumentation to a rhizomatic "digging potatoes" form of research. This is what Alberto Romele called the long road to a hermeneutic approach to digital technologies (Romele 2016). It is my hope that this chapter will lay the foundations for new postphenomenological models for the media that AI technologies produce.

NOTES

1. http://deepdreamgenerator.com/.

2. Created by GeorgiaTech's Gil Weinberg, see http://www.gtcmt.gatech.edu/projects/shimon.

3. https://www.narrativescience.com/; see also http://www.wired.com/2012/04/can-an-algorithm-write-a-better-news-story-than-a-human-reporter/.

4. Van Den Eede (2012) asserts that the word "interplay"—and not mediation—should be at the center of the analysis in order to underline the co-constitution and co-construction of humans and their technologies.

5. Van Den Eede (2012) explains that "the medium is the message" can be read as deterministic statement originating from a substantivist outlook, or as a relational statement that lays the foundations for a mediation theory. He suggests a third reading, based on another framework of McLuhan according to which "every new medium takes an older medium for its content—literally" (ibid., 165). This framework, he claims, overcomes the form-content dichotomy.

6. Ihde calls this "double translation process" (Ihde 1990, 92).

7. Verbeek had a somewhat different direction and set of examples. He describes a situation in which technological intentionality is not necessarily directed to an accurate representation of the world, but rather constructs a new way of seeing the world. He gives an example of an art work using a unique technique of photography to create an image of the world that is empty from anything that moves, leaving in the picture only what is constant and unmovable. The focus in this example is on the viewers, that is, the act of reading. Verbeek gives another example of composite intentionality; this time the world representation is based on input from a stereographic camera and some manipulation of the photographs so that the result is—again—an imaginary world picture. But this time it can be viewed only with the help of a 3D headset. He terms it "constructive intentionality" because the camera and the additional viewing technology construct a reality in such a way that the result is imaginary. It reminds me of Deep Dream Generator mentioned at the beginning of this chapter that generates dream-like images based on images the user uploads. Today, I believe, we can find practical digital technologies that produce such cyborg relations, for example, any Augmented Reality application. The direction I wish to pursue in this double arrow postphenomenology scheme is somewhat different. Instead of examining the viewer, I focus on the writer-author and instead of works of art based on digital media, I examine analog and digital everyday writings. It is not surprising that digital technologies led Verbeek to formulate new postphenomenology schemes. Once we reconfigure notions and structures to accommodate the new technologies, we realize that the new notions and structure can apply to existing technologies as well. Writing fits into Verbeek's composite intentionality scheme, with its double intentionality. It adds a dimension of leaving a trace in the world and thereby changing it.

8. Simondon notes that the overall design in such a case exceeds the designer's original intentions. Ihde provides a similar observation and terms it "the designer fallacy" (2008), though Ihde's notion is wider in scope and is applicable also to non-concrete technologies.

REFERENCES

Derrida, J. (1976). *Of Grammatology*. Trans. G. C. Spivak. Baltimore: Johns Hopkins University.

Feenberg, A. (2006). "Active and Passive Bodies: Don Ihde's Phenomenology of the Body." In E. Selinger (ed.), *Postphenomenology: A Critical Companion to Ihde*. Albany, NY: State University of New York Press, 189–196.

———. (2016). "Concretizing Simondon and Constructivism A Recursive Contribution to the Theory of Concretization." *Science, Technology & Human Values*.

Forss, A. (2012). "Cells and the (Imaginary) Patient: The Multistable Practitioner–Technology–Cell Interface in the Cytology Laboratory." *Medicine, Health Care and Philosophy* 15 (3): 295–308.

Hayles, N. K. (2002). *Writing Machines*. Cambridge, MA: MIT Press.

———. (2012). *How We Think: Digital Media and Contemporary Technogenesis*. Chicago: University of Chicago Press.

Ihde, D. (2010). *Heidegger's Technologies: Postphenomenological Perspectives*. New York: Fordham University Press.

———. (1990). *Technology and the Lifeworld: From Garden to Earth*. Bloomington/Indianapolis: Indiana University Press.

———. (2008). "The Designer Fallacy and Technological Imagination." In P. E. Vermaas, P. Kroes, A. Light, and S. E. Moore (eds.), *Philosophy and Design: From Engineering to Architecture*. Springer, 51–61.

Iliadis, A. (2015). "Two Examples of Concretization." *Platform: Journal of Media and Communication* 6: 86–95.

Irwin, S. O. (2016). *Digital Media: Human–Technology Connection*. Lanham: Lexington Books.

Liberati, N. (2016). "Augmented Reality and Ubiquitous Computing: The Hidden Potentialities of Augmented Reality." *AI & SOCIETY* 31 (1): 17–28.

Manovich, L. (2013). *Software Takes Command*. New York/London: Bloomsberry Academics.

Romele, A. (2016). "Toward a Digital Hermeneutics." *Techné: Research in Philosophy and Technology* 20 (1): 76–83.

Rosenberger, R. (2008). "Perceiving Other Planets: Bodily Experience, Interpretation, and the Mars Orbiter Camera." *Human Studies* 31: 63–75.

Simondon, G. (1958). *Du mode d'existence des objets techniques*. Paris: Aubier.

Stiegler, B. (1998). *Technics and Time, 1: The Fault of Epimetheus*. Trans. R. Beardsworth and G. Collins. Stanford: Stanford University Press.

Van Den Eede, Y. (2012). *Amor Technologiae: Marshall McLuhan as Philosopher of Technology—Toward a Philosophy of Human-Media Relationships*. Brussels: VUBPress.

Verbeek, P.-P. (2008). "Cyborg Intentionality: Rethinking the Phenomenology of Human–Technology Relations." *Phenomenology and Cognitive Science* 7: 387–395.

Wellner, G. (2014). "The Quasi-Face of the Cell Phone: Rethinking Alterity and Screens." *Human Studies* 37 (3): 299–316.

Wiltse, H. (2014). "Unpacking Digital Material Mediation." *Techné: Research in Philosophy and Technology* 18 (3): 154–182.

Chapter 12

The Mediumness of World

A Love Triangle of Postphenomenology, Media Ecology, and Object-Oriented Philosophy

Yoni Van Den Eede

In thinking about postphenomenology and media, one may eventually wind up asking: Where do media begin and where do they end? Or, one may begin the other way around and commence the inquiry from the widest angle possible: from a certain point of view, everything is a medium.

Chairs, tables, insurance companies, metro ticket stubs, Marxism, Taylor Swift, ... In the end, even the universe can be understood as a medium, Lance Strate concludes his survey of media ecology, *Echoes and Reflections* (2006, 91).[1] Indeed, for media ecology—the field of research that grew out of the work of Marshall McLuhan—no strict dividing line can be drawn between something that is a medium and something that is not. Media ecology is set to investigate the interactions between media: their "ecology." And surely, as one starts upon such an endeavor, one swiftly discovers how even "classic" media such as television, radio, or newspapers seamlessly flow over into other components (of social, political, economic, material, biological, psychological, ideological, ... character), that we thought independent of them, but that are actually part and parcel of those media and hence "medial" in nature just as much. With the terminology of media ecology: media are, and make, environments. And so, about everything in the universe can be said to be a medium.

But are we still saying something meaningful when we thus expand the scope of the term "medium"? Such a maneuver is reminiscent of talk of "the world": the world is unfair, the world is going mad, it's the way of the world, ... Really only on an abstract level can our minds span this kind of width. Abstractness does not preclude meaningfulness, however. In fact it's philosophy's core business to engage with immensely stretchable notions, like world. In phenomenology, of course, "world" has a special place, and a specific meaning. A good part of Heidegger's *Being and Time* is devoted to a systematic analysis of world, worldhood, and being-in-the-world. Ihde's postphenomenology sets out to study human-technology-world relations. Yet, only recently, a curious criticism has been voiced in this regard against the postphenomenological framework: Diane Michelfelder, in a commentary on the current state of the field (2015), argues that postphenomenology largely ignores "world." More than a criticism, perhaps, Michelfelder has raised a challenge. In what follows, I will look into her critique and take up the challenge—albeit without any reasonable hope of meeting it.

The key, I propose, is exactly the "medium" notion. The short summary of my argument goes as follows: if Michelfelder's worry is warranted, world can be reimported into postphenomenology by way of that other infinitely elastic term, that is, medium. Put otherwise: *mediation* alone is not sufficient; we also require *media*. Nevertheless, I need to put a triad of approaches in place to make this clear. Postphenomenology and media ecology are two of them; the third one is Graham Harman's object-oriented philosophy. My aim is to make clear how these three perhaps unlikely bedfellows fit together. But first, I must start to elaborate in more detail about Michelfelder's concerns.

MICHELFELDER'S CHALLENGE

It is in the *Postphenomenological Investigations* volume (Rosenberger and Verbeek 2015), which collects postphenomenological studies on a variety of subjects, that Michelfelder launches her critique in a part bearing the heading "Critical Interlocutors." Indeed critically interrogating the postphenomenological perspective, she charts two possible futures for it. In the first future, postphenomenologists keep on doing what they are already energetically involved in: further developing and fine-tuning the main conceptual instruments, and applying these to investigations of various human-technology relations. As such, this would already be a laudable undertaking, Michelfelder believes. But the second future—both futures do not exclude each other—is a bit more daring. Here, postphenomenologists would begin to account more for the notion of *world*, the component of human-technology-world relations that according to Michelfelder is at the moment in the postphenomenological corpus mostly taken for granted.

Postphenomenology has focused mainly on human-technology interactions, she finds, and has tended to disregard world. It has zoomed in on the ways in which humans embody and perceive technologies, and on how technologies mediate perception, interpretation, praxis, and even morality. But it has scarcely examined "how technology discloses the world as a whole" (Michelfelder 2015, 241). Michelfelder illustrates by referencing Peter-Paul Verbeek. Verbeek in his *Moralizing Technology* (2011) elucidates how a technology like the FoodPhone mediates eating experiences, behavior, and practices, but, as Michelfelder points out, that analysis is achieved without any reference to the world as a whole. It limits itself to the user's perspective plain and simple.

But why should it matter, one may ask, that "world" as such become more of a topic? Technologies and humans are *part of* world, so even if we only focus on those first two components, one might say, world is always already there, represented in our discussion. This is precisely what the notion of mediation is meant to convey in a sense: the human-technology relation is primordial in that it constitutes the relata and so calls something new into being. The user+FoodPhone constellation is not the sum of its parts—it creates its own reality, makes the existence of user and FoodPhone at all possible. But this is not what Michelfelder points to. She refers to the notion of world, analyzed by Heidegger in *Being and Time*, as the "wholeness" "within which our experience is disclosed to us in a familiar and trustworthy way" (Michelfelder 2015, 242). World is the non-thematic environment we are engaged in with our understanding and our practices. Or, in Maurice Merleau-Ponty's words, to which we are "geared-in." And Michelfelder is concerned that postphenomenology, by downplaying the importance of world as wholeness, will eventually be unable to make sense of technologies that endanger exactly that "gearing-in."

Specifically, she is thinking of emerging technologies that lie largely beyond the grasp of phenomenological attention because their operations—what they *do*, with the Verbeekian turn of phrase (2005)—escape the bounds of the immediately experientially given. The latter is what (post)phenomenology in the first instance attends to. A technology that does its work behind the scenes of everyday experience, in other words, risks staying invisible to postphenomenology, Michelfelder warns:

> A different way of putting this would be to say that if we were to talk about how an individual through this technology intends or is directed toward the world in a particular way, it would make no sense. But, such technologies can in fact work to co-shape human behavior in a way that could serve to help diminish overall trust in the world that one experiences. (Michelfelder 2015, 243)

Michelfelder offers the example of the American company Nordstrom which in 2012 started a project that involved tracking the customers in its stores through Wi-Fi. The project was terminated eventually due to customers' complaints about privacy invasion. Indeed one of the troublesome aspects was that customers were not—phenomenologically—aware of being tracked. This, Michelfelder argues, is a different kind of technology than Verbeek's example of the FoodPhone, which is more evidently based on "user-perceivable inputs leading to user-perceivable outcomes" (ibid., 245).

One can think of many other such—existing or possible—instances of technologies operating beyond the curtain of immediate, everyday experience, that still indirectly impact that experience. Postphenomenology does at least to some extent conceptualize such technologies, namely, in terms of "background relations" (Ihde 1990, 108ff.), but Michelfelder seems to talk about something more. The impact that these technologies have on everyday experience may be quite significant. Especially in our days of increasing, what I would call, "algorithmization" of daily life and society, we can expect this kind of phenomenon only to grow. The calculations, data analyzing, profiling, and targeting that one can imagine a future Internet of Things to be doing, for instance, is immense. I myself might just be having the experience of taking a piece of cheese out of the fridge. The fridge might, in a matter (still) analyzable by postphenomenology, suggest to me to eat less dairy because I already consumed my daily recommended amount. But somewhere, in a farm full of servers, an algorithm might be concluding that future employers should be informed about my alarming levels of craving for animal fat (in a not so unimaginable half-dystopian future world in which only the fittest find work). And that is a different thing. Not only would such a given escape my experience at that moment, I would have to undertake a whole lot of work to discover it. The more algorithms are operating, in such a way, behind the scenes and surreptitiously steering our courses of action and our thinking processes, the more Michelfelder's critique becomes pertinent, even acute.

Michelfelder puts forward a couple of potential reasons why postphenomenology has been cultivating this blind spot. The notion of world as a "whole" may be evoking dystopian critiques of technology such as the later Heidegger's, critiques that postphenomenology seeks to surpass. Also, postphenomenology's empirical disposition may cause it to look only into direct user-technology interactions and particular practices, since the aforementioned invisible "world" dynamics are much harder—even impossible, one may add?—to map empirically. In tandem with both these points, it is perhaps postphenomenology's "non-foundationalism" that prevents it from digging into deeper ontological terrain, Michelfelder adds. Her remarks at this point are much in line with recent debates going on within the larger context of the philosophy of technology about the status of the "empirical turn" (Achterhuis 2001) that was meant to correct the ills of all-encompassing, essentialist technology analyses, and that has defined the field in its contemporary guises. At the moment there is a concern, contrary to the "turn," that philosophy of technology has once more become too instrumentalist in trying to correct for classic essentialism, threatening to lose its critical clout in the process (cf. Van Den Eede, Goeminne, and Van den Bossche 2015; Scharff 2012; Rao et al. 2015). Calls are launched for among other things, a re-transcendentalization or "transcendental (re)turn" (Smith 2015a; Smith 2015b; Lemmens 2015). Postphenomenology, not unexpectedly, is often a target for these concerns, and so Michelfelder's considerations can to a large extent be inscribed into this stream of critical developments of late.

Nonetheless, with regard to her argument specifically, what to do then? Michelfelder leaves it largely up to postphenomenologists to work out an answer to her challenge. But she does give a couple of cues, some deliberate and others more "between the lines." Most particularly, she suggests that postphenomenology become more "speculative." She is not referring in particular to the branch of "speculative philosophy" that has arisen in recent decades, although she does quote Graham Harman, yet only as an aside (on the topic of how philosophies evolve). But why not take this cue literally and consult with the likes of speculative realism? Another cue along these lines, though certainly less deliberately, is given when she reverts to the—for postphenomenology—quintessential Heidegger passage, namely, *Being and Time*'s tool analysis, arguing that postphenomenology stresses its "tool use" (or praxical) aspect, rather than its function as part of Heidegger's investigation into worldhood. This leads us straight into, indeed, the "object-oriented philosophy" of Harman, for whom the tool analysis is also foundational, but exactly in the way that Michelfelder wants to see elucidated. Finally, and by all means in the least deliberative sense, the concept of world as environment, and the attending idea of technologies being able to disclose—or close off—worlds in an environmental manner, is reminiscent of McLuhan's notion of media-as-environments, and the idea of media ecology.

What emerges is a triangle of approaches—postphenomenology, McLuhanist media ecology, object-oriented philosophy—the combination of which, I propose, can help to account for world in the way Michelfelder envisions it. In the following sections, I will treat of them in consecutive order, but always in pairs, as the perspectives are related to each other in particular ways.

That said, the question will eventually remain to which extent Michelfelder's critique is accurate. First, does postphenomenology really ignore world in the sense described? Does it not already do what Michelfelder proposes it do to, and if so, to what extent? As said, there is for instance its treatment of technologies retreating from immediate awareness, in the elaboration of "background relations" ... Second, if Michelfelder's critique is correct, how should this essentially affect postphenomenology's status as an approach, a method, a field? Michelfelder seems to suggest that by neglecting world, it risks to stay superficial and even make itself obsolete—but is this so? Can postphenomenology not simply "survive" as a user-centered, use-centered approach? These questions will hover just beneath the surface of my survey, and in the closing section I will return to them in more detail.

POSTPHENOMENOLOGY AND MEDIA ECOLOGY

Let me start—appropriate in a volume such as this—with McLuhan's media theory, and see how it relates to postphenomenology. McLuhan is of course most famous for his aphorism "the medium is the message" (2003, 19ff.) and for the expression he coined of "the global village" (1962, 21ff.). The latter has perhaps a stronger foothold in the popular imagination—and certainly it has been picked up with renewed vigor in our days of globe-spanning information networks—but the former is more important in relation to the conceptual groundwork of his thought. In fact, it holds in condensed form the gist of his framework.

With "the medium is the message" McLuhan means to formulate the central insight that "media" are not what we believe or perceive them to be: they are not simple channels through which information is transported; in actuality they are *double-sided.* Or more precisely, our relation to them is double-sided.

In a first step, McLuhan defines media or technologies—the two are synonyms in his account—in a quite straightforward manner: they are extensions of a human sense or body part. The wheel is an extension of the foot, the hammer is an extension of the hand, ... The medium enhances a certain functionality, for example, the ability to move, materializing it in a form such that a device or tool helps us to achieve a specific goal faster, cheaper, more accurately, with less effort, more impact, and so on. Thus the wheel enables us to travel greater distances with less energy expenditure (in a direct sense on our part, that is; there is always energy spent, be it by the horse pulling the cart or the engine burning the fuel ...). Extension theory has been discussed now and then in recent years in the philosophy of technology (for overviews cf. Van Den Eede 2014; Steinert 2015), and surely there remains a lot of disagreement about the notion, but one of the fundamental ideas behind McLuhan's version of it is the almost ethical reminder that media "hail from us," they originate in "us." And subsequently we remain tethered to them, because once they are put "out there," they do not become neutral means-to-ends: they "feedback" upon us. With a phrase often attributed to McLuhan, but actually voiced by John Culkin: "We shape our tools and thereafter they shape us" (Culkin 1967, 38).

So much for the genesis of media; what happens then is a strange thing: we forget their origins. We start to look at them as if they are just things, standing apart from us. Specifically, this "Narcissus narcosis" (McLuhan 2003, 63ff.) implies in practice that we solely focus on a medium's content. Narcissus watched his mirror image in the water, entranced and numbed by it, but unaware that the image "hailed from him." He can only see the image, not the context of the reflection. Just like that, we are enthralled by the television's programs, deal only with the newspaper's articles (the "news"), read and write emails without any consideration of the wider machinations and dynamics of the technology. We see the content, but we neglect form: form being not so much the stylistic or visual-organizational aspects of a medium (the newspaper's layout, the television's screen and cables, et cetera), but the *effects* of that medium—the wider impact that it has on our perception, on society, on our ways of looking at the world. With an expression already cited: every medium makes an *environment* in this sense. It helps to create or confirm a certain way of doing things and of thinking about things. Television makes possible a world of fast news coverage from all over the world (indeed, it helps to install the "global village"), in which the boundary between reality and fiction becomes thinner or harder to pinpoint. Email brings into being an environment in which the speed of communication becomes paramount. And taken together, all media form a "media ecology" of media environments intersecting, crisscrossing, crashing, and fusing with each other. But we do not notice this immediately, as we are too busy working "within" media—just using them and no further questions asked.

So, media *themselves*, that is, their form, not their content, are the *real* message, the message we should be paying attention to. We are stuck in the middle of this dialectic of what immediately appears to us and what is lurking beyond—it should already be clear how this is pertinent for our topic here. Now does McLuhan's media-ecological approach differ in this sense from postphenomenology, does it attend more to "world," or not?

I have elaborated upon the convergences and divergences between the two perspectives elsewhere (Van Den Eede 2012, 175–9), but reiterate here briefly. Notwithstanding a certain "disconnect" between the fields of media ecology and philosophy of technology (Ralón 2016), Ihde and McLuhan do share some premises, analytical instruments, and methodological practices. McLuhan's "the medium is the message" can be compared to Ihde's concepts of "non-neutral acidity" (1993, 65), "instrumental inclination" (2012, 149), and "technological intentionality" (1990, 48, 103). Both tend to see relation as primordial. In McLuhan's case this is perhaps best epitomized in his riff on the book title of Richards and Ogden, *The Meaning of Meaning*: "'the meaning of meaning' is relationship" (McLuhan and Nevitt 1972, 3). In spite of suspicions about technological determinism, McLuhan's framework can be seen as a theory about mediation in the first instance, not so much about media as such (cf. Strate 2011, 60–61). Postphenomenology, of course, is often referred to as mediation theory (especially by Verbeek). Also, McLuhan's tension of extension or enhancement versus "feedback" finds a pendant in Ihde's amplification-reduction scheme. Both moreover look at perception and how the mediating effects of technologies can be felt all the way through to the cultural level; in Ihde's terminology, from microperception to macroperception.

Nevertheless, there are differences too, and these are just as relevant for our purposes, for they link up with Michelfelder's challenge. While postphenomenology limits itself mostly to an investigation of specific human-technology connections, one could say, McLuhan's media ecology takes off for a bird's-eye view, an across-the-board examination of cultural conditions. This endeavor is condensed into the content-form or—in a later phase of his work—the figure-ground dichotomy. Figure is what we pay attention to (content), ground is the background in our perception that does not become a focus (form), but that has influence on the figure. And McLuhan himself hints at the difference between his take and phenomenology's when he comments, somewhat mysteriously, about Heidegger: "Heidegger is using Husserl's rubric that 'the possible precedes the actual,' which is to observe abstractly that ground comes before figure. He has not noted that [...] its structure is entirely due to its interface with figures" (McLuhan and McLuhan 1988, 63). On the face of it, McLuhan would seem to an extent to echo Michelfelder's concern—the "bigger picture" (ground) or at least the way in which it interacts with the obviously given (figure) is disregarded—be it then toward Heidegger himself. I will not go into this apparent similarity (for more on McLuhan and phenomenology, cf. also Van Den Eede 2012), but simply take it as a slight suggestion that McLuhan's framework can help us with the problem at hand.

MEDIA ECOLOGY AND OBJECT-ORIENTED PHILOSOPHY

This, then, brings me to the next "pair": the intersection of media ecology and Graham Harman's object-oriented philosophy (henceforth OOP).[2] For in Harman's outlook, Heidegger returns full force. Harman is seen as one of the first representatives of "speculative realism" but has clearly carved out in the past decade his own niche: OOP. In this theory, Harman fuses various streams of continental philosophy into a brand new realist ontology. Beyond idealism, beyond materialism, he proposes the world to consist of objects. This might sound obvious to common sense, but for the history of philosophy, it is not. Throughout the "relational turn" of the 20th century, the notion of "substance," having been dominant for centuries on end, fell into grave disrepute, to be replaced by approaches such as process philosophy, systems thinking, (post)structuralism, and others stressing the primacy of some form of relation instead. The "in between" became predominant. Phenomenology and postphenomenology are part of this evolution.

Given this, it might seem strange that Harman has successfully morphed Heidegger's philosophy into an object-centered perspective in his development of OOP. The term "object-oriented" may be misleading in this regard:

relation does still have a place in Harman's theory. His objects are composites of substance and relation, but unlike any ontological model has previously suggested. They are *fourfold*, comprising a real object, a sensual object, and two kinds of qualities: real and sensual (Harman 2011). The innovation of this model concerns the real object: on the basis of Heidegger's tool analysis, Harman argues that this real object escapes all contact, perception, and conceptualization. But it is still there. And it can interact with other objects, but only indirectly, vicariously.

The bold move that Harman makes is to turn the orthodox Heidegger interpretation upside down. We simply have been looking at it the wrong way, he explains: "the hammer itself might easily be taken for something relational. But this is the central falsehood of mainstream Heidegger studies" (Harman 2009b, 141). Readiness-to-hand, he states—"tool-being" in his words (2002)—is not relation, but substance. In that capacity, tool-being is an autonomous, "subterranean realm," enigmatic and unattainable. In order for it to be visible, "unconcealed," it would have to be present-at-hand, that is, relational. Only relation is perceivable. But the "real object" stays forever "concealed." We can never grasp or perceive it directly. "Phenomena are only rare cases of visible things emerging from a dominant silent background of equipment" (Harman 2007, 63). Crucially, this counts for every object individually: tool-being is not one gigantic, plasma-like force or domain, in which all things in some or other way partake; no, every object harbors its own substance. Every object holds, within itself, its very own "mystery."

But Harman goes further. He contests Heidegger's anthropocentric viewpoint that casts *Dasein* as uniquely placed to reveal being. Not only is part of each object—its "real" core—always inaccessible in a direct way, this counts for *all* interactions between *all* objects: material, immaterial, organic, inorganic, … . Truly all things in the world are on equal ontological footing in this regard. All objects interact with each other across this chasm of "ingraspability." "[N]ot only *human* relations with a thing reduce it to presence-at-hand, but *any relations at all*" (Harman 2009b, 142; original emphasis). With one of Harman's well-known examples (derived from Islamic occasionalism): when fire burns cotton, the fire meets the cotton "as" cotton, but part of the latter remains hidden to the fire, as it remains hidden to all other things—its tool-being. The fire can only grasp the cotton as present-at-hand.

I mentioned that Harman's objects are fourfold. Two of the dimensions are thus ready-to-hand (substance, tool-being) and present-at-hand (relation). In the interest of focus I leave the other two (object versus qualities) undiscussed (but cf. Van Den Eede 2012, 192–4). More interesting here is Harman's special involvement with McLuhan. Intriguingly, Harman has interpreted McLuhan's work along the lines of his OOP, reading it as a full-blown ontology.[3] Also this meeting of frameworks I have treated of more fully in other places (cf. Van Den Eede 2012; Van Den Eede 2016). Above I have remarked how McLuhan can certainly be seen as a proponent of relationalism, of "network thinking." Surprisingly, however, Harman regards him as a kindred spirit who favors "objects" just as much. McLuhan can be read as an "object" thinker *as well*. His eventually very broad definition of "media"—encompassing all human-made things, including immaterial entities such as ideas and ideologies—foreshadows Harman's ontology, and retrospectively a substantivist bend can, in embryonic form, be discerned in his thought (Harman 2009a; Harman 2013; cf. Van Den Eede 2016). Harman reads McLuhan in this sense, equating the latter's media with his objects, and finding a pendant of the *Vorhandenheit-Zuhandenheit* dichotomy in McLuhan's figure-ground distinction. Everything, truly everything, is a medium, it can be said, creating its own "environment," in which something always stands out as prominent (content) while something else stays concealed (form, i.e., effects). (In the field of media ecology, analogous extensions of the medium notion can already be found. We are here reminded again of Strate's suggestion, referred to in the introduction, that even the universe is a medium. But no other approach does the broadening work so rigorously as Harman's.)

Here as well, there are differences between the two approaches, although in Harman's view they stay rather minor. Harman sees McLuhan as still too anthropocentric, looking at things too much from the standpoint of human perception and action, while that double-sided dynamic between figure (relation) and ground (real object; substance) actually plays out across the whole world of things, that is, among things in themselves just as well. One medium can never grasp, "perceive" or meet another medium fully, in its completeness; always only a part of each is exposed to another. So Harman's OOP may work here as an inducement to push even further away from a user-centered view. We have to take into account—at least the possibility—that what transpires between "us" and objects (i.e., technologies) and between us and the world, also goes on between objects among each other and between objects and the world.

OBJECT-ORIENTED PHILOSOPHY AND POSTPHENOMENOLOGY

Let us then complete the triad: How does OOP relate to postphenomenology? It does take some mental gymnastics to compare the two. They seem prima facie so removed from each other, even at odds with each other. Postphenomenology is relationalist, OOP takes substance on board. Postphenomenology looks at things from the human standpoint (as classic phenomenology did), OOP attempts to inhabit the viewpoint of objects.

As said, Harman deliberately goes against the grain of decades of "pragmatic" Heidegger readings that take the tool analysis to be about human praxis and experience. On the face of it, it would seem that postphenomenology can be categorized under the kind of approaches that Harman seeks to abandon. "Though Heidegger's tool analysis is usually glossed as 'unconscious practice vs. conscious seeing,' this hollow interpretation must be replaced by a duel of 'thing vs. relations'" (Harman 2009b, 142). To be sure, as far as Harman claims that the tool analysis does not only form the cornerstone of Heidegger's thought, but that it can also constitute if elaborated a bit further a completely new ontology and metaphysics, postphenomenology would probably largely concur. It also sees the tool analysis as central to Heideggerian phenomenology and embraces some of its ontological underpinnings (cf. Ihde 1979; 2010). Only, the words "completely new" would maybe repel postphenomenologists, as they rather seem to want to continue and consolidate relationalism's legacy. Also, postphenomenology does clearly understand the tool analysis as being mainly about the human use of tools and other materials, while Harman would forcefully assert that tool-being, that is, readiness-to-hand, "never becomes present to practical action any more than it does to theoretical awareness" (Harman 2002, 1).

Yet postphenomenology, if it were a person, would probably ask OOP: So what? Why do we need substance at all? And why should we take the standpoint of objects? We are concerned with how technologies affect "us." OOP, from its side, would scorn postphenomenology for its outworn, praxical interpretation of the tool analysis, making it unable to see beyond relation toward a deeper reality that has certain forces in store (more on this right away). Also, OOP would judge postphenomenology's stance to be anthropocentric.

The suspicion on both sides may be warranted, but since I am particularly concerned here with postphenomenology, we want to concentrate in the first instance on the (potential) skepticism of postphenomenology toward OOP. What fresh perspective could OOP bring to postphenomenology's study of technology? To answer that question, it serves to inquire into what actually connects both approaches. This connection can be found in the way they deal with transparent-opaque dynamics (cf. Van Den Eede 2011). Both are in a comparable degree concerned with the difference between that which appears and that which stays hidden. To this extent, they both strive to safeguard the distinction between readiness-to-hand and presence-at-hand (Ihde regrets that the later Heidegger collapses it, cf. 1979, 128; 2010, 54). For postphenomenology, the ready-to-hand "part" of human-technology-world relations is the transparent part that disappears from view in different ways depending on which type of relation is at stake (cf. Van Den Eede 2011). For OOP, there cannot be anything more distinguished from relation, that is, present-at-hand, than tool-being, the "real object."

Yet according to postphenomenology, the ready-to-hand is what we are "part of," in being enveloped within equipment. For Harman, by contrast, the ready-to-hand stays forever beyond our grasp: we can only "relate" in/with the mode of the present-at-hand. So the disagreement seems to be about *where* hiddenness is.

This is an unsolvable conundrum, it would seem at face value, given that indeed the hidden by definition can never be found. Even if it turns into something not hidden, it loses its status of being hidden. Exactly in this sense, the ready-to-hand and the present-at-hand *are* two mutually exclusive modes in between which a shift or switch happens—notwithstanding Verbeek's important observation that the two can perfectly be "present" together (2005); in fact in most human-technology-world relations, they naturally are. But something can only be either ready-to-hand or present-at-hand at any given point in time. And as long as the ready-to-hand stays hidden—and thus, in both postphenomenology and OOP, it can only *be* hidden—we can only make conjectures about its location.

Is this Harman's central move: to push the ready-to-hand further down the spectrum running from graspability to ungraspability? With postphenomenology, the ready-to-hand as relational network-of-concern stays immensely close to "us." Actually, it is primordial; it is what we in our assemblages with technologies *do*. Nothing could be more real, more tangible than practical engagement. Harman, conversely, pushes the real away behind the scenes of direct accessibility. What indeed could be the "use" of that, judging from the standpoint of the postphenomenological study into technology use?

Notwithstanding his distaste for practical-pragmatic explanations, Harman in fact continuously gives us hints as to the usefulness of the substance notion. His answer to the question "what is the use of posing substances beyond relational grasp?" could be paraphrased as follows: because of the little misty "extra" or surplus that substances offer. They are a sort of ontological vermiform appendix, of which it was once thought that it serves no particular function in the human body—yet it could still burst. It could still mess up the ordinary course of events. Substances are the puny "something more" that possibly disturb every present situation. They are, according to Harman, the "non-relational actuality" that offers the "material" for so many relevant or non-relevant shifts of direction: "Unless the thing holds something in reserve behind its current relations, nothing would ever change" (Harman 2009b, 187). Substance lurks beneath the surface, stays needed as a subliminal "engine of change" (Harman 2009a, 115), feeding and fueling, so to speak, relational constellations with a sort of actualizing "energy."

But, indeed, that engine stays hidden. "[S]ubstance is the ultimate underdog," Harman says (2009b, 49). Of course one could rebut that the idea of concealment does not automatically entail or even require the substance concept. Part of the relational network could be concealed to us too. But then the assumption would be that we could uncover, grasp, or perceive that specific part in some or other way. Whereas hidden substance stays hidden; it can only be perceived indirectly, through relation. Its capacity for surprise is total.

Important to remark in this context, is that in my experience it takes some practice, or maybe more precisely, some habituation, to really "feel" Harman's point. In that sense, it is much like phenomenological method: one also needs to acquaint oneself gradually with the "phenomenological" way of seeing before one can begin to "get it." This process might take years—like slowly getting to love a music album you have been listening to over and over. That might exactly be the key for unlocking Harman's OOP: it needs to be regarded as a prism through which one looks at the world—not simply a "theory"—and in which one must immerse oneself first before reaping any rewards, rather than as a bag of ideas. Eventually, one may start to realize that Harman is actually trying to convey a very simple, commonsensical insight: "experience"—as the generic interaction of all things with each other—can only be selective. The following longer quote from *Bells and Whistles* helps to grasp this:

> How could flames and ocean waves exhaust the reality of what they strike any more than we humans can? The fire interacts with the flammability of the cotton, not its whiteness and softness; the waves strike the sand as a feeble barrier, unaware of the odors that dogs have found there. The figure/ground interplay has nothing to do with the difference between conscious and unconscious and everything to do with how things are distorted and simplified by any relation whatsoever, whether with human or nonhuman things. (Harman 2013, 185)

But still, how does this impact upon postphenomenology? In fact, a couple of authors have already tried to link up the two perspectives. Golfo Maggini (2014) in a paper on the theme of technology in Heidegger's *Being and Time* compares Harman and Verbeek in light of their reading of that work. Somewhat surprisingly, she finds they have in common that they both aim to rise above the purely human standpoint. Indeed Verbeek works to give things and what they "do" their right due—an inclination definitely not present in Heidegger. But a bit later, Maggini goes on to observe that Harman wants things to be more "encountered in themselves" (ibid., 100). She also mentions how both in their endeavor of "dehumanizing" the tool analysis (ibid., 103) engage with the work of Latour. Yet they do it in different ways eventually: Verbeek reads Latour as a constructivist, while Harman interprets him as an ontologist or metaphysician (ibid., 105). All in all, nevertheless, Maggini's Harman-Verbeek comparison, though diligent, does not seem to go far enough for our purposes.

A more venturesome effort comes from Matt Hayler in his *Challenging the Phenomena of Technology: Embodiment, Expertise, and Evolved Knowledge*

(2015), a book first and foremost situated within the domain of cognitive science, but that has relevance for philosophy of technology as well. Hayler sets out to give an account of technology use, more precisely of expert use, by combining embodied cognition theory, Ihdean postphenomenology, pragmatism, and OOP. He defines technology as an *encounter* of an object in use, and this definition rests in part on Heidegger's tool analysis, and partly on the notion of expertise: a technology only really becomes a technology when it is used with a certain level of skill. Otherwise, it just appears as a—possibly complex—constellation of parts. For example, if you don't know how to use a computer, it is just an indistinct mass of components for you, not a technology.[4] In itself this makes for a fascinating and provocative account of technology, but I will not discuss it further here; what interests me most is how Hayler takes Harman on board. He does this exactly by contrasting him with postphenomenology in a manner similar to my foregoing comparison: while postphenomenology sticks to relation exclusively, OOP offers the addition of a "more," that always escapes. Verbeek, for instance, Hayler explains, reduces artifacts to "their relations with their human users" (ibid., 168). Conversely, OOP denies the primordiality of the human-world relation.

From there onward, it is precisely the "surprise" element of Harman's substance, also described above, that starts to play a central role in Hayler's enterprise. For in his view, the process of becoming expert at using a technology amounts to a continuous meeting and anticipating of the unexpected aspects or events that every technology—every object—has in store. An amateur is most daunted by all those surprises, while the expert has come to known many of them. The latter can still be surprised, since an object—in line with OOP—is never wholly exhausted. That is the slight, and interesting, ingredient that Hayler wants to add to Harman's outlook: according to Hayler, although the object will always harbor surprises, a progressive evolution is possible in getting to "know" an object better and better. In this context, the traditional interpretation of the tool analysis as an account about human praxical "fluency" still stands and should be preserved next to Harman's more idiosyncratic version of it. What is more, this way of encountering objects concerns a form of knowledge, in the pragmatist sense: "expertise is about the minimisation of surprise through knowing; to know is to be able to act successfully" (ibid., 187). But then logically thinking through Harman's argument, Hayler points out how technologies (objects) can also acquire that sort of knowledge about "us": the better we get at using a technology, the better that technology gets at being used, in turn.

Hayler thus neatly fuses postphenomenology and OOP by exploiting their respective differences. In the closing section of this chapter, I want to further build on this exercise, returning again to Michelfelder's challenge and to the questions surrounding it.

THE TRIANGLE

To reiterate: I set out to discuss and meet Michelfelder's challenge that postphenomenology should give more attention to world, beyond its mainly use-centered standpoint. I also already foreshadowed that *media*, in contrast to *mediation*, would play a central role in this endeavor. And indeed, with the postphenomenology-McLuhan-Harman constellation, we get a picture of a world in which something of what postphenomenology investigates as the human-technology relation touches *all* interactions between "media," that is, every object-object interaction.

One may still wonder what the fuss is all about. Can't we suffice with postphenomenology-as-we-know-it? There is the analysis of background relations in Ihde, even though this gets much less attention than embodiment and hermeneutic relations—but we could expand it. Yet the question remains whether this would be sufficient to meet Michelfelder's challenge. The triadic constellation outlined here exactly enables us to make sense of the kind of emerging technologies Michelfelder points to: the algorithmic infrastructures "behind the scenes" that, so to speak, are starting to lead their own lives, interacting with each other in ways we humans do not always control or even understand anymore. The classic account of background relations may not be able to sufficiently explicate these phenomena. We have not quite yet arrived at *Terminator* or *Her*-like scenarios, but algorithmic structures at times exhibit a behavior that can be at least perceived as autonomous. In other words: a matter of media, not merely of mediation. There might be a "core" escaping "us." This was illustrated probably most spectacularly by the "flash crash" of 2010. For about half an hour on May 6, the American stock market, grounded heavily in algorithm-driven high-frequency trading (cf. Lewis 2015), crashed for mysterious reasons—signaling, as would become clear, the degree to which algorithms and no longer so much human intention steer the stock exchange. More than simply an economic problem, it indicated that algorithms' rapid-fire interaction has outgrown human control (cf. Salmon and Stokes 2010). This, admittedly, is conjecture and speculation—although speculating was what Michelfelder encouraged us to do—but perhaps "our" control diminishes *because* algorithms interact among each other across the relation-substance divide: they too cannot grasp each other completely. In terms of our triad: we have to reckon with the possibility that the media environments created by technologies stay partly oblivious to each other; how should we then ever get a good grip on them? Taking into account the possibility of these, with a term from Ian Bogost (2012), *alien* black holes—not just the invisibilities or transparencies in "our" dealings with "them"—is pivotal with regard to our attempt at understanding new technological environments.

But why then this combination of approaches? Why these three? My answer would be that they need each other in a certain sense. They interlock neatly, complementing and reinforcing each other nicely. This becomes clear when one imagines how they would each do, on their own, in terms of meeting Michelfelder's challenge. With regard to postphenomenology, of course, Michelfelder has done the exercise. But OOP in itself would also not suffice. It brings two innovations to the phenomenological framework: the notion of the inaccessible or of "surprise," and the widening of ontological scope to all things. But in a sense one could perceive it to do exactly the same thing as postphenomenology: focus on the "user"-object interaction solely, or to a too large degree. "User" here does then denote possibly every thing, but still: "world" to a certain extent remains absent in Harman's outlook, too. Harman also looks mostly at *this* "instance," *this* interaction. Witness his, again with a Bogost term (2012), "Latour litanies," style: candles, diesel engines, bus drivers, Rihanna, dodecahedrons, ... In recent work, though, Harman seems to have begun to remediate this lack. *Immaterialism* (2016) for instance is a first systematic attempt at analyzing how large infrastructures come about as composites of objects, becoming eventually an object in the Harmanist sense (the Dutch East India Company is his fascinating case). But for now, we do well to supplement OOP in our triad with McLuhanist media ecology, more precisely, with the one component that Harman in fact often tends to overlook (because he focuses more on his favored figure-ground dynamic): the notion of media-as-environments.

This notion leads us to a *cultural* analysis. In times in which growing, powerful globe-spanning networks go lurking behind the veil of perceivability, we need an analysis of "cultural" allure like that. For, lest one too easily accepts McLuhan's "global village" idea that seems to suggest that more connectedness leads to more transparency—we are all tightly involved in each other's lives, McLuhan thinks, living in an intensely socially controlled contracted community that once again resembles a tribe—OOP is there to remind us that there always remains opacity. And surely, even though one can nowadays keep constantly in touch with a person on the other side of the planet, the shadow side—or counter-phenomenon—of this may be that the networks and algorithmic infrastructures stay hidden themselves. The Googles and Facebooks of this world are working hard to exploit this "other" invisibility.[5] So, the boundaries of transparency do shift, but this does not mean that the domain of opacity is diminished, at all: it simply moves elsewhere!

So why not simply revert then to Heidegger himself? As far as postphenomenology's concern about falling back into monolithic, essentialist technology accounts is warranted, though, we'd still need a safeguard against such a threat. That would be, thus, postphenomenology itself (attending to specific situations et cetera), as well as OOP with its microscopic lens on objects as "smallest units." And at the same time the McLuhanist environment notion is still there helping to remind us how we are always "geared-in" in the way Michelfelder, with Merleau-Ponty and Heidegger, describes … Logically thinking through the consequences of the triad, we might begin to wonder how we could apply Ihde's "phenomenology of technics" (1990) to technology-technology interactions. In fact, interestingly, Verbeek already started such a project in a 2008 article, adding two other types of relation to Ihde's overview: "hybrid" and "composite intentionality" (Verbeek 2008). In the case of hybrid intentionality—for example, a person with a brain implant—the technology is not simply used: user and technology merge to form a new entity, cultivating its own intentionality. With composite intentionality, Verbeek refers to the intentionality that a technology may have toward "its" world, like a cellphone relating to a cell tower—the human user stays largely outside of this interaction. Yet perhaps as Michelfelder feels, this initiative to transcend the user perspective on Verbeek's part has not been picked up widely within the postphenomenological workfield. Still, the work of Heather Wiltse (2014; Redström and Wiltse 2015) and of Galit Wellner (2016) are definitely other cases in point of attempts in such direction.

One may even ask to which extent postphenomenology does not already, not just in its applications but in its conceptual underpinnings, do what Michelfelder advises it to do. The notion of technological intentionality (Ihde 1990), on which Verbeek builds the two extra relation types, goes some way into making sense of the "supra-human"[6] level. But there is more. And the concept of multistability is the crux of the matter. In an essential way, multistability[7] already does for postphenomenology what substance or the "real object" notion does for OOP. Multistability offers us vistas onto possible "surprise" (Hayler, in his fusion of the two perspectives, overlooks this). Whereas Harman seeks to debunk "the notion that what is currently expressed in the world is all the world has to offer" (2016, 33), one could say that Ihde has always endeavored something similar with multistability: technologies in their development, the ways in which they are adopted and adapted by users, are open, in potentiality, to multiple trajectories. However, multistability has up until now been rather interpreted perhaps as a matter of perception, pertaining mostly to the human-technology link, while in fact, it also concerns the way(s) in which world discloses and hides itself.[8] This, automatically, brings postphenomenology more in line with an analysis of the cultural media ecology, and in fact also that is largely prefigured by Ihde, in his "cultural hermeneutics" (1990, 124ff.).

So, are the differences really that great, that we'd need the triad? To add insult to injury, what would actually be accomplished anyhow, by "adding" these perspectives to postphenomenology? Other attempts have been made to complement postphenomenology in this manner (as already mentioned,

I have done my fair share of that, cf. Van Den Eede 2012; cf. also Rosenberger 2014; Rao et al. 2015), and throughout all those efforts, the questions keep lingering whether (1) postphenomenology should be changed by these additions (merging in a sense with parts of the added components) or (2) we should just use the new amalgams to treat specific problems and issues, and leave postphenomenology as such untouched. Michelfelder appears to suggest that doing the latter, thus, leaving the discipline unaltered, might in the end threaten its existence, if the field turns out to become unable to account for new phenomena to which it is not tailored. But if we modify it, will it still remain postphenomenology? On the basis of our analysis, we can now say: why not? Moreover, theories have been adjusted, supplemented, extended, and reoriented countless times. In this specific case, the "objectification"—if I can use a misleading word—of mediation theory, that is, injecting it with a media-ecological + object-oriented notion of *media*, would perhaps entail such a reorientation. But as seen, it would be a modest one: some of these ideas are already embryonically present in the framework.

Why not let them emerge in all their vigor? It could be a love triangle. OOP can enrich and enhance multistability theory. A technology has always more sides to it than we can discover; Ihde would say "there are always multistabilities." Conversely, it is we who will still have to make sense of technologies, even if we are imagining, from "our" standpoint, medium-medium or medium-world interactions. It is *us* who have to be able to *feel* this. But opening up more to world, as far as I can suggest, means: making a jump beyond mediation to "the medium" in the McLuhanist sense. Everything is a medium, everything is "medial"—this broadness does not make the analysis trivial, it is the beginning of it. Infinitely elastic terms push us out of our conceptual comfort zone. Opening up more to world means: getting a taste for the mediumness of world. And that is in our account, quite simply really, the unexpected. Where this sort of experiment may lead us, is—and this should not be a surprise—unpredictable.

NOTES

1. More recently, John Durham Peters in his *The Marvelous Clouds: Toward a Philosophy of Elemental Media* argues, be it in a more specific sense: "the royal road to knowledge of the universe is reading its structure as a recording and transmitting medium" (2015, 362).

2. Harman is not really seen as a philosopher of technology per se, although some refer to him in that way (Maggini 2014) and he contributed, as also Ihde remarks (2010, 117), to the important volume *New Waves in Philosophy of Technology* (Olsen, Selinger, and Riis 2009). Others, such as Hayler (2015) and myself—here

and elsewhere—seek to make more clear and elaborate his (possible) contribution to philosophy of technology.

3. Harman reads him as a philosopher—and one of the most important philosophers in recent intellectual history at that. In one of his lectures on the topic, "McLuhan as Philosopher," Harman states: "I want to convince you that McLuhan is a figure of tremendous value for philosophy: not because McLuhan is more than just a media theorist, but because philosophy ultimately may be nothing more than media theory" (2013, 181).

4. For a detailed postphenomenologically inspired analysis of "lived experience" with the "Technological Other" of a computer (more specifically digital video editing applications), see Irwin 2005. It might be remarked that even if one knows how to use something, that does not necessarily imply one is skilled in using it. For Hayler, though, skill is a spectrum of "getting to know" a technology. From this perspective, it seems, even a novice is already "skilled" to a certain degree—but not as skilled as the pro.

5. In this context, I should remark that another kind of "world," though not unrelated to the notion provided here, can be sought out when looking into the political-economic conditions of technology. Especially the work of Andrew Feenberg and his *Critical Theory of Technology* (2002) are of pertinence in this regard. Unfortunately, and also in the interest of focus, I cannot go into this here, but I have discussed the meeting of McLuhanist media theory with Feenberg's outlook in Van Den Eede 2013.

6. Not to confuse with any Nietzschean or transhumanist notion of the "superhuman."

7. For a recent overview of the development of the notion and uses of the term, and also a reflection upon how the concept should be further developed in the future, cf. Rosenberger 2016.

8. As noted, Redström and Wiltse (2015) with their notion of "multi-instabilities" explore similar avenues, in this context, of moving beyond the exclusively "human" standpoint.

REFERENCES

Achterhuis, H. (2001). *American Philosophy of Technology: The Empirical Turn*. Trans. R. P. Crease. Bloomington: Indiana University Press.

Bogost, I. (2012). *Alien Phenomenology, or What It's Like to Be a Thing*. Minneapolis: University of Minnesota Press.

Culkin, John. (1967). "Each Culture Develops Its Own Sense-Ratio to Meet the Demands of Its Environment." In G. E. Stearn (ed.), *McLuhan Hot & Cool: A Primer for the Understanding of & a Critical Symposium with a Rebuttal by McLuhan*. New York: The Dial Press, 35–44.

Feenberg, A. (2002). *Transforming Technology: A Critical Theory Revisited*. Oxford: Oxford University Press.

Harman, G. (2002). *Tool-Being: Heidegger and the Metaphysics of Objects*. Chicago: Open Court.

———. (2007). *Heidegger Explained: From Phenomenon to Thing*. Chicago: Open Court.

———. (2009a). "The McLuhans and Metaphysics." In J. K. B. Olsen, E. Selinger, and S. Riis (eds.), *New Waves in Philosophy of Technology*. Basingstoke: Palgrave Macmillan, 100–122.

———. (2009b). *Prince of Networks: Bruno Latour and Metaphysics*. Melbourne: re.press.

———. (2011). *The Quadruple Object*. Winchester: Zero Books.

———. (2013). *Bells and Whistles: More Speculative Realism*. Winchester: Zero Books.

———. (2016). *Immaterialism: Objects and Social Theory*. Cambridge (UK): Polity.

Hayler, M. (2015). *Challenging the Phenomena of Technology: Embodiment, Expertise, and Evolved Knowledge*. Basingstoke: Palgrave Macmillan.

Ihde, D. (1979). *Technics and Praxis: A Philosophy of Technology*. Dordrecht: D. Reidel Publishing Co.

———. (1990). *Technology and the Lifeworld: From Garden to Earth*. Bloomington: Indiana University Press.

———. (1993). *Postphenomenology: Essays in the Postmodern Context*. Evanston (IL): Northwestern University Press.

———. (2010). *Heidegger's Technologies: Postphenomenological Perspectives*. New York: Fordham University Press.

———. (2012). *Experimental Phenomenology: Multistabilities*. Second Edition. Albany (NY): State University of New York Press.

Irwin, S. (2005). "Technological Other/Quasi Other: Reflection on Lived Experience." *Human Studies* 28 (4): 453–67.

Lemmens, P. (2015). "Love and Realism." *Foundations of Science* Online First (October): 1–6. doi:10.1007/s10699–015–9471–6.

Lewis, M. (2015). *Flash Boys: A Wall Street Revolt*. New York: W.W. Norton & Company.

Maggini, G. (2014). "On the Status of Technology in Heidegger's Being and Time." *Studia Philosophiae Christianae* 50 (1): 79–110.

McLuhan, M. (1962). *The Gutenberg Galaxy: The Making of Typographic Man*. Toronto: University of Toronto Press.

———. (2003). *Understanding Media: The Extensions of Man*. Critical Edition. Corte Madera: Gingko Press.

McLuhan, M. and E. McLuhan. (1988). *Laws of Media: The New Science*. Toronto: University of Toronto Press.

McLuhan, M. and N. Barrington. (1972). *Take Today: The Executive as Dropout*. New York: Harcourt Brace Jovanovich.

Michelfelder, D. P. (2015). "Postphenomenology with an Eye to the Future." In R. Rosenberger and P.-P. Verbeek (eds.), *Postphenomenological Investigations: Essays on Human–Technology Relations*. Lanham: Lexington Books, 237–46.

Olsen, J. K. B., E. Selinger, and S. Riis (eds.). (2009). *New Waves in Philosophy of Technology*. Basingstoke: Palgrave Macmillan.

Peters, J. D. (2015). *The Marvelous Clouds: Toward a Philosophy of Elemental Media*. Chicago: The University of Chicago Press.

Ralón, L. (2016). "The Media Ecology–Philosophy of Technology Disconnect: A Matter of Perception?" *Explorations in Media Ecology* 15 (2): 113–28.

Rao, M. B., J. Jongerden, P. Lemmens, and G. Ruivenkamp. (2015). "Technological Mediation and Power: Postphenomenology, Critical Theory, and Autonomist Marxism." *Philosophy & Technology* 28 (3): 449–74.

Redström, J. and H. Wiltse. (2015). "On the Multi-Instabilities of Assembled Things." Presentation at 4S 2015—annual meeting of the Society for Social Studies of Science. doi:10.13140/RG.2.1.2649.1924.

Rosenberger, R. (2014). "Multistability and the Agency of Mundane Artifacts: From Speed Bumps to Subway Benches." *Human Studies* 37 (3): 369–92.

———. 2016. "Husserl's Missing Multistability." *Techné: Research in Philosophy and Technology* 20 (2): 153–67.

Rosenberger, R. and P.-P. Verbeek (eds.). (2015). *Postphenomenological Investigations: Essays on Human–Technology Relations*. Lanham: Lexington Books.

Salmon, F. and J. Stokes. (2010). "Algorithms Take Control of Wall Street." *WIRED*. December 27. http://www.wired.com/2010/12/ff_ai_flashtrading/

Scharff, R. C. (2012). "Empirical Technoscience Studies in a Comtean World: Too Much Concreteness?" *Philosophy & Technology* 25 (2): 153–77.

Smith, D. (2015a). "Rewriting the Constitution: A Critique of 'Postphenomenology.'" *Philosophy & Technology* 28 (4): 533–51.

———. (2015b). "The Internet as Idea: For a Transcendental Philosophy of Technology." *Techné: Research in Philosophy and Technology* Online First. doi:10.5840/techne2015121140.

Steinert, S. (2015). "Taking Stock of Extension Theory of Technology." *Philosophy & Technology* 29 (1): 61–78.

Strate, L. (2006). *Echoes and Reflections: On Media Ecology as a Field of Study*. Cresskill (NJ): Hampton Press.

———. (2011). *On the Binding Biases of Time and Other Essays on General Semantics and Media Ecology*. Fort Worth: Institute of General Semantics.

Verbeek, P.-P. (2005). *What Things Do: Philosophical Reflections on Technology, Agency, and Design*. Trans. R. P. Crease. University Park (PA): The Pennsylvania State University Press.

———. (2008). "Cyborg Intentionality: Rethinking the Phenomenology of Human–Technology Relations." *Phenomenology and the Cognitive Sciences* 7 (3): 387–95.

———. (2011). *Moralizing Technology: Understanding and Designing the Morality of Things*. Chicago: University of Chicago Press.

Van Den Eede, Y. (2011). "In Between Us: On the Transparency and Opacity of Technological Mediation." *Foundations of Science* 16 (2–3): 139–59.

———. (2012). *Amor Technologiae: Marshall McLuhan as Philosopher of Technology—Toward a Philosophy of Human-Media Relationships*. Brussels: VUBPRESS.

———. (2013). "The Mailman Problem: Complementing Critical Theory of Technology by Way of Media Theory." *Techné: Research in Philosophy and Technology* 17 (1): 144–62.

———. (2014). "Extending 'Extension': A Reappraisal of the Technology-as-Extension Idea through the Case of Self-Tracking Technologies." In D. M. Weiss, A. D. Propen, and C. Emmerson Reid (eds.), *Design, Mediation, and the Posthuman*. Lanham: Lexington Books, 151–72.

———. (2017). "Formal Cause: McLuhan's 'Objective Turn'?" In C. Anton, R. K. Logan, and L. Strate (eds.), *Taking Up McLuhan's Cause: Perspectives on Media and Formal Causality*. Bristol: Intellect, 151–173.

Van Den Eede, Y., G. Goeminne, and M. Van den Bossche. (2015). "The Art of Living with Technology: Turning Over Philosophy of Technology's Empirical Turn." *Foundations of Science* Online First (December): 1–12. doi:10.1007/s10699–015–9472–5.

Wellner, G. P. (2016). *A Postphenomenological Inquiry of Cell Phones: Genealogies, Meanings, and Becoming*. Lanham: Lexington Books.

Wiltse, H. (2014). "Unpacking Digital Material Mediation." *Techné: Research in Philosophy and Technology* 18 (3): 154–82.

Index

About the Contributors

EDITORS

Yoni Van Den Eede is postdoctoral fellow of the Research Foundation—Flanders (FWO) and part-time assistant research professor, affiliated with the research groups Centre for Ethics and Humanism (ETHU) and Culture, Emancipation, Media & Society (CEMESO), both at the Free University of Brussels (Vrije Universiteit Brussel), Belgium. His research concerns the philosophy of technology, media theory, and media ecology, with an emphasis on phenomenological, cultural, existential, and political themes. He is the author of *Amor Technologiae: Marshall McLuhan as Philosopher of Technology* (Brussels, VUBPRESS, 2012) and of (in Dutch) *Mens en media* (Tielt, LannooCampus, 2014) and *Vanzelf* (Leuven, Acco, 2015). He has (co-)edited special issues of *Techné: Research in Philosophy and Technology*, *Foundations of Science*, and *Explorations in Media Ecology*. Since 2011 he is a member of the Board of Directors of the Society for Phenomenology and Media, and from 2014 to 2016 he served as president of that same organization.

Stacey O. Irwin is associate professor at Millersville University of Pennsylvania, where she teaches a variety of digital media production, writing, and theory classes. Her interest in studying media through philosophy began when she started teaching others how to use sophisticated media production editing and design tools in the classroom. This blossomed into critically studying the experiences of "making and doing" media through phenomenology and postphenomenology. Irwin's first book, *Digital Media: Human–Technology Connection*, was published as part of this "Postphenomenology and the Philosophy of Technology" series by Lexington Books in 2016. She has also published in *Explorations in Media Ecology*, *Human Studies: A Journal for Philosophy and the Social Sciences*, *Techné: Research in Philosophy and Technology*, and *Tamara: Journal for Critical Organization Inquiry*.

Galit Wellner is an assistant professor at the NB School of Design Haifa, Israel. She is also an adjunct professor at Tel Aviv University. Wellner studies digital technologies and their interrelations with humans. She graduated from the STS department at Bar-Ilan University in 2014. Her book *A Postphenomenological Inquiry of Cell Phones: Genealogies, Meanings, and Becoming* (Lexington Books) was published in 2016. She was a guest editor in *Techné*, editing "Celling While Driving" (2014) and "Techno-Anthropology" (2015), and published several peer-reviewed articles and book chapters. She is one of the lead authors of the Israeli National Ecosystem Assessment. Wellner was the vice-chair of Israeli UNESCO's Information For All Program (IFAP), a board member of the FTTH Council Europe, and a founder of a startup. Before that, she worked for hi-tech companies and startups in strategic marketing. Galit holds an LLB and LLM from Tel Aviv University and a certified software developer degree from IDF's Mamram.

CONTRIBUTORS

Lars Botin is associate professor at the Department of Planning at Aalborg University (Denmark). He has during the past decade investigated the intersection between art, science, and technology in the domains of media, health informatics, and hospital design. He is the instigator of a new research domain: techno-anthropology in postphenomenological perspective.

Pieter Lemmens teaches philosophy and ethics at the Radboud University in Nijmegen, The Netherlands. He has published on themes in the philosophy of technology and innovation (open source and commons-based), on the work of Martin Heidegger, Peter Sloterdijk, and Bernard Stiegler, as well as on post-autonomist Marxism (Hardt, Negri, Berardi) and themes from philosophical anthropology. He translated work of Stiegler in Dutch and co-edited a book on the philosophy of landscape and place and one on contemporary German philosophy (both in Dutch). Current interests are the philosophical and politico-economic aspects of cognitive enhancement technologies, trans- and posthumanism, philosophical aspects of psychedelics, and philosophy of technology in the age of the Anthropocene.

Nicola Liberati is a postdoctoral researcher at the Universiteit Twente (University of Twente), The Netherlands, supported by The Netherlands

Organisation for Scientific Research (NWO). He works on postphenomenology and new computer technologies such as Augmented Reality, wearable computers, and teledildonics in order to highlight their knock-on effects on our society.

Shoji Nagataki is professor of philosophy at the School of International Liberal Studies, Chukyo University, Japan. His research interests include phenomenology, philosophy of embodiment, philosophy of mind, and cognitive robotics. He is author of among others "Phenomenology and the Third Generation of Cognitive Science" (in *Human Studies*, 2007) and of contributions in *The Evolution of Social Communication in Primates* (Springer, 2014) and *Technoscience and Postphenomenology* (Lexington Books, 2015).

Robert Rosenberger is an associate professor of philosophy in the School of Public Policy at the Georgia Institute of Technology. For the first part of 2016, he took an unexpected turn as the world's foremost expert on "phantom vibration syndrome," that feeling that your smartphone has vibrated when it actually has not. His long-term lines of research explore topics such as driver distraction, laboratory imaging, computer interface, frog dissection simulation, and hostile architecture. He serves as the editor-in-chief of the series "Postphenomenology and the Philosophy of Technology," which he co-founded with Don Ihde and Peter-Paul Verbeek for Lexington Books, and for which this current volume on media is the latest entry. His edited and co-edited books include *Postphenomenological Investigations* and *Philosophy of Science: 5 Questions*, and he is the author of the forthcoming polemical pamphlet *Guilty Technology*, which critiques anti-homeless law and design.

Fernando Secomandi holds a PhD in design from Delft University of Technology (The Netherlands) and is currently adjunct professor at the Higher School of Industrial Design of the State University of Rio de Janeiro (Brazil). His research explores areas of intersection between industrial design, postphenomenology, and service research, and it has been published in design journals, such as *Design Issues* and *Design Philosophy Papers*, and other books from the series "Postphenomenology and the Philosophy of Technology."

Robert N. Spicer is assistant professor of digital journalism at Millersville University. His primary area of research is in media and political culture. His dissertation, which he defended in June of 2014 at the Rutgers University School of Communication & Information, is titled *The Discourses and Practices of Political Deception: From Campaigns to Cable to the Courts*. Spicer's secondary area of research is in emerging media and philosophy of technology. His most recent publications are "Long-Distance Caring Labor: Fatherhood, Smiles, and Affect in the Marketing of the iPhone 4 and Face-Time" in the journal *Techné: Research in Philosophy and Technology* and "When More Speech is not Enough: An Argument for the Regulation of Political Falsehoods" in *The Jefferson Journal of Science and Culture*.

Daniel Susser is assistant professor of philosophy at San Jose State University. Previously, he was a research fellow at the Information Law Institute at New York University's School of Law. He works in philosophy of technology, with a focus on its normative (social/political/ethical) dimensions, and has published on such issues as the nature and function of privacy, how big data is changing the sciences, and the relationship between artificial intelligence and the body.

Heather Wiltse is assistant professor at Umeå Institute of Design, Umeå University (Sweden), where she is also currently serving as director of PhD studies. Her research centers around trying to understand and critique the role of (digital) things in experience and society in ways that can inform design, and it sits at the intersection of design studies, philosophy of technology, and critical technology studies. She has published and/or presented refereed work in philosophy of technology, science and technology studies, human-computer interaction, and design research. She is currently writing a book in collaboration with Johan Redström, to be published by Bloomsbury, that investigates and articulates what has become of things as computational processes, dynamic networks, and contextual customization now emerge as factors as important as form, function, and material were for designing, using, and understanding objects in the industrial age.

Ingram Content Group UK Ltd.
Milton Keynes UK
UKHW041619070323
418181UK00002B/18